Lecture Notes in Computer Science 16520

The series Lecture Notes in Computer Science (LNCS), including its subseries Lecture Notes in Artificial Intelligence (LNAI) and Lecture Notes in Bioinformatics (LNBI), has established itself as a medium for the publication of new developments in computer science and information technology research, teaching, and education.

LNCS enjoys close cooperation with the computer science R & D community, the series counts many renowned academics among its volume editors and paper authors, and collaborates with prestigious societies. Its mission is to serve this international community by providing an invaluable service, mainly focused on the publication of conference and workshop proceedings and postproceedings. LNCS commenced publication in 1973.

Numan Saeed · Shahad Hardan · Salma Hassan ·
Mohammad Yaqub
Editors

Head and Neck Tumor Lesion Segmentation, Diagnosis and Prognosis (HECKTOR)

4th Challenge, HECKTOR 2025
Held in Conjunction with MICCAI 2025
Daejeon, South Korea, September 23, 2025, Proceedings

Springer

Editors
Numan Saeed
Mohamed bin Zayed University of Artificial Intelligence
Abu Dhabi, Abu Dhabi, United Arab Emirates

Shahad Hardan
Mohamed bin Zayed University of Artificial Intelligence
Abu Dhabi, Abu Dhabi, United Arab Emirates

Salma Hassan
Mohamed bin Zayed University of Artificial Intelligence
Abu Dhabi, Abu Dhabi, United Arab Emirates

Mohammad Yaqub
Mohamed bin Zayed University of Artificial Intelligence
Abu Dhabi, Abu Dhabi, United Arab Emirates

ISSN 0302-9743 ISSN 1611-3349 (electronic)
Lecture Notes in Computer Science
ISBN 978-3-032-25765-9 ISBN 978-3-032-25766-6 (eBook)
https://doi.org/10.1007/978-3-032-25766-6

This Springer imprint is published by the registered company Springer Nature Switzerland AG
The registered company address is: Gewerbestrasse 11, 6330 Cham, Switzerland

Preface

This volume presents the proceedings of the HEad and neCK TumOR Lesion Segmentation, Diagnosis and Prognosis (HECKTOR) 2025 Challenge, held in conjunction with the International Conference on Medical Image Computing and Computer-Assisted Intervention (MICCAI) in 2025. The proceedings feature papers submitted by participants that describe their cutting-edge methods for segmentation of primary tumor and lymph node metastasis, prognosis using risk-free survival, and HPV classification, based on the official HECKTOR 2025 dataset released for this challenge.

Head and neck (H&N) cancers continue to impose a considerable impact on global health systems, where precise identification of tumor boundaries is fundamental for high-quality radiotherapy planning. The anatomical intricacy of the oropharyngeal region, together with the diverse radiographic characteristics of lesions, renders manual contouring both labor-intensive and vulnerable to differences between observers. In parallel with segmentation, estimating recurrence-free survival (RFS) and inferring human papillomavirus (HPV) status directly from imaging data remain difficult yet clinically important tasks. The HECKTOR 2025 challenge sought to advance this field by providing a structured benchmark for automated, multimodal PET/CT-based analysis of head and neck cancers.

Extending the scope of the earlier editions (2020–2022), this year's challenge introduced a substantially enlarged, multi-center cohort. Competitors were invited to address three interconnected tasks: (1) automated delineation of primary tumors (GTVp) and nodal metastases (GTVn), (2) estimation of recurrence-free survival (RFS), and (3) prediction of HPV status. To support these aims, a diverse, real-world dataset was curated, consisting of PET/CT scans from 1,123 patients acquired at 10 different centers. Imaging data were obtained using multiple scanners and acquisition protocols to reflect routine clinical variability. Reference segmentations for primary and nodal disease were manually annotated by experienced clinicians. In addition, the dataset provided structured clinical information, including HPV status and recurrence-free survival outcomes, with radiotherapy dose distributions available for a subset of cases. Participants were required to develop fully automated approaches spanning lesion segmentation, RFS prediction, and HPV classification. Performance was assessed using mean Dice for primary tumors and aggregated Dice for lymph node metastases, balanced accuracy for HPV classification, and the concordance index for survival prediction.

The challenge attracted 35 active teams with 347 total submissions, from more than 50 countries around the world. Fifteen papers were submitted and accepted; these were single-blind reviewed by two reviews each. The top nine teams presented their methods at a Satellite event at the MICCAI 2025 conference. Top-performing solutions spanned strong nnU-Net–based baselines, architecture innovations (e.g., hierarchical, multi-stage, coarse-to-fine, and multi-task models), molecular- and anatomy-guided strategies, and systematic analyses of preprocessing and augmentation.

Across its successive editions, the HECKTOR initiative has progressively expanded in both scale and clinical scope: from the 2020 focus on primary tumor segmentation in PET/CT, to the 2021 introduction of survival prediction with and without expert contours, and the 2022 extension to joint segmentation of primary tumors and metastatic lymph nodes alongside recurrence modeling, with datasets growing from a few hundred to more than 1000 multi-institutional cases. This steady increase in cohort size, task complexity, and integration of imaging with clinical variables reflects a shift toward more realistic, end-to-end modeling of head and neck cancer management. HECKTOR 2025 strengthened the clinical relevance of the benchmark by promoting comprehensive, fully automated pipelines that address lesion delineation, outcome prediction, and biologically meaningful stratification such as HPV status within large, heterogeneous, multi-center datasets. Such efforts are critical for advancing reproducible, data-driven tools that can support staging, treatment planning, and personalized risk assessment in head and neck oncology.

We extend our gratitude to all participants, reviewers, and the organizing committee, including clinicians and AI researchers worldwide, for their commitment to advancing head and neck cancer studies. Special thanks to the sponsors of the challenge: Mohamed bin Zayed University of Artificial Intelligence, the Society of Nuclear Medicine and Molecular Imaging, and NVIDIA. Thanks to the centers that supported the data collection: Centre Hospitalier Universitaire de Sherbrooke (CHUS), Centre Hospitalier de L'Université de Montréal (CHUM), Centre Hospitalier Universitaire de Poitiers (CHUP), Hôpital Général Juif (HGJ), Hôpital Maisonneuve-Rosemont (HMR), MD Anderson Cancer Center (MDA), University Hospital of Zürich (USZ), Centre Henri Becquerel (CHB), Centre Hospitalier Universitaire de Brest (CHUB), and Centre Hospitalier Universitaire de Nantes (CHUN).

February 2026

Numan Saeed
Shahad Hardan
Salma Hassan
Mohammad Yaqub

Organization

Organizing Committee

Numan Saeed	Mohamed bin Zayed University of Artificial Intelligence, UAE
Shahad Hardan	Mohamed bin Zayed University of Artificial Intelligence, UAE
Salma Hassan	Mohamed bin Zayed University of Artificial Intelligence, UAE
Mohammad Yaqub	Mohamed bin Zayed University of Artificial Intelligence, UAE

Program Committee

Ronan Abgral	University Hospital of Brest, France
Alaa Mohamed Shawky Ali	MD Anderson Cancer Center, USA
Ahmed Aly	Mohamed bin Zayed University of Artificial Intelligence, UAE
Vincent Andrearczyk	HES-SO Valais-Wallis University of Applied Sciences and Arts Western Switzerland, and Lausanne University Hospital (CHUV), Switzerland
David Bourhis	University Hospital of Brest, France
Catherine Cheze Le Rest	Centre Hospitalier Universitaire de Poitiers (CHUP), France
Pierre Decazes	Laboratoire AIMS, Université de Rouen Normandie, Rouen, France
Cem Dede	MD Anderson Cancer Center, USA
Gregory Delpon	Institut de Cancérologie de l'Ouest, France
Adrien Depeursinge	HES-SO Valais-Wallis University of Applied Sciences and Arts Western Switzerland, and Lausanne University Hospital (CHUV), Switzerland
Mélanie Dore	Institut de Cancérologie de l'Ouest, France
Hesham Elhalawani	Brigham and Women's Hospital, Dana Farber Cancer Institute, Harvard Medical School, USA
Thomas Eugene	Nantes Université, CHU Nantes, France
Romain Floch	University Hospital of Brest, France

Clifton D. Fuller	MD Anderson Cancer Center, USA
Mathieu Hatt	University Hospital of Brest, France
Mario Jreige	Lausanne University Hospital (CHUV), Switzerland
Kevin Kerleguer	University Hospital of Brest, France
Ufaq Khan	Mohamed bin Zayed University of Artificial Intelligence, UAE
Jean-Christophe Leclere	University Hospital of Brest, France
Maelle Mauguen	University Hospital of Brest, France
Raphaël Metz	Nantes Université, CHU Nantes, France
Mohamed Naser	MD Anderson Cancer Center, USA
Umair Nawaz	Mohamed bin Zayed University of Artificial Intelligence, UAE
Valentin Oreiller	HES-SO Valais-Wallis University of Applied Sciences and Arts, Switzerland
Vijay Ram Kumar Papineni	Sheikh Shakhbout Medical City, UAE
John O. Prior	Lausanne University Hospital (CHUV), Switzerland
Arman Rahmim	BC Cancer Research Institute, Canada
Muhammad Ridzuan	Mohamed bin Zayed University of Artificial Intelligence, UAE
Su Ruan	Laboratoire AIMS, Université de Rouen Normandie, Rouen, France
Amandine Sambourg	University Hospital of Brest, France
Ulrike Schick	University Hospital of Brest, France
Carlos Sjogreen	MD Anderson Cancer Center, USA
Stephanie Tanadini-Lang	University Hospital Zürich, Switzerland
Olena Tankyevych	Centre Hospitalier Universitaire de Poitiers (CHUP), France
Darya Taratynova	Mohamed bin Zayed University of Artificial Intelligence, UAE
Martin Vallières	Medical Physics Unit, Department of Oncology, McGill University, Montreal, Canada
Kareem Wahid	MD Anderson Cancer Center, USA
Yutong Xie	Mohamed bin Zayed University of Artificial Intelligence, UAE
Panagiotis Balermpas	University Hospital Zürich, Switzerland

Additional Reviewers

Mai A. Shaaban	Hussain Alasmawi
Roba Al Majzoub	Alya Almsouti

Mubarak G. Abdu-Aguye
Asif Hanif
Ainur Khamitova
Umaima Rahman
Tausifa Jan Saleem
Mostafa Salem
Amal Saqib
Ikboljon Sobirov
Hu Wang
Aigerim Zhusubalieva

Contents

Tumor and Lymph Node Segmentation

HectoMixNet: Advancing Automated Head and Neck Tumor Segmentation with Multicenter PET/CT Data

Moona Mazher[1], Steven A. Niederer[2], and Abdul Qayyum[2](✉)

[1] Hawkes Institute, Department of Computer Science, University College London, London, UK
[2] Faculty of Medicine, Imperial College London, National Heart and Lung Institute, London, UK

a.qayyum@imperial.ac.uk

Abstract. Head and Neck (H&N) cancers represent one of the most prevalent malignancies worldwide, with accurate delineation of primary tumors and metastatic lymph nodes being essential for radiotherapy planning and treatment outcome prediction. Manual segmentation, though standard, is time-consuming and prone to inter-observer variability, motivating the development of automated deep learning–based methods. In this study, we propose HectoMixNet, a novel 3D encoder–decoder framework augmented with a bidirectional quasiseparable mixing module for robust segmentation of primary tumors and lymph nodes in multimodal PET/CT imaging. The proposed module efficiently integrates local anatomical detail with global volumetric context, addressing the challenges of heterogeneous and spatially complex lesions. We evaluate HectoMixNet on the HECKTOR 2025 Task 1 dataset, the largest multicentric benchmark for H&N cancer analysis to date, comprising over 1,200 patients from 11 international centers. Our model achieved strong performance, with a GTVp Dice score of 0.8812, GTVn Dice of 0.8246, and GTVn F1 of 0.7273 on the validation and leaderboard sets. Compared to state-of-the-art baselines such as 3D Mamba and xLSTM, HectoMixNet demonstrated superior lymph node segmentation accuracy, highlighting the importance of bidirectional quasiseparable mixing for modeling long-range spatial dependencies. These results establish HectoMixNet as an effective and clinically relevant tool for automated H&N cancer segmentation in large-scale, heterogeneous imaging cohorts.

Keywords: Bidirectional Quasiseparable Mixing · State-Space Models · Head and Neck Cancer Tumor Segmentation · Lymph Node Detection · PET/CT Imaging · Radiotherapy Planning · HECKTOR Challenge

1 Introduction

Head and Neck (H&N) cancers represent the fifth most common malignancy worldwide, with a substantial global disease burden and significant clinical management challenges [1]. Accurate delineation of primary tumors and metastatic lymph nodes plays a crucial role in radiotherapy planning, treatment monitoring, and outcome prediction.

N. Saeed et al. (Eds.): HECKTOR 2026, LNCS 16520, pp. 3–15, 2026.
https://doi.org/10.1007/978-3-032-25766-6_1

Conventionally, segmentation is performed manually by expert radiation oncologists, a process that is both time-consuming and subject to high inter-observer variability. As a result, there is a growing demand for robust, automated segmentation algorithms that can generalize across heterogeneous, multicenter datasets. The HECKTOR (Head and Neck Tumor Segmentation and Outcome Prediction) challenge, organized annually in conjunction with the International Conference on Medical Image Computing and Computer-Assisted Intervention (MICCAI), has become the leading benchmark for automated H&N cancer analysis on multimodal Positron Emission Tomography (PET) and Computed Tomography (CT) data. Following the success of the 2020–2022 editions [1–5], the 2025 HECKTOR challenge expands the dataset to more than 1,200 patients from 11 international centers, making it the largest multicentric cohort available for this task. The 2025 edition introduces refined evaluation metrics to better assess detection and segmentation of multiple distinct lesions, thereby improving clinical relevance. In recent years, numerous segmentation models have been developed for medical image analysis [5–17], demonstrating the potential of deep learning to accurately delineate complex anatomical structures and lesions.

In this work, we present HectoMixNet, a novel deep learning framework for automatic segmentation of primary tumors and lymph nodes in H&N cancer patients. The model builds upon a classical 3D encoder–decoder design but incorporates a specialized bidirectional quasiseparable mixing module at the network bottleneck, enabling effective modeling of both local detail and global spatial context. By integrating fine anatomical information with long-range dependencies across volumetric scans, HectoMixNet is tailored to address the challenges of detecting irregular, heterogeneous tumor structures. We evaluate our method on the HECKTOR 2025 Task 1 dataset and demonstrate its ability to achieve precise and robust segmentation in a challenging multicenter setting.

2 Proposed Method

In this section, we describe the dataset used for training and evaluation, followed by the architecture and implementation details of the proposed HectoMixNet framework.

2.1 Dataset

The dataset used in this study is provided by the HECKTOR 2025 challenge, which focuses on automatic detection and segmentation of head and neck primary tumors and lymph nodes from multimodal PET/CT imaging. The training cohort consists of approximately 850 patients drawn from the HECKTOR 2022 database [5], updated with additional clinical variables including HPV status and extended follow-up information. For the 2025 challenge, two new French cohorts have been added, forming an unseen test set of ~400 patients. Altogether, the dataset comprises more than 1,200 patients from at least 11 medical centers, ensuring significant heterogeneity in imaging protocols and patient demographics [18].

Each patient study contains co-registered FDG-PET and CT scans, with corresponding expert-annotated segmentation masks for the primary tumor (GTVp) and metastatic lymph nodes (GTVn). PET images provide complementary metabolic information to the anatomical details visible in CT, enabling more reliable lesion identification. The segmentation task requires the model to accurately detect and delineate both lesion types, including cases with multiple, spatially distinct lymph node metastases. For evaluation, the challenge employs updated metrics that measure both overall volumetric overlap (e.g., Dice similarity) and lesion-wise detection performance, reflecting the clinical importance of identifying all tumor sites for accurate treatment planning.

2.2 Preprocessing

For preprocessing, we followed the standardized pipeline provided by the challenge organizers. CT and PET scans were stacked as two-channel volumes and processed as follows:

- Resampling & Alignment: All scans were resampled to an isotropic resolution of 1 mm^3 and aligned using bounding-box coordinates to ensure PET–CT correspondence.
- Region-of-Interest Cropping: A fixed box of $200 \times 200 \times 310$ voxels centered on PET-intensity landmarks was extracted to capture the head and neck region while reducing irrelevant background.
- Normalization: CT intensities were clipped to $[-250, 250]$ HU and scaled to $[-6, 6]$, while PET images were normalized to zero mean and unit variance.
- Reorientation & Padding: All images were reoriented to the RAS convention, foreground-cropped, and padded to the target size to ensure uniform input dimensions.

This preprocessing pipeline, implemented with SimpleITK and MONAI, standardizes resolution, orientation, and intensity distributions across the cohort, while preserving anatomical fidelity and ensuring compatibility with deep learning workflows.

2.3 Postprocessing

To restore predictions to the native imaging space, we applied a structured inverse transformation pipeline. First, symmetric padding introduced during preprocessing was removed, followed by reinsertion into the cropped foreground and neck region of interest. The reconstructed mask in the standardized 1-mm isotropic space was then resampled back to the original CT resolution using nearest-neighbor interpolation to preserve label integrity. This ensured voxel-level alignment of the predicted segmentation with the scanner-resolution images, facilitating accurate evaluation and downstream clinical usability.

2.4 Model

1. **HectoMixNet: Proposed Model for 3D heterogeneous H&N tumors and lymph nodes**

To address the challenges of segmenting heterogeneous H&N tumors and lymph nodes, we propose HectoMixNet, a 3D convolutional encoder–decoder network augmented with a bidirectional quasiseparable mixing module. The architecture is designed to combine local feature extraction with global spatial context modeling, a critical requirement for distinguishing small, irregular lesions as well as capturing large-scale disease patterns.

The encoder consists of hierarchical 3D convolutional blocks with strided convolutions, batch normalization, and non-linear activations. This stage progressively reduces spatial resolution while extracting rich multi-scale representations of tumor and anatomical structures. Skip connections are preserved to ensure high-fidelity recovery of spatial details. At the network bottleneck, feature maps are passed through the HectoMix module, which reshapes the volumetric features into a sequence and applies bidirectional quasiseparable mixing using semiseparable state-space models. This operation efficiently propagates information from both past (causal) and future (anti-causal) spatial positions, while preserving self-connections for stability. In doing so, each voxel representation integrates contextual knowledge from the entire 3D volume (Fig. 1).

The decoder mirrors the encoder, using 3D transposed convolutions to restore spatial resolution. Mixed global features from the bottleneck are fused with skip-connected encoder features at multiple scales, allowing fine-grained lesion boundaries to be reconstructed while maintaining global consistency. This design enables HectoMixNet to adaptively handle both small, isolated lymph nodes and larger, diffused primary tumors.

By unifying multi-scale local features with efficient long-range dependency modeling, HectoMixNet offers an effective and computationally scalable solution for volumetric medical image segmentation. Its ability to capture global relationships while preserving anatomical detail makes it particularly well-suited for the complexity of head and neck tumor segmentation in the HECKTOR 2025 dataset.

The core mechanism of mixing aggregates information from three sources for each sequence position: past positions (causal context), future positions (anti-causal context), and the current position itself. In the causal pass, a semiseparable SSM operation accumulates information from all preceding positions, with the output shifted to align with the current position. The anti-causal pass reverses the sequence and applies the same causal SSM operation; the result is shifted and reversed back to propagate information from future positions. This bidirectional processing ensures every spatial location benefits from both preceding and succeeding spatial context.

Additionally, a self-connection term applies learnable diagonal parameters to each position's features, preserving local information and stabilizing the mixing process. Mathematically, this operation corresponds to a quasiseparable mixing matrix M structured as follows: the diagonal entries represent self-connection weights, the lower triangular part encodes causal mixing weights for past positions, and the upper triangular part encodes anti-causal mixing weights for future positions. The quasiseparable structure implies a low-rank representation that enables efficient computation without explicitly forming a large dense matrix [19].

Together, this bidirectional quasiseparable mixing yields a powerful, context-aware feature representation that integrates global spatial relationships effectively. This makes mixing highly suitable for 3D medical imaging tasks like TBI, where modeling both local details and global spatial dependencies is critical for precise and reliable analysis.

The equation below describes how the output at each sequence position i is computed by combining three components: contributions from all past positions $j < i$, contributions

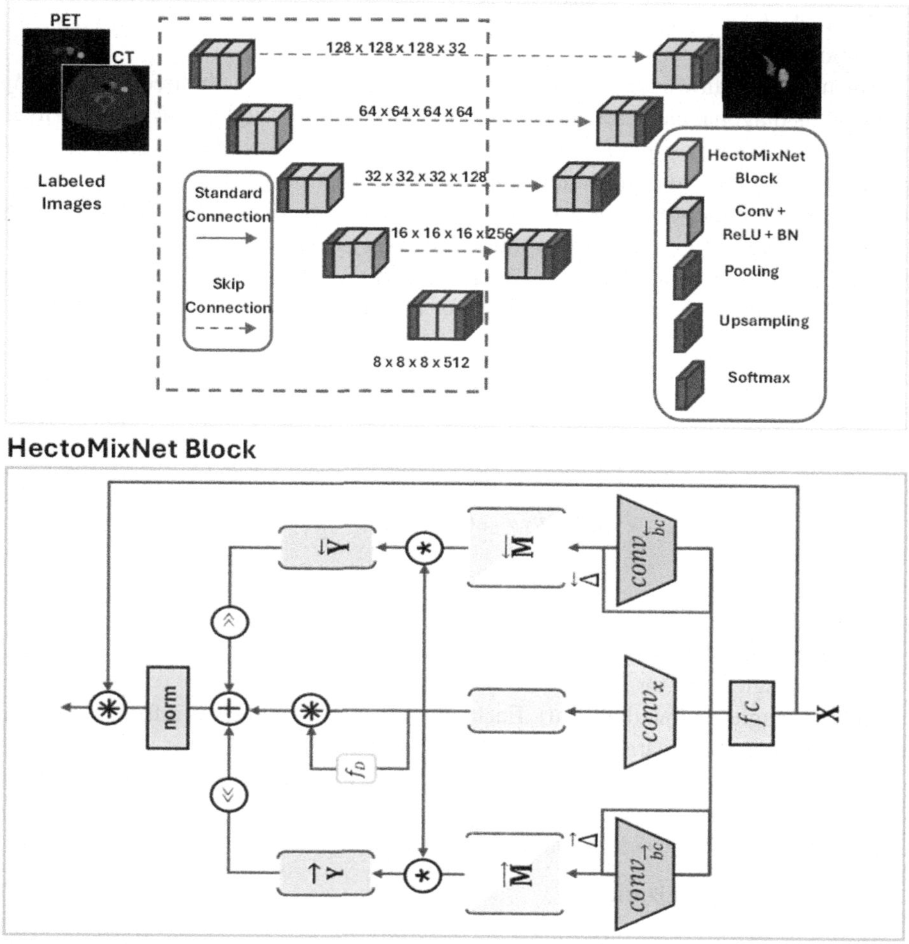

Fig. 1. Architectural framework of HectoMixNet, designed for segmentation of complex and heterogeneous head and neck tumors.

from all future positions $j > i$, and direct self-connection at the position i. The matrix M organizing these parameters is structured so that their diagonal elements δ_i represent self-connections preserving local features. The lower triangle contains parameters $A_i b_j$ that govern how information flows causally from past positions to the current one, while the upper triangle contains parameters $A_i' b_j'$ for anti-causal mixing, aggregating information from future positions. This quasiseparable structure enables efficient modeling of bidirectional dependencies without explicitly storing a full dense matrix.

For each batch b, position i:

$$Y_{b,i} = \sum_{j<i} A_i b_j X_{b,j} + \sum_{j>i} A_i' b_j' X_{b,j} + \delta_i X_{b,i}$$

Where A_i, b_j: causal parameters, A_i', b_j': anti-causal parameters and δ_i: diagonal/self-connection

The matrix M shown for sequence length 16 illustrates how the bidirectional mixing operates. Its diagonal elements δ_i represent self-connection weights that preserve local information at each position i. The lower triangular part (below the diagonal) contains parameters $A_i b_j$ that mix information causally from past positions $j < i$ to the current position iii. Conversely, the upper triangular part (above the diagonal) holds parameters $A_i' b_j'$ responsible for mixing information anti-causally from future positions $j > i$ back to position i. This structured matrix efficiently captures dependencies in both directions while maintaining a sparse, low-rank form for fast computation.

$$M = \begin{bmatrix} \delta_1 & A_1'b_2' & A_1'b_3' & \cdots & A_1'b_{16}' \\ A_2b_1 & \delta_2 & A_2'b_3' & \cdots & A_2'b_{16}' \\ A_3b_1 & A_3b_2 & \delta_3 & \cdots & A_3'b_{16}' \\ \vdots & \vdots & \vdots & \ddots & \vdots \\ A_{16}b_1 & A_{16}b_2 & A_{16}b_3 & \cdots & \delta_{16} \end{bmatrix}$$

Where,

- Diagonal: δ_i for $i = 1, \ldots, 16$
- Lower triangle: $A_i b_j$ for $i > j$
- Upper triangle: $A_i' b_j'$ for $i < j$
- Lower triangle (below diagonal): Each entry M_{ij} for $i > j$ mixes information from past positions using parameters A_i and b_j (causal direction).
- Upper triangle (above diagonal): Each entry M_{ij} for $i < j$ mixes information from future positions using parameters A_i' and b_j' (anti-causal direction).
- Diagonal: Each M_{ii} is a self-connection parameter δ_i.

2. **Training and optimization**

HectoMixNet is a 3D UNet-based architecture implemented in PyTorch, specifically designed for the segmentation of primary tumors and lymph nodes in head and neck PET/CT scans. The network integrates a bidirectional quasiseparable mixing module at the bottleneck, enabling it to capture both local features through convolutional layers and long-range spatial dependencies across the entire volume. All convolutional layers are initialized using He initialization, and the model uses $3 \times 3 \times 3$ convolution kernels across five encoding and five decoding levels, with skip connections preserved to maintain high-resolution spatial information.

For training, input patches of size $160 \times 160 \times 160$ were used, and the AdamW optimizer was applied with a cosine annealing learning rate schedule starting at 0.0002. The loss function combines Dice and Cross-Entropy losses, balancing volumetric overlaps and boundary accuracy. Training was conducted for 1000 epochs on all labeled HECKTOR2025 cases, with a batch size of 2 due to GPU memory limitations. A five-fold cross-validation scheme (~80% training, 20% validation per fold) was employed for robustness, and final predictions were obtained through ensemble averaging across folds. Extensive data augmentation, including rotations, flipping, scaling, Gaussian blur, and additive noise, was applied to improve generalization. Hyperparameters, such as learning rate, batch size, and network depth, were tuned via grid search, and each fold required approximately 24 h of training on a single NVIDIA A6000 GPU.

The advantages of HectoMixNet stem from its combination of local convolutional feature extraction with global context modeling via the bidirectional quasiseparable mixing module. This design enables accurate segmentation of both small, irregular lymph nodes and large, diffuse primary tumors. Coupled with standardized preprocessing, extensive data augmentation, and ensemble predictions, HectoMixNet demonstrates robust generalization and high segmentation fidelity. Its architecture ensures precise boundary delineation, effective detection of multiple lesions, and efficient use of multi-modal PET/CT information, making it particularly well-suited for the challenges posed by the HECKTOR 2025 Task 1 dataset.

3 Results

Table 1. Segmentation Performance on HECKTOR2025 Task 1

Model	GTVp Dice	GTVn Aggregate Dice	GTVnAggregate F1
HectoMixNet (Validation)	0.7381	0.8021	0.7015
HectoMixNet (Sanity Check)	0.8812	0.8246	0.7273
3D Mamba (Sanity Check)	0.8831	0.8169	0.6667
3D xLSTM (Sanity Check)	0.8626	0.6937	0.4286

HectoMixNet demonstrates strong segmentation performance on HECKTOR2025 Task 1 as shown in Table 1. On the validation set, it achieved a GTVp Dice score of 0.7381, indicating good overlap with the ground truth for primary tumors, while the GTVn aggregate Dice of 0.8021 and F1 score of 0.7015 reflect accurate identification of lymph nodes. In a sanity check on the leaderboard, HectoMixNet further improved, reaching 0.8812 GTVp Dice, 0.8246 GTVn Dice, and 0.7273 GTVn F1, demonstrating its robustness under different test splits. Compared to other models, 3D Mamba slightly outperformed HectoMixNet on GTVp Dice (0.8831 vs. 0.8812), but HectoMixNet achieved higher lymph node segmentation scores (GTVn Dice 0.8246 vs. 0.8169, F1 0.7273 vs. 0.6667). The 3D xLSTM model, while competitive on primary tumor segmentation, lagged significantly in lymph node detection (GTVn Dice 0.6937, F1 0.4286), highlighting the advantage of HectoMixNet's bidirectional quasiseparable mixing module for capturing long-range spatial context. Overall, HectoMixNet provides a balanced and robust segmentation performance for both primary tumors and lymph nodes, making it particularly well-suited for the HECKTOR2025 Task 1 challenge.

Figures 2 and 3 present segmentation results for three validation subjects from the Hector dataset, comparing ground truth (GT) with predictions from HectoMixNet, 3D Mamba, and 3D xLSTM. Columns show GT (first), HectoMixNet (second), 3D Mamba (third), and 3D xLSTM (fourth), with red representing the primary tumor volume (GTVp) and green indicating lymph nodes (GTVn). Rows show axial slice overlays (odd) and

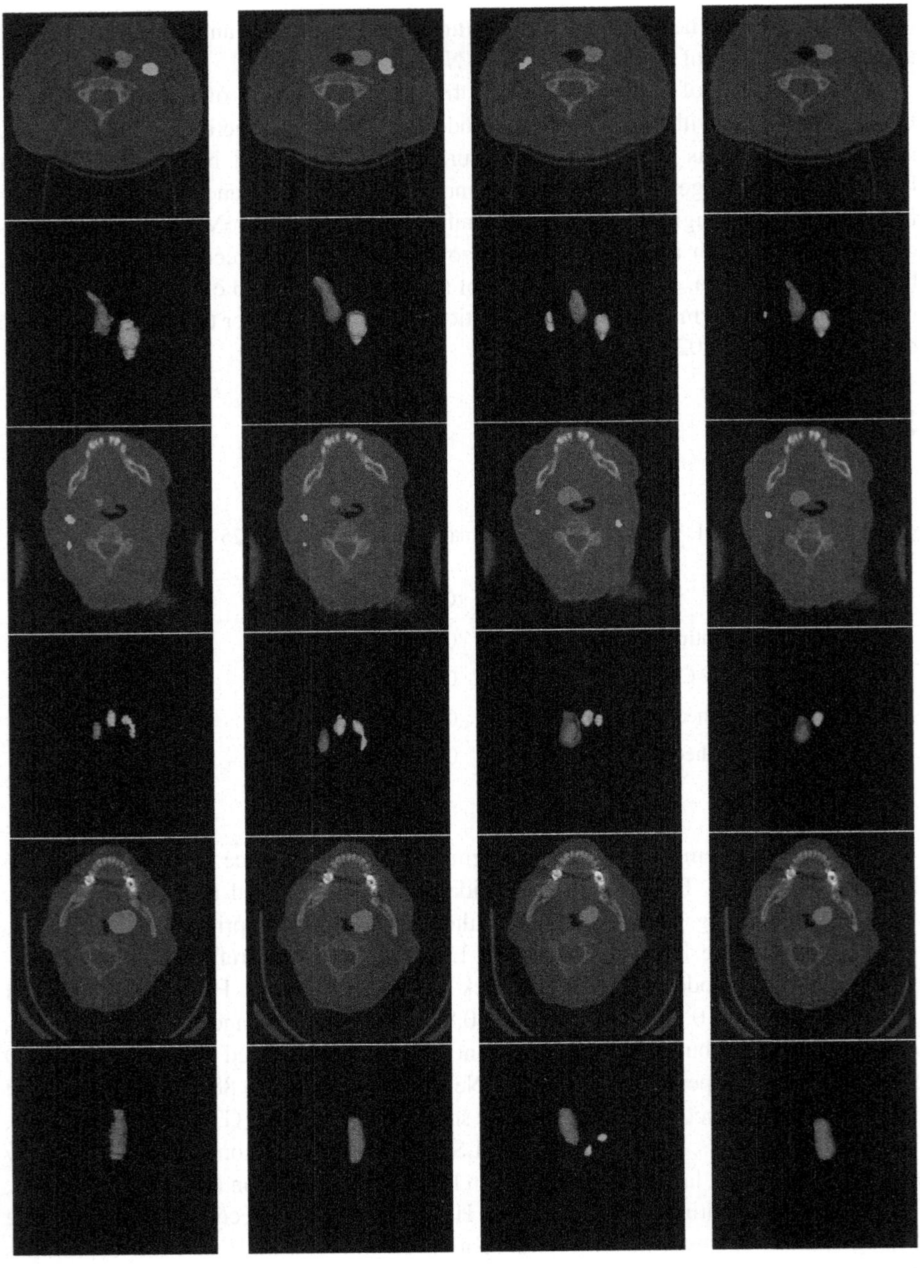

Fig. 2. Columns display CT axial overlays with corresponding segmentations. The first column shows the ground truth (GT), followed by predictions from the proposed HectoMixNet, 3D Mamba, and 3D xLSTM. Red highlights the primary tumor volume (GTVp), while green denotes lymph nodes (GTVn).

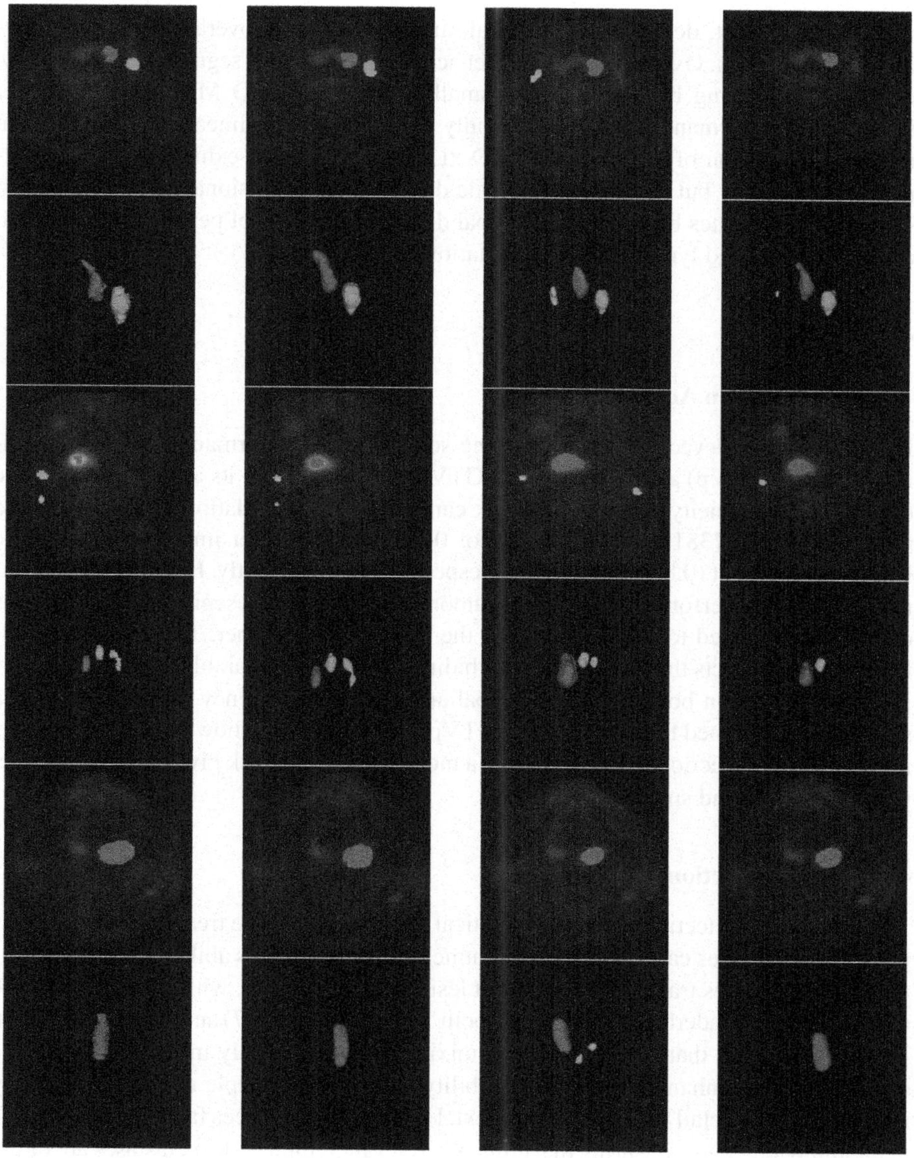

Fig. 3. Columns display PET axial overlays with corresponding segmentations. The first column shows the ground truth (GT), followed by predictions from the proposed HectoMixNet, 3D Mamba, and 3D xLSTM. Red indicates the primary tumor volume (GTVp), and green represents lymph nodes (GTVn).

corresponding 3D volumetric reconstructions (even) for CHUM-014 subject (rows 1–2), HMR-013 subject (rows 3–4), and USZ-003 subject (rows 5–6). Axial slices provide local segmentation detail, highlighting differences in tumor boundary delineation and lymph node detection, particularly for smaller or isolated nodes. 3D views offer volumetric context, demonstrating spatial alignment, tumor coverage, and connectivity of lymph nodes. Overall, HectoMixNet achieves the highest segmentation accuracy, effectively capturing both tumors and small lymph nodes; 3D Mamba provides the second-best performance, showing generally accurate tumor delineation but occasional under-segmentation of smaller nodes; 3D xLSTM ranks third, exhibiting smooth volumetric continuity but less consistent node detection and occasional shape deviations. This figure illustrates both local and global differences in model performance for head and neck tumor and lymph node segmentation.

4 Discussion

4.1 Segmentation Accuracy

HectoMixNet achieved consistently strong segmentation performance across both primary tumors (GTVp) and lymph nodes (GTVn), demonstrating its ability to handle the complex heterogeneity of head and neck cancers. On the validation set, it achieved a GTVp Dice of 0.7381 and GTVn Dice of 0.8021, with further improvements on the leaderboard test set (0.8812 and 0.8246, respectively). Importantly, HectoMixNet maintained balanced performance between tumor and lymph node segmentation, whereas other models tended to favor one task at the expense of the other. The superior voxel-level overlap reflects the effectiveness of bidirectional quasiseparable mixing in capturing both fine lesion boundaries and global anatomical consistency. While 3D Mamba slightly outperformed HectoMixNet on GTVp Dice, our model showed clear advantages in lymph node detection and delineation, a more challenging task given their small size, variable shapes, and spatial dispersion.

4.2 Lesion Detection

Accurate lesion detection is clinically critical for comprehensive treatment planning, as missed lymph nodes can lead to undertreatment. HectoMixNet's ability to capture long-range dependencies translated into robust lesion-wise detection, with a GTVn F1-score of 0.7273 on the leaderboard, surpassing both 3D Mamba (0.6667) and xLSTM (0.4286). This demonstrates that the bidirectional mixing module not only improves volumetric overlap but also enhances the model's ability to identify multiple distinct lesions. By integrating local detail with broader context, HectoMixNet reduces false negatives while maintaining precision, ensuring that clinically relevant lymph node metastases are rarely overlooked.

4.3 Role of State Space Models

Both HectoMixNet and competing SSM-based architectures highlight the value of state space modeling for volumetric medical imaging. Traditional CNNs and recurrent architectures are limited by local receptive fields or vanishing memory, constraining their ability to model the irregular and dispersed nature of H&N lesions. By contrast, HectoMixNet's bidirectional quasiseparable mixing extends SSM capabilities, enabling efficient propagation of contextual information across the entire 3D volume while preserving local fidelity. The performance gap between HectoMixNet and 3D Mamba underscores that architectural design choices, particularly the integration of self-connections and dual causal/anti-causal processing, are critical for fully exploiting the potential of state space models in medical image segmentation.

4.4 Clinical Implications

From a clinical standpoint, HectoMixNet offers significant advantages. Its high Dice scores and strong lesion-wise detection make it particularly well-suited for radiotherapy planning, where complete and precise delineation of both primary tumors and lymph nodes is essential. The model's robustness across multicenter data also suggests potential for real-world deployment, where imaging protocols and patient characteristics vary widely. Compared to manual segmentation, which is labor-intensive and prone to inter-observer variability, HectoMixNet provides a scalable and reproducible alternative. Importantly, its ability to detect small, spatially separated lymph nodes enhance clinical safety by reducing the likelihood of missed lesions that could compromise treatment outcomes.

4.5 Limitations and Future Work

Despite its promising performance, HectoMixNet has several limitations. First, evaluation was restricted to the HECKTOR 2025 dataset, which, while large and multicentric, may not capture the full variability of clinical practice, such as motion artifacts, rare tumor subtypes, or unusual imaging conditions. Second, the current framework focuses solely on PET/CT; integrating additional modalities such as MRI could provide a richer anatomical and functional context. Third, although quasiseparable mixing is computationally efficient relative to dense global attention, training requirements remain substantial, potentially limiting accessibility for institutions with limited computational resources.

Future directions include extending HectoMixNet for different data fusion, exploring self-supervised pretraining strategies to improve cross-institutional generalization, and developing interpretability mechanisms tailored to state space models to better align automated outputs with clinical decision-making. In addition, longitudinal extensions for outcome prediction could further enhance its value in personalized oncology workflows.

5 Conclusion

In this work, we introduced HectoMixNet, a deep learning framework specifically designed for automatic segmentation of primary tumors and lymph nodes in head and neck cancer patients using multimodal PET/CT imaging. By incorporating a bidirectional quasiseparable mixing module within a 3D encoder–decoder architecture, the model successfully combines fine anatomical detail with efficient global context modeling, enabling robust performance across heterogeneous patient cohorts. Evaluation on the HECKTOR 2025 Task 1 dataset demonstrated that HectoMixNet achieves competitive segmentation accuracy, with particularly strong performance in lymph node detection and delineation—an area where existing methods often underperform. Compared with state-of-the-art models, HectoMixNet provides a more balanced performance between tumor and lymph node segmentation, underlining the effectiveness of bidirectional quasiseparable mixing in capturing long-range spatial dependencies. Given its scalability and generalization capability, HectoMixNet represents a promising step toward reliable, automated segmentation tools that can reduce inter-observer variability and support precision radiotherapy planning in clinical practice.

References

1. Parkin, D.M., et al.: Global cancer statistics, 2002. CA A Cancer J. Clin. **55**(2), 74–108 (2005)
2. Bonner, J.A., et al.: Radiotherapy plus Cetuximab for Locoregionally advanced head and neck cancer: 5-year survival data from a phase 3 randomised trial, and relation between Cetuximab-induced rash and survival. Lancet Oncol. **11**(1), 21–28 (2010)
3. Chajon, E., et al.: Salivary gland-sparing other than parotid-sparing in definitive head-and-neck intensity-modulated radiotherapy does not seem to jeopardize local control. Radiat. Oncol. **8**(1, 1), –9 (2013)
4. Bogowicz, M., et al.: Comparison of PET and CT radiomics for prediction of local tumor control in head and neck squamous cell carcinoma. Acta Oncol. **56**(11), 1531–1536 (2017)
5. Andrearczyk, V., et al.: Overview of the HECKTOR challenge at MICCAI 2021: automatic head and neck tumor segmentation and outcome prediction in PET/CT images. In: Head and Neck Tumor Segmentation and Outcome Prediction, pp. 1–37 (2022)
6. Mazher, M., et al.: Self-supervised spatial–temporal transformer fusion based federated framework for 4D cardiovascular image segmentation. Inf. Fusion. **106**, 102256 (2024)
7. Wang, K., et al.: Extreme Cardiac MRI Analysis under Respiratory Motion: Results of the CMRxMotion Challenge. arXiv preprint https://arxiv.org/abs/2507.19165 (2025).
8. Yang, K., et al.: Benchmarking the cow with the topcow challenge: Topology-aware anatomical segmentation of the circle of willis for cta and mra. ArXiv arXiv-2312 (2024).
9. de la Rosa, E., et al.: ISLES'24: Improving final infarct prediction in ischemic stroke using multimodal imaging and clinical data. arXiv preprint https://arxiv.org/abs/2408.10966 (2024).
10. Payette, K., et al.: Multi-center fetal brain tissue annotation (feta) challenge 2022 results. IEEE Trans. Med. Imaging. (2024)
11. Imran, M., et al.: Multi-class segmentation of aortic branches and zones in computed tomography angiography: The aortaseg24 challenge. arXiv preprint https://arxiv.org/abs/2502.05330 (2025).
12. Qayyum, A., et al.: Transforming Heart Chamber Imaging: Self-Supervised Learning for Whole Heart Reconstruction and Segmentation. arXiv preprint https://arxiv.org/abs/2406.06643 (2024).
13. Nan, Y., et al.: Hunting imaging biomarkers in pulmonary fibrosis: benchmarks of the AIIB23 challenge. Med. Image Anal. **97**, 103253 (2024)
14. de la Rosa, E., et al.: A robust ensemble algorithm for ischemic stroke lesion segmentation: Generalizability and clinical utility beyond the isles challenge. arXiv preprint https://arxiv.org/abs/2403.19425 (2024).
15. de la Rosa, E., et al.: DeepISLES: a clinically validated ischemic stroke segmentation model from the ISLES'22 challenge. Nat. Commun. **16**(1), 7357 (2025)
16. Zhu, L., B. Liao, Q. Zhang, X. Wang, W. Liu, X. Wang: Vision mamba: Efficient visual representation learning with bidirectional state space model. arXiv preprint https://arxiv.org/abs/2401.09417 (2024).

17. Qayyum, A., et al.: Hybrid 3D-ResNet deep learning model for automatic segmentation of thoracic organs at risk in CT images. In: 2020 International Conference on Industrial Engineering, Applications and Manufacturing (ICIEAM), pp. 1–5. IEEE (2020)
18. Saeed, N., Hassan, S., Hardan, S., et al.: A Multimodal and Multi-centric Head and Neck Cancer Dataset for Tumor Segmentation and Outcome Prediction (2025).
19. Hwang, S., Lahoti, A., Puduppully, R., Dao, T., Albert, G.: Hydra: bidirectional state space models through generalized matrix mixers. Adv. Neural Inf. Proces. Syst. **37**, 110876–110908 (2024)

nnU-Net v2 for Head-and-Neck PET/CT Primary Tumor and Lymph Node Segmentation: A Simple, Strong Baseline

Yansong Bu[1,2], Zihao Wang[1,2], Yuwan Wang[1,2], Jiexin Jiang[1], Yuhan Chen[1], and Mengye Lyu[1,2(✉)]

[1] College of Health Science and Environmental Engineering, Shenzhen Technology University, Shenzhen, China
lvmengye@sztu.edu.cn

[2] College of Applied Sciences, Shenzhen University, Shenzhen, China

Abstract. Accurate segmentation of primary tumors (GTVp) and nodal lesions (GTVn) is essential for radiotherapy planning in head and neck cancer (HNC). The HECKTOR 2025 challenge provides a large-scale multi-center PET/CT dataset for benchmarking automated tumor segmentation. In this study, we developed a segmentation pipeline based on the nnU-Net v2 framework without architectural modifications. The model was trained using 5-fold cross-validation on the complete training cohort and deployed in a Docker container for submission. On the official validation leaderboard, our approach achieved a GTVp Dice of 0.7444, a GTVn Dice of 0.7956, and a GTVn F1-score of 0.5868, securing seventh place overall in Task 1. These results demonstrate that nnU-Net v2 remains a competitive baseline for multi-center PET/CT segmentation tasks, providing robust tumor delineation performance across heterogeneous datasets. We ranked third overall in the HECKTOR 2025 Challenge (Task 1).

Keywords: Medical image segmentation · nnU-Net · tumor segmentation · MRI-guided radiation therapy

1 Introduction

Head and neck cancer (HNC) remains one of the most challenging malignancies to treat due to its complex anatomical structures and the close proximity of tumors to critical organs at risk [1]. Radiation therapy (RT) plays a central role in the management of HNC, and accurate delineation of gross tumor volumes (GTVs) is essential for effective treatment planning and outcome optimization, especially with the increasing adoption of MRI-guided RT, which offers superior soft-tissue contrast [2]. In recent years, the HEad and neCK TumOR Lesion Segmentation (HECKTOR) challenge series has provided large-scale, multi-center

Y. Bu and Z. Wang—These authors contributed equally to this work.

N. Saeed et al. (Eds.): HECKTOR 2026, LNCS 16520, pp. 16–23, 2026.
https://doi.org/10.1007/978-3-032-25766-6_2

datasets with standardized evaluation protocols, enabling the benchmarking of automated tumor segmentation methods in PET/CT imaging [3]. The multi-institutional nature and heterogeneous data distributions of HECKTOR make it a valuable testbed for developing clinically robust algorithms.

Manual delineation of primary tumors (GTVp) and involved lymph nodes (GTVn) from PET/CT is time-consuming, labor-intensive, and prone to inter-observer variability [4]. Deep learning methods, especially fully convolutional neural networks, have shown promise in automating this task and alleviating the burden on clinicians [5]. Among them, nnU-Net has emerged as a widely adopted framework due to its self-configuring design and strong performance across diverse medical image segmentation challenges [6]. Its ability to automatically adapt preprocessing, architecture, and training parameters to the target dataset makes it a strong and reproducible baseline. Therefore, we present a simple, fully documented nnU-Net v2 baseline for the HECKTOR 2025 challenge, aiming to maximize reproducibility and provide a strong reference for PET/CT-based HNC segmentation.

We evaluate this baseline on the HECKTOR 2025 Task 1 segmentation benchmark. Without introducing architectural modifications or large-scale pre-training, we demonstrate that the default nnU-Net v2 pipeline achieves competitive performance on this multi-center dataset. On the official validation leaderboard, our approach reached an overall rank of seventh place, highlighting that nnU-Net v2 remains a strong baseline for PET/CT-based HNC tumor segmentation. In the final test phase, our method ranked third overall in Task 1, further reinforcing this message.

2 Dataset

The dataset used in this study originates from the HEad and NeCK TumOR Lesion Segmentation (HECKTOR) 2025 challenge [3]. It is a large-scale, multi-institutional collection of FDG-PET/CT scans from over 1,100 patients with histologically confirmed head and neck cancer, acquired across 10 international medical centers. The training cohort consists of approximately 700 cases from 8 centers, while the test cohort includes about 450 previously unseen cases from 3 centers. Notably, a subset of the 2022 test set was incorporated into the 2025 training cohort. The estimated HPV status distribution in the test set is approximately 80 HPV-positive and 20 HPV-negative.

Each patient case includes co-registered CT and PET images. PET images were normalized to standardized uptake values (SUVs), and CT scans were provided as low-dose non-contrast-enhanced images. Ground-truth segmentation masks, available only for Task 1, delineate primary tumors (GTVp) and involved lymph nodes (GTVn). All images underwent standardized preprocessing to ensure cross-center comparability and facilitate model training.

3 Method

3.1 Model Architecture

For Task 1, we selected the nnU-Net v2 [6] framework as our segmentation model and trained it on the HECKTOR 2025 dataset. nnU-Net is a widely adopted, self-configuring deep learning framework for medical image segmentation, which automatically adapts preprocessing, network architecture, data augmentation, and training hyperparameters to the target dataset. This flexibility allows it to serve as a robust and reproducible baseline across a variety of imaging tasks.

In our study, we used the 3D full-resolution configuration, which determines patch size, network depth, loss function (a combination of Dice and cross-entropy), and learning rate schedule automatically according to the dataset properties. No manual modifications were made to the network architecture. For multi-modal input, CT and PET images were concatenated as separate channels, following the default nnU-Net v2 implementation.

3.2 Pre-processing

The raw dataset was provided in a patient-wise folder structure, where each folder contained a CT scan, a PET scan, and the corresponding segmentation mask. To comply with the nnU-Net v2 input format, the data were reorganized into a standardized directory layout, including a dataset description file and modality-indexed inputs (with CT assigned to channel 0000 and PET to channel 0001). During this step, we identified a small number of invalid cases where the CT and label volumes were not aligned in size; these cases were excluded from training. Furthermore, discrepancies in voxel dimensions between CT and PET images were corrected by resampling the PET volumes using the SimpleITK library to ensure voxel-wise correspondence. The final dataset consisted of paired CT and PET inputs with corresponding labels, ready for training with nnU-Net v2.

3.3 Training and Inference

Model training was performed with 5-fold cross-validation to maximize the use of the available training cohort and assess robustness across different partitions. Each fold was trained independently for 1000 epochs using mixed-precision training. All other hyperparameters were kept as default in nnU-Net v2. During inference, the framework's standard strategy was employed, namely sliding-window prediction with overlapping patches, followed by Gaussian weighting to fuse patch-level outputs into the final segmentation map. For the official submission, results from the cross-validation models were aggregated and evaluated on the challenge validation set.

3.4 Implementation Details

All experiments were implemented using Python and the PyTorch deep learning library, and training was conducted on a GPU server. The nnU-Net v2 (3D full-resolution) framework was used for both training and inference. During inference, single-case predictions were performed using a sliding-window strategy with Gaussian weighting, and the predicted segmentation masks were resampled to the original CT geometry to preserve label integrity. The final outputs were saved in the required format according to HECKTOR challenge guidelines. Training protocols are summarized in Table 1, and hardware configuration and development environments are presented in Table 2.

Table 1. Training protocols.

Network initialization	normal initialization
Batch size	2
Patch size	$96 \times 160 \times 160$
Total epochs	1000
Optimizer	SGD with Nesterov momentum ($\mu = 0.99$)
Weight decay	3e−5
Loss function	Dice + cross-entropy loss
Initial learning rate (lr)	0.001

Table 2. Development environments and requirements.

System	Ubuntu 22.04
CPU	Intel(R) Xeon(R) CPU E5-2680 v4
RAM	256 GB
GPU (number and type)	8× Tesla P40
CUDA version	12.0
Programming language	Python 3.10.18
Deep learning framework	PyTorch 2.7.1; torchvision 0.22.1

4 Results

The performance of the proposed pipeline based on nnU-Net v2 was evaluated on the HECKTOR 2025 Task 1 segmentation benchmark. To ensure robustness, we conducted a 5-fold cross-validation on the training cohort. This strategy allowed us to assess the variability of the model across different data partitions and reduce the risk of overfitting to a single split. The cross-validation results demonstrated stable segmentation performance for both primary tumors (GTVp) and lymph nodes (GTVn), highlighting the reliability of the nnU-Net v2 framework in a multi-center PET/CT setting. As illustrated in Fig. 1 and Table 3, the predicted segmentations show good agreement with the ground-truth annotations, further confirming the effectiveness of nnU-Net v2.

For the official submission, the trained nnU-Net v2 model was applied to the challenge validation set. On the official leaderboard, our method achieved a GTVp Dice of 0.7444 (rank 9), a GTVn aggregated Dice of 0.7956 (rank 2), and a GTVn F1-score of 0.5868 (rank 14), resulting in a mean position of 8.3 and an overall rank of 7th among all participating teams. These results indicate that the default nnU-Net v2 configuration, without any architectural modifications or external pre-training, remains a strong and competitive baseline for automatic segmentation of head and neck tumors in PET/CT images.

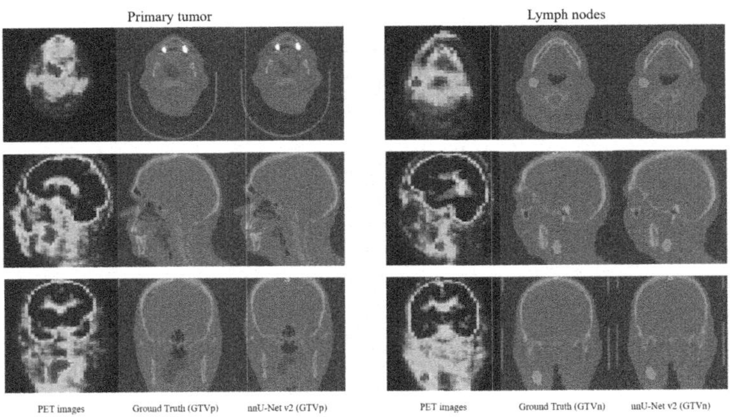

Fig. 1. Qualitative visualization of the segmentation results. For ease of comparison, only representative cropped regions of the original images are shown.

Table 3. Cross-validation Dice scores (training cohort, 5-fold).

Fold	Mean Validation Dice
0	0.6913
1	0.6958
2	0.6933
3	0.6800
4	0.6650

Table 4 summarizes the quantitative performance of our method on the official validation leaderboard.

Table 5 reports the official test results, where our team ranked third overall in Task 1.

Table 4. Official validation leaderboard results (team `sztu_bme2025`, HECKTOR 2025 Task 1).

Metric	Score	Rank	Description
GTVp Dice	0.7444	9	Primary tumor segmentation
GTVn Dice (agg)	0.7956	2	Nodal tumor segmentation
GTVn F1-score	0.5868	14	Detection sensitivity
Mean Position	8.3	–	Averaged ranking across metrics
Overall Rank	–	7	Leaderboard standing

Table 5. Official test leaderboard results (team `sztu_bme2025`, HECKTOR 2025 Task 1).

Metric	Score	Rank	Description
GTVp Dice	0.7308	–	Primary tumor segmentation
GTVn Dice (agg)	0.7641	–	Nodal tumor segmentation
GTVn F1-score (agg)	0.6320	–	Detection sensitivity
Mean Position	–	–	Averaged ranking across metrics
Overall Rank	–	**3**	Leaderboard standing

5 Discussion

In this study, we investigated the performance of nnU-Net v2 on the HECKTOR 2025 Task 1 segmentation benchmark. Without introducing architectural modifications or external pre-training, the standard 3D full-resolution configuration of nnU-Net v2 achieved a competitive 7th place on the official validation leaderboard and maintained comparable accuracy on the hidden test set, ultimately placing third overall in the final Task 1 ranking.

These results highlight the robustness of nnU-Net v2 as a strong baseline for head and neck tumor segmentation in multi-center PET/CT data, particularly reflected in the high DSCagg score for nodal disease (GTVn).

Despite these promising results, several limitations should be noted. First, the relatively low F1-score for GTVn suggests that the model tends to miss smaller or less distinct lesions, indicating limited sensitivity in challenging cases. This may be partly due to the absence of advanced post-processing strategies, such as threshold optimization or connected-component filtering, which could improve recall. Second, unlike recent large-scale models that leverage transfer learning, our approach did not incorporate external pre-training or domain adaptation techniques. As a result, the model may be less effective at handling inter-institutional variability across unseen test centers. In addition, our internal experiments indicated that using STU-Net [7,8] might further improve the F1-score, especially for nodal disease. However, due to time constraints, we were not able to submit this approach for official evaluation.

Future research can address these limitations in several ways. Semi-supervised learning strategies could leverage the unannotated test-center data to improve generalization. Domain adaptation methods may further reduce the performance gap across centers with heterogeneous imaging protocols. A two-stage pipeline combining lesion detection and fine-grained segmentation could help capture small-volume nodal disease more effectively [9,10]. In addition, uncertainty-aware post-processing may provide more reliable outputs for clinical use. Finally, training with larger patch sizes or more complex architectures could be explored on hardware with higher memory capacity, such as TPUs or high-memory GPUs, to better capture long-range spatial context.

In summary, this study demonstrates that nnU-Net v2, even in its default configuration, provides a strong and reproducible baseline for automatic tumor segmentation in PET/CT images of head and neck cancer. These findings suggest that while more advanced models may further improve accuracy, nnU-Net v2 remains a reliable starting point for clinical and research applications in radiation therapy planning.

Acknowledgments. This work was in part supported by Shenzhen Science and Technology Program (Shenzhen Higher Education Stable Support Program, No. 20220716111838002) and a university–industry collaborative project (No. HT20 241125001).

Disclosure of Interests. The authors have no competing interests.

References

1. Anderson, G., Ebadi, M., Vo, K., Novak, J., Govindarajan, A., Amini, A.: An updated review on head and neck cancer treatment with radiation therapy. Cancers **13**(19), 4912 (2021)
2. Lavigne, D., et al.: Magnetic resonance-guided radiation therapy for head and neck cancers. Curr. Oncol. **29**(11), 8302–8315 (2022)
3. Saeed, N., et al.: A multimodal and multi-centric head and neck cancer dataset for segmentation, diagnosis, and outcome prediction (2025)
4. Gudi, S., et al.: Inter-observer variation in head and neck gross tumour volume delineation on CT and PET-CT: comparison between radiation oncologists and radiologists from the same institution. Radiother. Oncol. **122**(2), 300–304 (2017)

5. Naser, M.A., et al.: Tumor segmentation in patients with head and neck cancers using deep learning based on multi-modality PET/CT images. Cancers **13**(3), 615 (2021)
6. Isensee, F., Jaeger, P.F., Kohl, S.A., Petersen, J., Maier-Hein, K.H.: nnU-Net: a self-configuring method for deep learning-based biomedical image segmentation. Nat. Methods **18**(2), 203–211 (2021)
7. Huang, Z., et al.: STU-Net: scalable and transferable medical image segmentation models empowered by large-scale supervised pre-training, arXiv preprint arXiv:2304.06716 (2023)
8. Wang, Z., Lyu, M.: Head and neck tumor segmentation for MRI-guided radiation therapy using pre-trained STU-Net models. In: Wahid, K.A., Dede, C., Naser, M.A., Fuller, C.D. (eds.) Head and Neck Tumor Segmentation for MR-Guided Applications. LNCS, vol. 15273, pp. 65–74. Springer, Cham (2025)
9. Huang, S., et al.: Abdominal CT organ segmentation by accelerated nnUNet with a coarse to fine strategy. In: Ma, J., Wang, B. (eds.) Fast and Low-Resource Semi-supervised Abdominal Organ Segmentation. LNCS, vol. 14221, pp. 23–34, Springer, Cham (2022)
10. Huang, S., Yang, H., Mei, L., Zhang, T., Liu, S., Lyu, M.: From whole-body to abdomen: Streamlined segmentation of organs and tumors via semi-supervised learning and efficient coarse-to-fine inference. In: Ma, J., Wang, B. (eds.) Fast, Low-resource, and Accurate Organ and Pan-cancer Segmentation in Abdomen CT. LNCS, vol. 14904, pp. 283–292. Springer, Cham (2024)

The Impact of Preprocessing, Augmentation, and Architecture on Head and Neck Tumor and Lymph Node Segmentation in PET/CT: A HECKTOR 2025 Challenge Report

Sébastien Quetin[1,2](✉) and Shirin A. Enger[1,2,3]

[1] Medical Physics Unit, Department of Oncology, McGill University, Montreal, QC, Canada
sebastien.quetin@mail.mcgill.ca

[2] Montreal Institute for Learning Algorithms, Mila, Montreal, QC, Canada

[3] Lady Davis Institute for Medical Research, Jewish General Hospital, Montreal, QC, Canada

Abstract. The HECKTOR 2025 challenge provides a platform to benchmark automatic segmentation methods for Head and Neck (H&N) primary tumors and lymph nodes in FDG-PET and CT scans (Task 1). This study presents a challenge submission based on a Residual Encoder U-Net within the nnU-Net framework, enhanced with modality-specific preprocessing and data augmentations. The proposed solution, submitted under the user name sebquet, achieved mean Dice scores of 71.81% for primary tumors and 74.54% for metastatic lymph nodes on the test set. These results demonstrate competitive performance and highlight the effectiveness of combining residual encoder architectures with tailored preprocessing for H&N tumor segmentation. The implementation is available at https://github.com/sebquetin/Hecktor2025.git.

Keywords: Head and Neck tumor · Deep Learning segmentation · PET and CT scans

1 Introduction

Head and Neck (H&N) cancer ranks among the most common cancers worldwide and remains a major cause of cancer-related morbidity and mortality. Accurate tumor delineation is essential for treatment planning, particularly in radiotherapy, where precise localization directly impacts clinical outcomes. Positron Emission Tomography (PET) has proven to be a valuable modality for guiding H&N cancer management, as it provides metabolic information that complements the anatomical detail of Computed Tomography (CT) [3]. However, PET suffers from lower spatial resolution compared to CT, making the integration of both modalities crucial for reliable tumor and lymph node segmentation.

N. Saeed et al. (Eds.): HECKTOR 2026, LNCS 16520, pp. 24–36, 2026.
https://doi.org/10.1007/978-3-032-25766-6_3

Several recent works have explored radiomics approaches based on PET and CT, with the goal of predicting prognosis in a non-invasive manner while utilizing routinely available diagnostic and treatment-planning scans [2,4,13]. While radiomics approaches based on PET and CT have shown considerable promise, most studies to date have been conducted on relatively small patient cohorts. To ensure robust generalization and avoid overestimating predictive performance, validation on large, multi-institutional datasets is essential [1]. The HECKTOR 2025 challenge addresses this need by providing more than 1,200 PET/CT scans collected across multiple centers, enabling both reliable benchmarking and the development of clinically relevant models [11]. Three different tasks are proposed to tackle in the Hecktor 2025 challenge. This study addresses the first task which consists in segmenting the primary tumor volume (GTVp) and the metastatic lymph nodes (GTVn).

Building upon the HECKTOR 2025 dataset, we propose an nnU-Net–based approach [6,7] that integrates customized preprocessing strategies and augmentations to enable accurate automatic segmentation of tumor regions in H&N cancer patients. Our implementation is available at https://github.com/sebquetin/Hecktor2025.git.

2 Materials and Methods

The following methods describe the approach submitted to the test phase of the challenge. Alternative solutions previously explored during the validation phase are reported in the Results and Ablation sections.

2.1 Dataset

Our work was based solely on the HECKTOR 2025 training dataset [11] composed of 680 examinations from seven different centers with CT and registered PET scans along with manual expert contours for the GTVp and GTVn. No external dataset was used to develop our solution. Figure 1 shows a CT and a registered PET scan for a patient from the training dataset.

2.2 Data Preprocessing

Resampling. For training, ground truth masks and PET scans were resampled to the CT original resolution using a nearest neighbor and a Bspline interpolation, respectively, with the SimpleITK toolkit [9].

Cropping. To train the deep learning model with the most informative signal, a preprocessing method was designed to crop the volumes around the head and neck region. The procedure consisted of two main steps: identifying the brain using PET Standardized Uptake Values (SUVs) and CT Hounsfiled Units (HUs) to define cropping in the x and y axes, and refining the z-axis cropping based on anatomical priors derived from the training dataset. Brain localization was

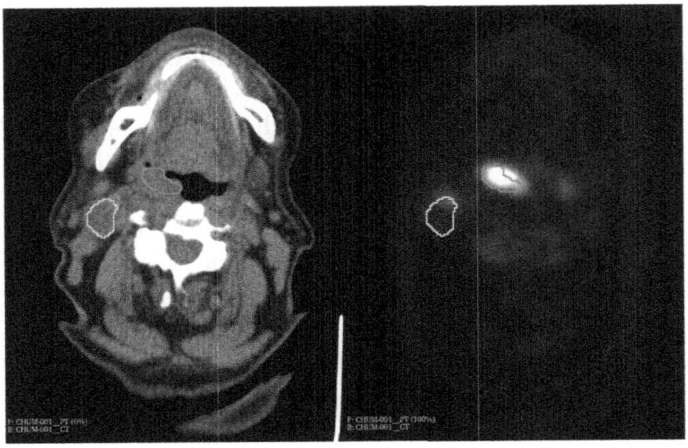

Fig. 1. CT and registered PET scans from a HECKTOR 2025 training case with overlaid ground-truth masks: GTVp in green and GTVn in yellow. (Color figure online)

achieved by first studying PET SUVs within the patient body, defined as values of PET scan voxels registered with CT scan voxels whose HUs were between –500 and 1000. This range reliably captured soft tissue while excluding background air. The 95th percentile of these SUVs was used as a threshold, as it consistently separated high-uptake brain regions from the rest of the body. Voxels above this threshold formed a high-SUV mask that was split into connected components; components smaller than 100 mm^3 were discarded because they represented noise or isolated hotspots. Among the remaining components, the one with the highest z-coordinate was selected as the brain, avoiding confusion with other high-uptake regions such as the bladder. Volumes were cropped above this brain component, and laterally around its x-y boundaries with a 50 mm margin to ensure the full head was encompassed.

To define the inferior boundary of the z-axis, we measured the distances between the top of the brain component and all ground-truth contours (GTVp and GTVn) across the training set. The maximum observed distance was used to crop along the z-axis below the brain, with an additional 10 mm margin for safety. The overall cropping process is illustrated in Fig. 2.

2.3 Model Training

Normalization. The CT scans were normalized using the nnU-Net CT normalization scheme. Foreground voxels, defined as voxels within regions where the ground-truth mask was non-zero, were used to compute the mean, standard deviation, and the 0.5^{th} and 99.5^{th} percentiles across the entire training dataset. Each CT scan was then normalized using these dataset-specific statistics by first clipping voxel intensities to the range defined by the 0.5th and 99.5th percentiles, followed by z-score normalization using the defined mean and standard deviation.

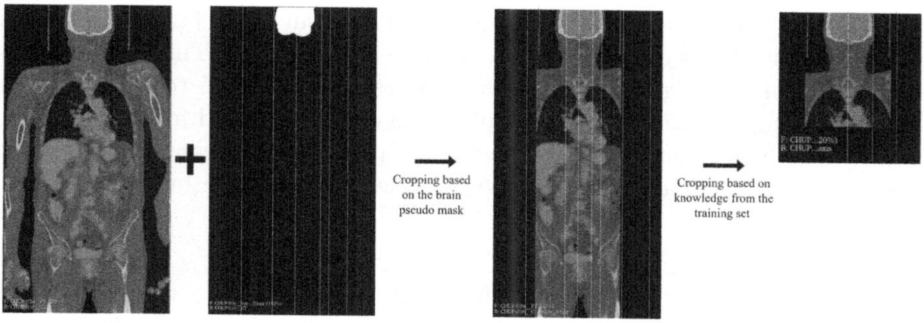

Fig. 2. Cropping process: a pseudo mask is derived from PET SUVs to define an initial crop, followed by removal of the lower body informed by training contour positions.

For the PET scans, the default nnU-Net image-based z-score normalization was not used. Instead, we applied the same dataset-specific approach as for the CT scans. Specifically, the mean and standard deviation of the foreground PET SUVs were estimated across the training dataset. However, instead of percentile-based clipping, custom thresholds were applied: SUV values were clipped to the range [0, 15] before z-score normalization, which provided a favorable performance trade-off, as shown in Tables 1 and 4.

Model Architecture. Although the benchmarking of different augmentations, clipping boundaries, and normalization strategies was conducted using a standard convolutional U-Net architecture (see Sect. 4), the final test-phase submission employed a Residual Encoder U-Net model. In both cases, the architectures were implemented using the nnU-Net framework with the 3D full-resolution configuration.

The standard U-Net has a symmetric encoder–decoder structure with skip connections between corresponding layers, propagating high-resolution features directly to the decoder, and uses two convolutions per stage in both encoder and decoder. The Residual Encoder U-Net replaces the encoder's convolutional blocks with residual blocks containing identity shortcuts, which improve gradient flow and enable training of deeper networks [5]. In this architecture, the encoder has 1, 3, 4, 6, 6, 6 convolutions per stage while the decoder has only 1 convolution per stage, resulting in an overall asymmetric design.

For the Residual Encoder U-Net, the default parameters were modified by setting the GPU VRAM target to 16 GB, matching the hardware constraints of the HECKTOR 2025 challenge. Both U-Net variants were trained with six resolution levels comprising 32, 64, 128, 256, 320, and 320 feature maps.

Augmentations. The default nnU-Net augmentation settings were strengthened by empirically modifying both the augmentation probabilities and their application ranges. Specifically, the probability of applying rotations and scalings was increased from 0.2 to 0.5, while their parameter ranges remained unchanged.

For Gaussian noise, the probability was increased from 0.1 to 0.25 for CT scans and to 0.5 for PET scans, with the variance left unchanged. The probability of the multiplicative brightness transform was raised from 0.15 to 0.75 for both modalities. For PET scans, the multiplier range was expanded from (0.75, 1.25) to (0.6, 1.4), while the default range was retained for CT scans. The contrast transform underwent the same changes as the multiplicative brightness transform.

Optimization. For training, all volumes were resampled to the median CT voxel spacing of 0.98 mm × 0.98 mm × 3.27 mm, as computed from the training dataset. The plain convolutional U-Net model was trained with a patch size of 160 × 192 × 64 voxels, while the Residual Encoder U-Net used a larger patch size of 192 × 224 × 80 voxels. Default nnU-Net training hyperparameters were applied: a learning rate of 0.01, batch size of two, and a total of 1000 training epochs. Models were trained with five-fold cross-validation to minimize the Dice–Cross Entropy loss, each fold using 80% of the training set for optimization and 20% as an internal validation set. For each fold, the model checkpoint that maximized the exponential moving average of the pseudo-Dice score, computed by the nnU-Net framework on the internal validation set during training, was selected and used for inference.

2.4 Inference

At inference time, the PET scan was resampled to the CT scan as described in Sect. 2.2 followed by application of the cropping strategy outlined in Sect. 2.2. The distance to crop the inferior portion of the body in the z-axis was the one defined used in the training dataset.

Ensembling was performed using the five cross-validation models trained within the nnU-Net framework. For each fold, test-time augmentation was applied by flipping the input volumes along all three axes. The corresponding model outputs (logits) were then realigned by resetting the original axes and subsequently averaged. This procedure was repeated for the best-performing model from each fold. The mean logits across all five models were ultimately averaged and converted into segmentation masks using the argmax operation.

Finally, the predicted mask volume was padded back to match the original CT scan dimensions. No further post-processing was applied.

2.5 Evaluation

Challenge Evaluation. Two earlier versions of this work were submitted to the HECKTOR 2025 challenge platform for evaluation during the validation phase. These versions differed slightly from the methodology described in the previous sections. Specifically, both validation submissions employed the default nnU-Net augmentations rather than the customized augmentations described in Sect. 2.3, used a batch size of eight instead of two, and were based on the plain convolutional U-Net architecture.

Additionally, both submissions employed a different PET normalization strategy than that described in Sect. 2.3. In the first submission, PET scans were normalized using the nnU-Net CT normalization scheme, with clipping performed at the 0.5th and 99.5th percentiles of foreground voxels rather than using fixed boundaries. The second submission applied the default nnU-Net PET normalization, consisting of standard image-specific z-score normalization without any clipping.

The HECKTOR 2025 challenge platform evaluated our submission on a withheld testing set of 50 patients using the Dice score for the GTVp, an aggregated Dice score for the GTVn adapted from the Aggregated Jaccard Index [8], and a custom aggregated F1-score for GTVn. For the latter, true positives (TP), false negatives (FN), and false positives (FP) were accumulated across correctly detected lesions, with a detection considered correct if the intersection-over-union (IoU) exceeded 30%.

Local Evaluation. To optimize the segmentation pipeline, the training dataset, already partitioned into five folds using an 80–20% split, was evaluated fold by fold on each respective internal validation set (n = 136). Performance metrics were subsequently averaged across folds. Unlike the challenge submission, no ensemble predictions were performed.

To benchmark the trained models, the HECKTOR 2025 challenge evaluation metrics were replicated to the best of our ability; however, they may differ from the metrics computed by the official challenge platform. Segmentation performance for GTVp was assessed using the Dice score. For GTVn, both an aggregated Dice score and a custom aggregated F1-score were computed. For the aggregated Dice score, TP, FP, and FN were summed across all patients in the internal validation set of each fold, and the final metric was calculated using the standard Dice formula: $AggregatedDice = 2 * TP/(2 * TP + FP + FN)$.

For the GTVn F1-score, both the ground-truth and predicted masks were separated into connected components. For each predicted component, if its IoU with a ground-truth GTVn component exceeded 30%, the corresponding TP, FP, and FN were accumulated. If the IoU did not meet this threshold, the sum of voxels in the predicted component was added to the FP count. If a ground-truth component had no overlapping predicted component, the sum of its voxels was added to the FN count. The final metric was then computed using the same formula as for the Aggregated Dice.

3 Results

3.1 Challenge Evaluation on the Validation Set

Table 1 summarizes the results of our two submissions to the HECKTOR 2025 challenge validation phase using earlier versions of our pipeline, and the results of our submission to the test phase.

It can be seen that the normalization strategy applied to PET scans significantly affects the pipeline's performance on new patients. Specifically, using the

Table 1. Results from our validation-phase submissions and our final test submission to the HECKTOR platform. Challenge metrics are averaged over patients in the challenge validation set. Local metrics are computed on each fold's internal validation set and averaged across folds. Values are reported as mean ± standard deviation, with minimum and maximum fold scores in brackets.

Submission	PET processing	Network	Evaluation	GTVp Dice Score (%)	GTVn Aggregated Dice Score (%)	GTVn Aggregated F1-score (%)
1	CT normalization	U-Net	Challenge Validation	**75.09**	77.04	62.07
2	z-score normalization	U-Net	Challenge Validation	73.72	**77.86**	62.07
1	CT normalization	U-Net	Local	**72.59 ±** **1.47 [70.77, 75.1]**	76.70 ± 0.67 [75.43, 77.25]	61.54 ± 3.41 [57.76, 66.44]
2	z-score normalization	U-Net	Local	72.21 ± 1.15 [70.75, 73.66]	**77.03 ±** **0.61 [76.44, 78.11]**	62.22 ± 3.58 [56.93, 67.46]
3	CT norm., clip [0, 15]	ResU-Net	Challenge Test	71.87	74.54	**65.07**

nnU-Net CT normalization scheme for PET scans improves the Dice score for GTVp (75.09 vs 73.72%), whereas an image-based z-score normalization yields a higher aggregated Dice score for GTVn (77.86 vs 77.04%). Additionally, the pipeline showed a performance drop on the test set compared with the validation set: the GTVp Dice score decreased from 75.09% to 71.87%, and the aggregated GTVn Dice score from 77.04% to 74.54%, while the GTVn aggregated F1-score increased from 62.07% to 65.07%. These differences cannot be explained solely by the choice of architecture (see Table 5).

3.2 Local Evaluation on Internal Validation Sets

The two pipelines submitted to the validation phase were also evaluated locally. Table 1 reports the performance of each pipeline using a single fold, averaged across folds. Metrics for each fold were computed on the corresponding internal validation set, which included 136 patients. Overall, the locally computed metrics generally correlated with the results obtained during the validation phase. In particular, a higher average Dice score across folds for GTVp, 72.59% against 72.21%, corresponded to a higher GTVp Dice score in the challenge, with a similar trend observed for the aggregated GTVn Dice score. For the aggregated F1-score, although our local implementation produced an average value close to that obtained in the challenge, higher values for one submission did not translate to a higher score with the challenge platform evaluation.

Table 2. Pipeline performance using nnU-Net or custom augmentations, averaged over all patients in fold 0's internal validation set.

Augmentations used for training and inference	GTVp Dice Score (%)	GTVn Aggregated Dice Score (%)	GTVn Aggregated F1-score (%)
nnU-Net default	**75.20**	78.46	58.65
Custom	74.90	**78.84**	**61.64**

4 Ablation Study

To optimize our pipeline prior to submission for the HECKTOR challenge test phase, we empirically evaluated and benchmarked its components, resulting in the final configuration presented in Sect. 2. Unless otherwise specified, all results reported below were obtained using the plain convolutional U-Net described in Sect. 2.3. Performance metrics were computed locally and follow the definitions in Sect. 2.5.

Batch Size and Augmentations. Data augmentation strategies were benchmarked using the pipeline from our first validation-phase submission, which employed the nnU-Net CT normalization scheme for PET scans and a batch size of two instead of eight. Table 2 presents the performance of the pipeline on the internal validation set of fold 0, comparing default nnU-Net augmentations with our custom augmentation scheme. The custom augmentations resulted in lower Dice scores for GTVp with 74.90% against 75.20%, but improved performance for both the aggregated GTVn Dice score and the aggregated F1-score. Although evaluation on the remaining four folds is needed to confirm this trend, the substantially stronger performance on the aggregated F1-score, from 58.65% to 61.64%, combined with the challenge timeline, motivated the selection of the custom augmentation strategy.

Figure 3 presents the training and validation losses for pipelines trained with custom augmentations and different batch sizes. Training with a batch size of two, compared to eight, produced a noisier validation loss curve suggestive of greater model exploration and ultimately resulted in a lower validation loss. Moreover, a batch size of two reduced overfitting, as indicated by the closer alignment between training and validation losses.

Table 3 reports the pipeline performance averaged across the five folds, comparing training with nnU-Net default augmentations and a batch size of eight against training with custom augmentations and a batch size of two. The latter configuration produced substantially higher Dice scores for GTVp as well as improved aggregated Dice scores for GTVn, but at the cost of a markedly lower aggregated F1-score for GTVn. Based on these results, we selected the combination of custom augmentations and a batch size of two for subsequent experiments. All further ablation studies were conducted under this configuration.

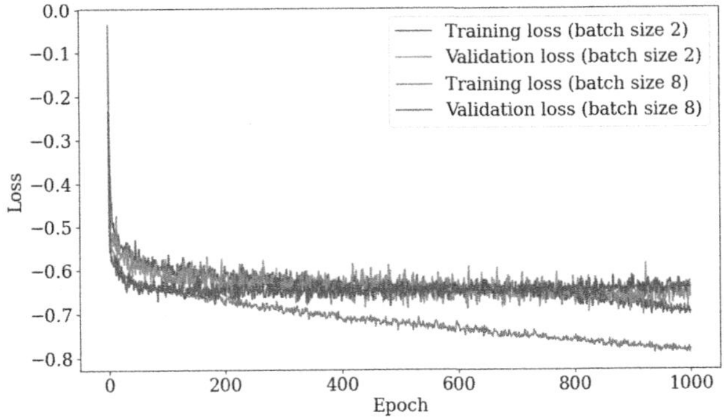

Fig. 3. Loss curves obtained when training our pipeline with different batch sizes.

Table 3. Pipeline performance with different augmentations, batch sizes, and spacings. Metrics are averaged over the internal validation set of each fold, with mean ± standard deviation and fold-wise minimum and maximum in brackets.

Augmentations used for training and inference	Batch size	Spacing	GTVp Dice Score (%)	GTVn Aggregated Dice Score (%)	GTVn Aggregated F1-score (%)
nnU-Net default	8	Median	72.59 ± 1.47 [70.77, 75.1]	76.70 ± 0.67 [75.43, 77.25]	**61.54** ± 3.41 [57.76, 66.44]
Custom	2	Median	**74.70** ± 0.89 [73.77, 76.30]	**77.30** ± 1.00 [75.91, 78.84]	58.68 ± 5.90 [47.72, 64.95]
Custom	2	Isotropic 1mm	73.14 ± 2.0 [69.19, 74.47]	74.57 ± 4.4 [65.81, 77.59]	51.98 ± 15.78 [20.66, 63.48]

The effect of voxel spacing on model performance was benchmarked using a similar pipeline from our first validation-phase submission, which applied the nnU-Net CT normalization scheme to the PET scans, with a batch size of two instead of eight and with our custom augmentations. Motivated by previous work [10,12] reporting the use of an isotropic 1 mm resolution, we investigated resampling each CT scan to a 1 mm isotropic resolution, followed by resampling the corresponding PET and mask to this new CT resolution as a preprocessing. In this experiment, models were trained on isotropic 1 mm volumes, and at inference, the predicted masks were resampled back to the original CT resolution using nearest-neighbor interpolation. Table 3 summarizes the performance of the pipeline under both settings, averaged across folds. It can be seen that a model trained using the median CT spacing performs consistently better across the different metrics than a model whose inputs were resampled to a 1mm isotropic spacing.

Clipping. As part of the ablation study, different empirically defined clipping boundaries for PET normalization were evaluated: [0–5], [0–8], [0–10], and [0–15]. These experiments were conducted using the custom augmentations described in Sect. 2.3 and a batch size of two. Table 4 reports the performance on the internal validation set of each fold, averaged across the five folds. A clear trend was observed for the GTVp Dice score: a stronger clipping consistently reduced the average performance. For the GTVn metrics, no consistent trend emerged; however, custom clipping with lower maximum boundaries than the 99.5th percentile appeared to improve the segmentation performance. Considering the trade-off between GTVp and GTVn performance, the [0–15] clipping range was selected for submission to the test phase.

Table 4. Pipeline performance using nnU-Net CT normalization for PET with different clipping boundaries. Metrics are first average over all patients in the internal validation set of each fold then averaged across folds and are reported as mean ± standard deviation [minimum, maximum fold value].

Clipping boundaries	GTVp Dice Score (%)	GTVn Aggregated Dice Score (%)	GTVn Aggregated F1-score (%)
[0, 5]	74.43 ± 1.53 [72.67, 76.47]	**77.61** ± 1.05 [75.73, 78.66]	61.07 ± 6.27 [48.99, 66.89]
[0, 8]	74.69 ± 1.19 [72.79, 76.34]	77.14 ± 0.92 [75.5, 78.05]	59.36 ± 4.62 [51.51, 65.92]
[0, 10]	74.71 ± 1.33 [73.02, 76.06]	77.51 ± 0.73 [76.4, 78.46]	**61.88** ± 6.37 [50.72, 68.58]
[0, 15]	**74.80** ± 0.96 [73.26, 75.81]	77.54 ± 1.07 [75.62, 78.65]	61.49 ± 6.74 [49.02, 68.84]
[0.81, 22.66] (0.5, 99.5 percentile)	74.70 ± 0.89 [73.77, 76.3]	77.30 ± 1.00 [75.91, 78.84]	58.68 ± 5.9 [47.72, 64.95]

Model Architecture. The final pipeline parameter evaluated was the model architecture. Both the Residual Encoder U-Net and the plain convolutional U-Net described in Sect. 2.3 were trained using the configuration detailed in Sect. 2. Table 5 summarizes the performance of the two architectures. Although the Residual Encoder U-Net resulted in a slight decrease in the average GTVp Dice score which went from 74.80% to 74.22%, it yielded improvements in the GTVn metrics. In particular, the aggregated F1-score increased from 61.49% to 63.59%, identifying the Residual Encoder U-Net as the stronger candidate for our test-phase submission.

Table 5. Pipeline performance with different model architectures. Results are first average over all patients in the internal validation set of each fold then averaged across folds and are reported as mean ± standard deviation [minimum, maximum fold value].

Model architecture	GTVp Dice Score (%)	GTVn Aggregated Dice Score (%)	GTVn Aggregated F1-score (%)
Plain Convolutional U-Net	**74.80** ± 0.96 [73.26, 75.81]	77.54 ± 1.07 [75.62, 78.65]	61.49 ± 6.74 [49.02, 68.84]
Residual Encoder U-Net	74.22 ± 1.55 [72.18, 76.56]	**78.18** ± 1.0 [76.94, 79.6]	**63.59** ± 4.83 [55.93, 69.83]

5 Discussion

This study presents a pipeline submitted to the HECKTOR 2025 challenge for the automatic segmentation of primary tumor volumes and lymph nodes from CT and PET scans. We empirically evaluated various training strategies to identify those that improve segmentation performance. In particular, clipping, voxel spacing, batch size, and model architecture were found to have a substantial impact on the overall segmentation performance.

The learning rate was kept constant across experiments with different batch sizes, and the number of iterations per epoch was identical in all settings. Increasing the learning rate for a batch size of eight could potentially enhance the exploratory capacity of training and reduce the overfitting observed, thereby providing a more reliable comparison between batch sizes.

Our experiments indicate that resampling to 1 mm isotropic resolution does not improve performance, in contrast to the approach reported by [10]. A possible explanation is that the initial resampling excessively increased the PET resolution relative to the original spacing along the z-axis, which may have hindered effective feature learning during training.

The proposed segmentation task exhibits substantial variability across data splits, as reflected by the wide range of fold-wise performance metrics. This variability may explain why ensembling numerous models, as performed by the HECKTOR 2022 winning team [10], is beneficial for improving performance. Moreover, the challenge test set appears to differ from the validation data distribution, since improvements observed in our ablation study did not translate into higher performance on the test set.

A notable finding from our ablations is that preprocessing and architectural choices affect GTVp and GTVn segmentation differently. Strategies that improved GTVn performance often reduced GTVp accuracy, and vice versa, reflecting the distinct imaging characteristics of lymph nodes and primary tumors. Clinically, this suggests that model design should be aligned with the priorities of the intended application. Workflows where comprehensive nodal detection is critical may favor configurations optimized for GTVn sensitivity, whereas treatment planning requiring precise primary tumor boundaries may benefit from settings tuned for GTVp accuracy.

Acknowledgments. This work was supported by the Canada Research Chair Program (grant #252136) and partly supported by Mitacs through the Mitacs Accelerate program. This research was partly enabled by support provided by Calcul Quebec https://www.calculquebec.ca/en/ and the Digital Research Alliance of Canada https://alliancecan.ca/. Deep learning models were trained on the Narval cluster. We thank Yujing Zou for valuable discussions.

Disclosure of Interests. The authors have no competing interests to declare that are relevant to the content of this article.

References

1. HEad and neCK TumOR Lesion Segmentation, Diagnosis and Prognosis - Grand Challenge. https://hecktor25.grand-challenge.org/
2. Bogowicz, M., et al.: Comparison of PET and CT radiomics for prediction of local tumor control in head and neck squamous cell carcinoma. Acta Oncol. **56**(11), 1531–1536 (2017). https://doi.org/10.1080/0284186X.2017.1346382.https://medicaljournalssweden.se/actaoncologica/article/view/25070
3. Caldarella, C., et al.: Role of 18f-FDG PET/CT in head and neck squamous cell carcinoma: current evidence and innovative applications. Cancers **16**(10) (2024). https://doi.org/10.3390/cancers16101905. https://www.mdpi.com/2072-6694/16/10/1905
4. Castelli, J., et al.: A PET-based nomogram for oropharyngeal cancers. Eur. J. Cancer **75**, 222–230 (2017). https://doi.org/10.1016/j.ejca.2017.01.018. https://linkinghub.elsevier.com/retrieve/pii/S095980491730076X
5. He, K., Zhang, X., Ren, S., Sun, J.: Deep residual learning for image recognition. In: Proceedings of the IEEE Conference on Computer Vision and Pattern Recognition (CVPR) (2016)
6. Isensee, F., Jaeger, P.F., Kohl, S.A.A., Petersen, J., Maier-Hein, K.H.: nnU-Net: a self-configuring method for deep learning-based biomedical image segmentation. Nat. Methods **18**(2), 203–211 (2021). https://doi.org/10.1038/s41592-020-01008-z. https://www.nature.com/articles/s41592-020-01008-z
7. Isensee, F., et al.: nnu-Net revisited: a call for rigorous validation in 3d medical image segmentation. arXiv preprint arXiv:2404.09556 (2024)
8. Kumar, N., Verma, R., Sharma, S., Bhargava, S., Vahadane, A., Sethi, A.: A dataset and a technique for generalized nuclear segmentation for computational pathology. IEEE Trans. Med. Imaging **36**(7), 1550–1560 (2017). https://doi.org/10.1109/TMI.2017.2677499
9. Lowekamp, B.C., Chen, D.T., Ibáñez, L., Blezek, D.: The Design of SimpleITK. Front. Neuroinform. **7**, 45 (2013). https://doi.org/10.3389/fninf.2013.00045
10. Myronenko, A., Siddiquee, M.M.R., Yang, D., He, Y., Xu, D.: Automated head and neck tumor segmentation from 3D PET/CT Hecktor 2022 challenge report. In: Andrearczyk, V., Oreiller, V., Hatt, M., Depeursinge, A. (eds.) Head and Neck Tumor Segmentation and Outcome Prediction, pp. 31–37. Springer, Cham (2023)
11. Saeed, N., et al.: A multimodal and multi-centric head and neck cancer dataset for segmentation, diagnosis, and outcome prediction (2025). https://arxiv.org/abs/2509.00367

12. Sun, X., An, C., Wang, L.: A coarse-to-fine ensembling framework for head and neck tumor and lymph segmentation in CT and PET images. In: Andrearczyk, V., Oreiller, V., Hatt, M., Depeursinge, A. (eds.) Head and Neck Tumor Segmentation and Outcome Prediction, pp. 38–46. Springer, Cham (2023)
13. Vallières, M., et al.: Radiomics strategies for risk assessment of tumour failure in head-and-neck cancer. Sci. Rep. **7**(1), 10117 (2017). https://doi.org/10.1038/s41598-017-10371-5. https://www.nature.com/articles/s41598-017-10371-5

Head-and-Neck PET/CT Lesion Segmentation via SSIMH and SegResNet

Shuai Huang, Yuqi Cheng, Shilin Yu, and Hongtu Zhu(✉)

University of North Carolina at Chapel Hill, Chapel Hill, NC, USA
{shuaishu,htzhu}@email.unc.edu, {yuqic,shiliny}@unc.edu

Abstract. We present a simple and effective pipeline for automatic detection and segmentation of primary tumors and lymph nodes in FDG-PET/CT for HECKTOR 2025 Task 1. The method starts with an anatomy-aware pre-crop of the head-and-neck region to suppress irrelevant context, followed by modality-specific intensity normalization with soft clamping. To mitigate cross-center domain shift, we apply single-subject, SSIM-guided spectrum swapping (SSIMH) on CT in the frequency domain without external references. For segmentation, we use a residual U-Net–style SegResNet with deep supervision and a combined Dice + Cross-Entropy loss. Training employs stratified five-fold cross-validation with foreground-centered sampling to emphasize small lesions. At inference, we use sliding-window tiling on the cropped volumes, lightweight post-processing to remove small isolated components, and a five-model ensemble by averaging per-voxel logits before softmax. On the official HECKTOR 2025 evaluation, our pipeline provides a concise and reproducible baseline for multi-center PET/CT tumor and lymph-node segmentation under domain shift. The overall recipe is concise and reproducible, providing a strong and transparent baseline for multi-center head-and-neck PET/CT segmentation under domain shift. (Team name: BIGS2)

Keywords: HECKTOR 2025 · Head and neck cancer · PET/CT segmentation · Domain adaptation · SegResNet

1 Introduction and Task Motivation

Head and neck (H&N) cancers remain a major global burden and are prone to loco-regional failure despite modern therapy [1–3]. PET captures glycolytic activity while CT provides anatomy; their complementarity is crucial for accurate delineation of primary tumors and nodal disease [4]. HECKTOR 2025 extends prior editions with a larger, multi-center cohort ($>$1200 patients across $\geq$11 centers) and refined metrics that emphasize both segmentation quality and *lesion detection* [5,7]. Task 1 targets fully automatic detection and segmentation of the primary tumor (GTVp) and metastatic lymph nodes (GTVn) on pre-treatment FDG-PET/CT, with evaluation combining instance-aware aggregated

N. Saeed et al. (Eds.): HECKTOR 2026, LNCS 16520, pp. 37–46, 2026.
https://doi.org/10.1007/978-3-032-25766-6_4

Dice (DSC_{agg}) and lesion-level F1 at IoU > 0.3 to reward methods that both *find* and *delineate* multiple lesions [6,7]. Standardized nomenclature (AAPM TG-263) ensures consistency and clinical interoperability [7].

2 Data Description

The dataset comprises paired pre-treatment FDG-PET and low-dose, non-contrast-enhanced CT for each case, collected on combined PET/CT systems from multiple centers [4,5]. Expert-drawn voxel-wise annotations provide a single label map with three classes: background (0), GTVp (1), and GTVn (2), following harmonized guidelines and centralized quality control; TG-263 naming (*GTVp*, *GTVn*) is adopted [7]. By design, imaging-defined targets may include contourable GTVn even when TNM reports N0, reflecting clinical practice in radiotherapy planning. The expanded 2025 cohort increases diversity and statistical power for benchmarking multimodal, multi-lesion segmentation under realistic domain shifts [5,7]. The dataset builds upon previous HECKTOR editions [4,5] and is now released as a unified multi-centric PET/CT resource [10].

3 Methods

3.1 Pre-processing

Data Preparation. We first resample both CT and PET volumes to an isotropic resolution of $1\times1\times1$ mm and register them to a common voxel grid. To restrict the input to the clinically relevant head-and-neck (H&N) field-of-view while keeping the procedure fully automatic, we adopt a simple anatomy-aware cropping strategy: (i) detect the superior head boundary by applying a coarse PET threshold to locate metabolically active cranial tissue; (ii) estimate a 2D H&N center in the axial plane from the average foreground mask across superior slices; and (iii) extract a fixed-size $200\times200\times310$ mm bounding box centered at this point. In practice, this deterministic crop consistently covers the full H&N region across the training cohort while reducing the typical volume size from $\sim500\times500\times900$ to $200\times200\times310$ voxels and eliminating irrelevant anatomy such as the thorax and couch.

Data Normalization. After spatial standardization, we normalize CT and PET independently and then concatenate them into a 2-channel input (CT, PET):

- CT: intensities are linearly mapped from a predefined HU window to [0,1] and then passed through a sigmoid nonlinearity, which softly clamps outliers while preserving local contrast.
- PET: values are standardized to zero mean and unit variance across the cropped volume and similarly transformed by a sigmoid to dampen extreme uptake values.

This modality-specific normalization stabilizes optimization across centers and scanners while maintaining the relative CT/PET contrast that is crucial for joint tumor and lymph-node delineation (Fig. 1).

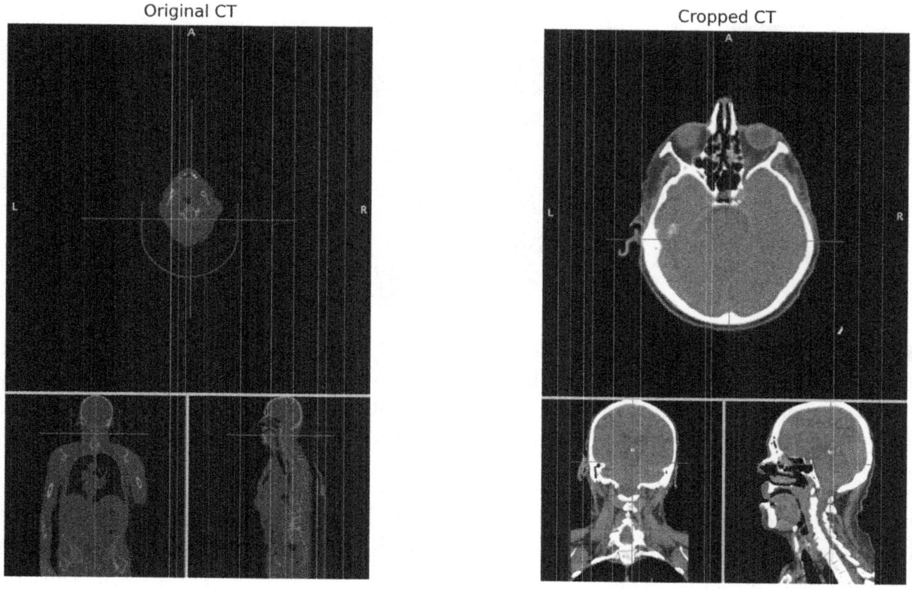

Fig. 1. Example of the pre-processing pipeline on a CHUM case. Left: original CT in scanner coordinates. Right: standardized head-and-neck crop after resampling to 1 mm isotropic spacing. The crop removes irrelevant anatomy while preserving the full tumor and nodal extent.

Domain Adaptation via SSIMH. To mitigate inter-center appearance shifts, we adopt the Spectrum Swapping-based Image-level Harmonization (SSIMH) method [8,9]. SSIMH operates in the frequency domain: given a source CT volume X_s and a reference (target) CT volume X_t, we compute their discrete cosine transforms (DCT), $F_s = \mathrm{DCT}(X_s)$ and $F_t = \mathrm{DCT}(X_t)$. Let $\Omega_{\mathrm{LF}}(\tau)$ denote the low-frequency band defined by a radius (threshold) τ; SSIMH replaces the source low-frequency coefficients with those of the reference,

$$F'_s[\Omega_{\mathrm{LF}}(\tau)] \leftarrow F_t[\Omega_{\mathrm{LF}}(\tau)], \quad X'_s = \mathrm{IDCT}(F'_s),$$

thereby transferring scanner/site-specific intensity/style while preserving high-frequency anatomical detail [8]. In practice, we apply SSIMH *slice-wise* with a 2D DCT on axial slices for efficiency and robustness [9]. Unless otherwise specified, we use the toolbox default $\tau = 3$ for the swapped low-frequency region. SSIMH is training-free and is executed after cropping but before normalizations; PET is left unchanged.

A qualitative example of SSIMH is shown in Fig. 2, demonstrating that low-frequency scanner/style statistics are aligned to the reference while anatomical high-frequency structures remain preserved.

Reference Strategy. We fix a single reference subject from the training cohort and adapt each source CT to this reference (*one-to-one* harmonization). For scenarios

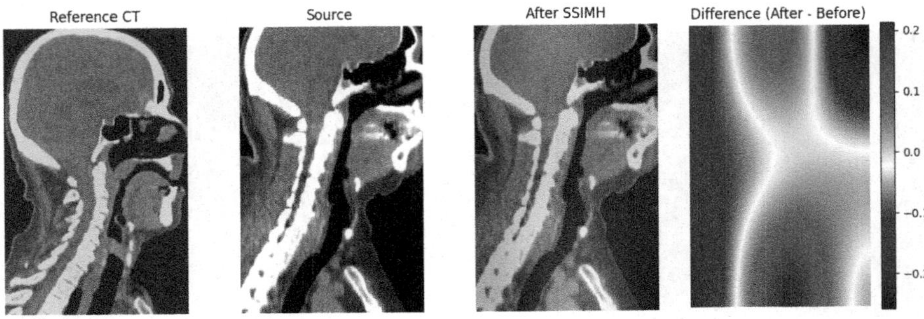

Fig. 2. SSIMH harmonization example. (CHUP-000) From left to right: (1) reference CT, (2) source CT before harmonization, (3) source CT after SSIMH, (4) intensity difference map (after – before). SSIMH selectively transfers low-frequency scanner/site appearance while preserving anatomical structures.

with multiple incoming scans per site, SSIMH also supports *batch* harmonization by adapting all source scans to a chosen site/template reference [9]. This yields a consistent intensity/style space across centers while leaving structural contrast largely intact.

Notes. (1) SSIMH is conceptually different from SSIM-guided histogram matching; our implementation follows frequency-domain spectrum swapping. (2) We clip X_s' to valid HU ranges and retain original voxel spacing/geometry so downstream resampling and segmentation are unaffected.

3.2 Network and Training

Architecture. We use SegResNet (residual U-Net) from MONAI as the backbone, with encoder–decoder residual blocks and deep supervision on decoder scales.

Patch Sampling. From each pre-cropped H&N volume, we sample 192×192×192 voxel patches. Sampling is biased toward lesions to emphasize detection:

- probability 0.45 to center on primary tumor,
- probability 0.45 to center on lymph nodes,
- probability 0.10 to sample background.

Data Augmentation. We apply spatial augmentations to both CT and PET: random affine transforms and random flips along all axes. For CT only, we apply intensity augmentations (random scale, shift, Gaussian noise, and blur). PET intensities are not perturbed.

Objective and Optimization. The training loss is Dice + Cross-Entropy computed at the main output and summed over all deep-supervision heads. Optimization uses standard stochastic gradient descent variants (e.g., Adam/AdamW) with cosine or step-decay scheduling; exact hyper-parameters are provided in code (omitted here for brevity).

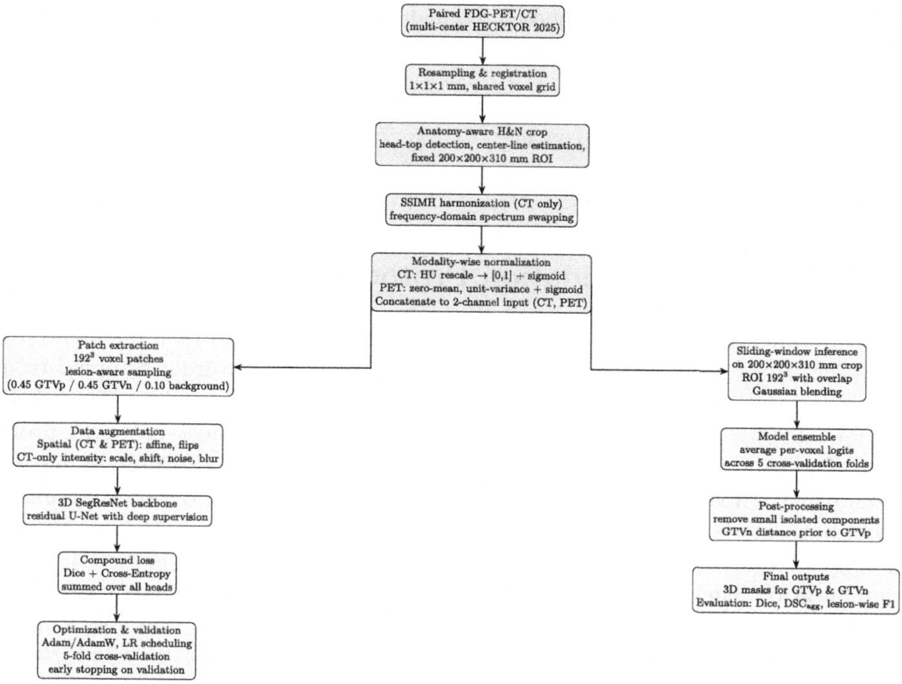

Fig. 3. Overview of the proposed pipeline for HECKTOR 2025 Task 1: shared pre-processing (blue), training pipeline (green), and inference/ensemble with post-processing (orange). (Color figure online)

Cross-validation protocol. We perform 5-fold cross-validation with stratification by center and lesion presence where possible. Model selection is based on mean validation performance over folds. The final submission can be an ensemble (averaging logits) across the five fold-specific models (Fig. 3).

4 Inference and Post-processing

At inference, we run sliding-window evaluation on the 200×200×310 mm crop using ROI size 192×192×192 with overlap and Gaussian blending. We take argmax over classes to obtain labels. We apply minimal post-processing: (i) connected-component "island" removal for both classes, discarding components smaller than a voxel-count threshold; and (ii) a distance-based prior on lymph nodes. Specifically, we compute a 3D Euclidean distance transform of the predicted GTVp and remove any GTVn component whose minimum surface-to-surface distance to GTVp exceeds a fixed threshold. This suppresses anatomically implausible, isolated node predictions far from the primary tumor while preserving contiguous or nearby nodal disease. No test-time augmentation is used unless specified.

Table 1. Performance of the proposed method on the internal validation split and the official HECKTOR 2025 Task 1 test set.

Split	GTVp Dice ↑	DSC_{agg} ↑	GTVn Lesion-F1 ↑
Validation (BIGS2)	0.8393	0.7657	0.5455
Test (BIGS2)	0.5779	0.5280	0.3207

5 Training and Validation Protocol

All experiments were conducted using the MONAI framework implemented in PyTorch. Prior to model training, CT and PET volumes were resampled to an isotropic resolution of 1 mm and cropped to a standardized head-and-neck field-of-view of $200 \times 200 \times 310$ mm using the official HECKTOR neck-cropping procedure. To mitigate inter-center variability, CT volumes were additionally harmonized using SSIM-guided spectrum swapping (SSIMH) in the frequency domain, while both modalities were normalized using a sigmoidal intensity transform.

We adopted the 3D SegResNet architecture with deep supervision as the segmentation backbone. Training samples were generated by extracting 192^3 voxel patches according to a lesion-aware sampling strategy that oversamples tumor regions and challenging hard negatives (probabilities: 0.45/0.45/0.10). Data augmentation included spatial transformations applied to both CT and PET (random affine, elastic deformation, and flipping), supplemented with CT-specific intensity perturbations to reflect modality characteristics. Optimization was performed using a compound loss combining Dice and Cross-Entropy terms summed across all supervision scales.

Model development followed a 5-fold cross-validation scheme, with early stopping based on the validation loss to prevent overfitting. Consistent with the HECKTOR 2025 evaluation protocol, model performance was assessed using lesion-wise detection F1 score, Dice similarity coefficient for primary tumors and lymph nodes, surface-distance–based measures, and the aggregated Dice (DSC_{agg}) computed across all predicted lesions.

6 Results

Table 1 summarizes our performance on the internal validation split and the official HECKTOR 2025 Task 1 test set. On validation, we obtained a GTVp Dice of 0.8393, a GTVn aggregated Dice of $DSC_{agg} = 0.7657$, and a GTVn aggregated lesion-wise F1 of 0.5455. Unless otherwise noted, all metrics were computed after sliding-window inference on the standardized $200 \times 200 \times 310$ mm head-and-neck crop with minimal post-processing and five-fold logit ensembling.

On the official test set, the same pipeline achieved a GTVp Dice of 0.5779, $DSC_{agg} = 0.5280$, and a GTVn lesion-wise F1 of 0.3207, indicating a pronounced validation–test gap particularly for lymph-node detection.

Figure 4 summarizes the validation–test gap for the three challenge metrics, highlighting the impact of domain shift on lymph-node detection.

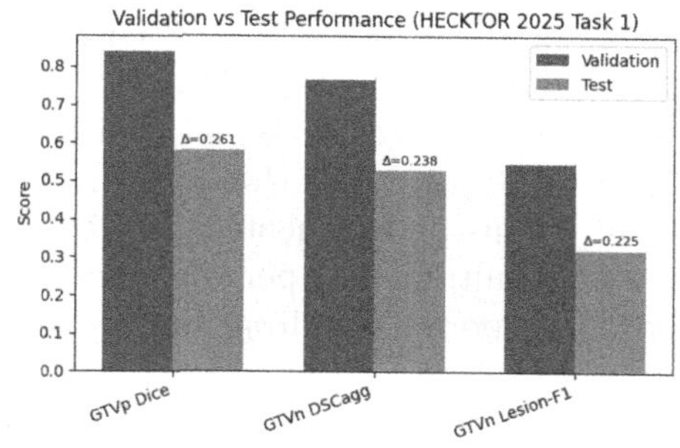

Fig. 4. Comparison of validation and test performance on HECKTOR 2025 Task 1.

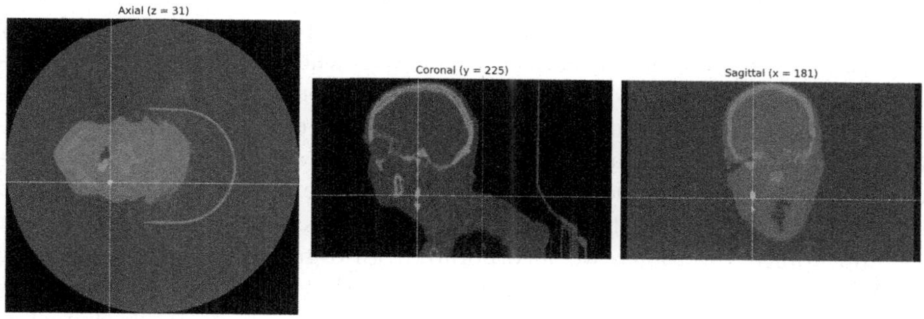

Fig. 5. Qualitative prediction example on case CHUM-001. The triplanar visualization overlays the predicted segmentation (red: GTVp, green: GTVn) onto the original CT volume. The model delineates the primary tumor clearly, while small, isolated nodal regions remain challenging. (Color figure online)

In addition to the quantitative metrics, Fig. 5 provides a qualitative visualization on a representative CHUM case. The triplanar view suggests that the model can localize both the primary tumor and involved lymph nodes, while most failure modes occur in small or low-uptake nodal regions, consistent with the drop in lesion-wise F1 under domain shift.

7 Discussion and Interpretation

The primary tumor (GTVp) Dice of 0.8393 reflects accurate voxel-wise delineation in metabolically and morphologically conspicuous regions, where the joint PET uptake pattern and CT anatomy provide consistent cues for boundary localization. For lymph nodes (GTVn), the aggregated Dice of 0.7657 indicates good overlap quality once nodal lesions are detected, whereas the aggregated lesion-wise F1 of 0.5455 highlights residual challenges in identifying small, scattered, or low-contrast nodal metastases. This discrepancy—relatively strong voxel-wise overlap but weaker lesion-level detection—is expected in multi-lesion head-and-neck PET/CT, where nodal disease often appears as multiple small instances with heterogeneous uptake and subtle anatomical contrast, and can be easily missed or confused with physiologic uptake. Moreover, the HECKTOR 2025 Task 1 evaluation explicitly emphasizes instance awareness through aggregated Dice and lesion-wise F1 at an IoU threshold (IoU >0.3), which is inherently more sensitive to missed small lesions or fragmented predictions than conventional voxel-wise Dice alone. As a result, modest per-voxel errors or slight localization shifts can translate into disproportionate drops in lesion-level scores, especially for tiny nodal targets. [5,7]

The pronounced validation–test gap further suggests a non-trivial multi-center domain shift, a known issue in medical imaging benchmarks where acquisition protocols, scanner vendors, reconstruction parameters, and site-specific intensity characteristics vary across institutions. Such shifts can alter low-frequency appearance statistics and noise/texture patterns in CT, and may indirectly affect multimodal feature fusion even when PET remains informative, thereby impairing generalization to unseen centers. [5,11,12] Our anatomy-aware crop and lesion-aware sampling likely improved optimization by focusing capacity on the clinically relevant field-of-view and by repeatedly exposing the model to foreground and hard-negative contexts, which benefits GTVp delineation and stabilizes training for sparse targets. To mitigate cross-center CT appearance variations, we incorporated SSIM-guided spectrum swapping (SSIMH), an image-level harmonization strategy that operates in the frequency domain by replacing low-frequency components to align scanner/style characteristics while preserving high-frequency anatomical structures. [8] This design is intended to reduce site-dependent intensity/style discrepancies without requiring target-domain labels or additional training. Nevertheless, lesion discovery—particularly for small nodes with weak uptake or ambiguous morphology—remains the dominant bottleneck reflected by lesion-wise F1. Future improvements may therefore prioritize strategies that explicitly target nodal recall and calibration under domain shift (e.g., stronger hard-negative mining and false-positive control, uncertainty-aware filtering, or cascaded detection-and-segmentation), while maintaining the transparency and reproducibility of the current pipeline.

8 Limitations and Future Work

First, our deterministic fixed-size cropping strategy, while robust in most cases, may be sub-optimal for extreme anatomies or scans where the primary tumor or nodal disease extends close to the superior or inferior bounds of the field-of-view. Misses near volume boundaries can be particularly costly under instance-aware evaluation, motivating adaptive or anatomy-conditioned cropping (e.g., landmark- or organ-guided ROIs) to better accommodate outlier cases.

Second, SSIMH is applied with a single fixed reference subject, which may not fully represent the diversity of acquisition protocols and scanner characteristics across centers. Although SSIMH aims to align low-frequency appearance statistics while preserving high-frequency anatomical structures, a single-reference strategy can introduce reference bias or underfit certain domains. Multi-reference or center-aware reference selection, as well as lightweight on-the-fly reference updates, could improve robustness without sacrificing structural fidelity.

Third, the pronounced drop in GTVn lesion-wise F1 from validation to test indicates that lesion-level detection for small nodes remains the main limitation. This is consistent with the HECKTOR 2025 Task 1 emphasis on lesion discovery (lesion-wise F1 at IoU > 0.3) in addition to overlap-based scores, where small, low-uptake, or fragmented nodal predictions are penalized more strongly than by voxel-wise Dice alone. Future work will therefore focus on improving nodal recall while controlling false positives, for example via hard-negative mining, cascaded detection-and-segmentation schemes, and uncertainty-aware filtering or score calibration at inference.

Finally, we have not explored test-time augmentation, more advanced ensembling strategies, or foundation-model initialization tailored to PET/CT, all of which may further enhance generalization in multi-center settings.

9 Conclusion

We presented a compact and reproducible baseline for HECKTOR 2025 Task 1 that combines a MONAI SegResNet backbone with anatomy-aware pre-processing and SSIMH-based CT harmonization. The pipeline is intentionally simple—standardized resampling and head-and-neck cropping, frequency-domain CT harmonization, modality-specific normalization, lesion-aware patch sampling, and a five-model logit ensemble with minimal post-processing—yet provides a transparent reference recipe for multi-center PET/CT tumor and lymph-node segmentation under domain shift.

On the official HECKTOR 2025 test set, the method achieved a GTVp Dice of 0.5779, a GTVn aggregated Dice of $\text{DSC}_{\text{agg}} = 0.5280$, and a GTVn aggregated lesion-wise F1 of 0.3207. These results suggest that voxel-level delineation of primary tumors is feasible with a streamlined approach, while lesion-level detection of small lymph nodes remains the key challenge. We release this pipeline as an easily reproducible baseline to support future work on robust head-and-neck PET/CT segmentation and domain adaptation in large multi-center cohorts.

References

1. Parkin, D.M., Bray, F., Ferlay, J., Pisani, P.: Global cancer statistics, 2002. CA Cancer J. Clin. **55**(2), 74–108 (2005). https://doi.org/10.3322/canjclin.55.2.74
2. Bonner, J.A., Harari, P.M., Giralt, J., et al.: Radiotherapy plus cetuximab for locoregionally advanced head and neck cancer: 5-year survival data from a phase 3 randomised trial, and relation between cetuximab-induced rash and survival. Lancet Oncol. **11**(1), 21–28 (2010). https://doi.org/10.1016/S1470-2045(09)70311-0
3. Chajon, E., Lafond, C., Louvel, G., et al.: Salivary gland-sparing other than parotid-sparing in definitive head-and-neck intensity-modulated radiotherapy does not seem to jeopardize local control. Radiat. Oncol. **8**, 132 (2013). https://doi.org/10.1186/1748-717X-8-132

4. Oreiller, V., Andrearczyk, V., Jreige, M., et al.: Head and neck tumor segmentation in PET/CT: the HECKTOR challenge. Med. Image Anal. **77**, 102336 (2022). https://doi.org/10.1016/j.media.2021.102336
5. Andrearczyk, V., Oreiller, V., Abobakr, M., et al.: Overview of the HECKTOR challenge at MICCAI 2022: automatic head and neck tumor segmentation and outcome prediction in PET/CT. In: Andrearczyk, V., Oreiller, V., Hatt, M., Depeursinge, A. (eds.) HECKTOR 2022, LNCS, vol. 13626, pp. 1–30. Springer, Cham (2023). https://doi.org/10.1007/978-3-031-27420-6_1
6. Kumar, N., Verma, R., Anand, D., et al.: A multi-organ nucleus segmentation challenge. IEEE Trans. Med. Imaging **39**(5), 1380–1391 (2020). https://doi.org/10.1109/TMI.2019.2947628
7. HECKTOR Challenge Homepage. https://hecktor.grand-challenge.org/, Accessed 12 Sep 2025
8. Guan, H., Liu, S., Lin, W., Yap, P.-T., Liu, M.: Fast image-level MRI harmonization via spectrum analysis. In: Machine Learning in Medical Imaging (MLMI) 2022, LNCS, vol. 13583, pp. 201–209. Springer, Cham (2022). https://doi.org/10.1007/978-3-031-21014-3_21
9. Guan, H., Liu, M.: Domain adaptation toolbox for medical data analysis. Neuroimage **268**, 119863 (2023). https://doi.org/10.1016/j.neuroimage.2023.119863
10. Saeed, N., et al.: A Multimodal and Multi-centric Head and Neck Cancer (2025). Dataset for Segmentation, Diagnosis, and Outcome Prediction
11. Hu, F., et al.: Image harmonization: a review of statistical and deep learning methods for removing batch effects and evaluation metrics for effective harmonization. Neuroimage **274**, 120125 (2023). https://doi.org/10.1016/j.neuroimage.2023.120125
12. Mali, S.A., et al.: Making Radiomics More Reproducible across scanner and imaging protocol variations: a review of harmonization Methods. J. Pers. Med. **11**(9), 842 (2021). https://doi.org/10.3390/jpm11090842

Multi-phase Mandible-Anchored Automated Segmentation of Oropharyngeal GTVs in FDG-PET/CT

Dominic Labella[1(✉)], Keshav Jha[2], Kevin Goff[1], Esther Yu[1], and Jared Robbins[1]

[1] Department of Radiation Oncology, Duke University Medical Center, Durham, NC 27710, USA
dominic.labella@duke.edu
[2] Duke University, Durham, NC 27710, USA

Abstract. Accurate delineation of gross tumor volumes (GTVs) in oropharyngeal carcinoma remains central to radiotherapy (RT) planning, and recent advances in automated segmentation are beginning to influence multi-ple aspects of clinical workflow. However, automated segmentation of head and neck primary tumors and nodal metastases in multi-modal FDG-PET/CT is challenging due to anatomical complexity and varying image resolution. We describe the DLaBella29 team's approach for Task 1 of the MICCAI 2025 HECKTOR challenge, which involves a multi-phase deep learning pipeline for GTVp and GTVn segmentation. Our method leverages the MONAI Auto3DSeg framework with a 3D SegResNet backbone, trained on co-registered PET/CT scans using a cross-validation strategy (3/7/15 folds across Phases). Key innova-tions include a mandible-anchored region-of-interest cropping strategy derived from automated mandible segmentation to focus the model on the oropharyngeal region and improve efficiency. A multi-phase seg-mentation pipeline was employed: an initial Phase infers GTVp and GTVn in the focused anatomical region-of-interest, and a second Phase independently refines these predictions. Post-processing ensues to merge GTVp and GTVn outputs to the original image coordinates. On the HECKTOR 2025 test set, our more limited and resource-constrained algorithm achieved a primary tumor Dice Similarity Coefficient (DSC) of 0.5289, an aggregated nodal DSC of 0.6156, and a GTVn detection F1-score of 0.5561, indicating fair performance in the challenge. This paper details the clinical context, methodology, cross-validation and testing results, and the implications of PET/CT-guided automated segmentation for oropharyngeal carcinoma.

Keywords: Oropharyngeal Cancer · FDG-PET/CT · Automated Segmentation · MONAI · Auto3DSeg · SegResNet · Radiotherapy Planning · Dose De-escalation

1 Introduction

Head and neck cancers are a major global health burden, motivating continuous efforts to optimize radiation therapy (RT) effectiveness while minimizing treatment morbidity [1]. Studies have shown that intensity-modulated RT with deliberate organs-at-risk (OAR)

N. Saeed et al. (Eds.): HECKTOR 2026, LNCS 16520, pp. 47–60, 2026.
https://doi.org/10.1007/978-3-032-25766-6_5

sparing techniques achieved toxicity reduction without compromising local control, underscoring the importance of anatomy-guided dose sculpting and target delineation [2–4].

Fludeoxyglucose positron emission tomography (FDG PET) and computed tomography (CT) are now integral across the head and neck cancer (HNC) care continuum, from staging and RT planning to response assessment, and quantitative PET signals have been linked to prognosis and treatment tailoring [5, 6]. PET-derived and CT-derived radiomics features capture complementary aspects of tumor biology relevant to local control modeling; in comparative studies, PET-based models often provide more reliable risk estimates for adverse outcomes [7]. Multi-feature radiomics strategies have also been shown to stratify failure risk in HNC, reinforcing the promise of image-derived biomarkers for individualized therapy [8].

These advances have motivated selective de-escalation strategies in HPV-associated oropharyngeal squamous cell carcinoma (OPSCC), designed to reduce late effects without compromising disease control. Prospective data indicate that thoughtfully implemented de-escalation can maintain excellent oncologic outcomes while improving quality of life [9]. Building on this, a recent phase II trial used mid-treatment FDG-PET response as a biomarker to selectively reduce RT dose in early-stage HPV-positive OPSCC, reporting feasibility with encouraging disease-control and toxicity profiles [10]. Together, these data frame FDG-PET as both a planning tool and a dynamic response indicator to guide patient-specific de-intensification.

Adaptive radiation therapy (ART) provides a paradigm for customized daily radiotherapy. By accommodating day-to-day anatomic and volumetric variation, ART can improve target coverage while reducing dose to OARs which may ultimately improve outcomes [11–13]. ART workflows require frequent on-treatment imaging, deformable mapping, and rapid plan adaptation; their clinical scalability increasingly depends on accurate, automated contouring of both gross tumor volumes (GTVs) and OARs to shorten decision cycles [14]. In this context, daily deep-learning automated segmentation of GTVs, ideally integrated with routine image guidance, could enable response-adapted thresholds and ART triggers while maintaining consistency in normal-tissue delineation [14].

Community challenges have been pivotal in stress-testing these technologies on a large scale. The HEad and neCK TumOR (HECKTOR) series, initiated at MICCAI, standardized multicenter FDG-PET/CT datasets and performed objective evaluation to benchmark automatic tumor segmentation [15, 16]. The MICCAI 2021 edition combined primary-tumor segmentation with progression-free survival prediction, accelerating translation of robust PET/CT pipelines [17]. More recently, HEad and neCK TumOR Lesion Segmentation, Diagnosis and Prognosis Using Multimodal Data Fourth Edition Challenge (HECKTOR25) extends this agenda on the Grand-Challenge platform, focusing on multimodal PET/CT lesion segmentation (including primary and nodal disease) with containerized submissions and standardized metrics to ensure fair, reproducible comparison across methods [15, 16]. This iteration emphasizes clinical applicability through large, multi-institutional data and harmonized evaluation protocols [15, 16].

We present *Multi-Phase Mandible-Anchored Automated Segmentation of Oropharyngeal GTVs in FDG-PET/CT*, an algorithm designed for HECKTOR25 that aims to produce anatomically consistent, high-fidelity delineations suitable for PET-guided de-escalation studies and ART workflows. Using a CT-based mandible segmentation to define a stable oropharyngeal anchor, our approach crops to a biologically and anatomically focused field-of-view; a subsequent multimodal PET/CT model performs joint coarse GTVp and GTVn segmentation, followed by dedicated refinement models for primary and nodal disease, with fusion back to canonical space. This design is intended to: (i) improve localization stability across heterogeneous acquisitions, (ii) reduce silent failure modes in high-complexity neck anatomy, and (iii) furnish daily-ready GTV contours that can be paired with automated OAR delineation to support ART decision-making. The method is implemented with open-source components (MONAI, Auto3DSeg, and SegResNet) and evaluated in the HECKTOR25 framework; methodological details and analyses are provided in the subsequent sects [18, 19].

2 Methods

2.1 Dataset Selection

The training set consisted of co-registered CT and FDG-PET scans from patients with head and neck cancer, with expert contours for the primary gross tumor volume (GTVp) and any pathologic gross lymph nodes (GTVn); the data were provided as part of the HEad and neCK TumOR Lesion Segmentation, Diagnosis and Prognosis Using Multimodal Data Fourth Edition Challenge (HECKTOR25) [15, 16]. Every CT and FDG-PET case included the patient's head and neck within the field of view, and a subset of cases also included the chest, abdomen, and pelvis. All CT and FDG-PET image pairs were already registered, as provided by the challenge, but we resampled all images to a consistent and common sampling of $0.9766 \times 0.9766 \times 1.5$ mm. We preserved the original images origin and direction metadata such that predictions made on resampled and cropped images could be transformed back to the original CT space for submission without loss of spatial correspondence.

Additionally, we generated a synthetic reference standard mandible label for all cases in the training set. The synthetic reference standard mandible label was generated using TotalSegmentator on each case's CT to first segment major anatomical structures, from which we extracted the mandible (jaw bone) mask [20]. TotalSegmentator is a robust, pretrained model capable of segmenting over 100 structures on CT, and upon qualitative review, it provided a reliable mandible label in the training set data [20]. We did not manually modify any mandible label within the training set, as this would have created an unallowable expert annotated private dataset for training, contradictory to challenge rules.

2.2 Mandible Segmentation and Cropping Strategy

A key aspect of our method is focusing the Phase 1 segmentation task on a specific anatomical region-of-interest (aROI) around the mandible-anchor-point, since the oropharyngeal primary tumors in this dataset typically occur in anatomical proximity to the mandible (e.g. tonsillar region, base of tongue) and involved lymph nodes are often in levels II-III of the neck. We therefore hypothesized that using the mandible-anchor-point as a landmark could define a cropped volume that still contains all relevant targets (GTVp and GTVn) while excluding irrelevant areas (e.g. chest, abdomen) that increase complexity and inference time.

To define a reproducible anatomical landmark for Phase 1 cropping, we utilized the aforementioned synthetic mandible label. From this mandible label, we identified the most anterior midline voxel, which corresponds to the anterior symphyseal point of the mandible. This voxel, termed the mandible-anchor-point, was chosen because (i) it is highly consistent across subjects and (ii) it lies immediately anterior to the oropharynx, providing a stable reference for downstream aROI placement.

To ensure that the Phase 1 cropped field-of-view always encompassed the full aROI, we compute, for every training subject, the 3D Euclidean distance between the mandible-anchor-point and the minimum/maximum coordinates of all expert-annotated GTVp and GTVn contours. These distances (left/right, anterior/posterior, cranial/caudal) were aggregated across the 682 training cases. We then selected fixed, symmetric safety margins that exceeded the largest observed GTV extent in each direction. The resulting expansions (Table 1) defined a standardized mandible-anchored aROI that covered all primary tumors and nodal levels II-III without including irrelevant thoracic or abdominal structures.

Table 1. Fixed margin expansions for cropped Phase 1 images from the mandible-anchor-point in the initial resampled uncropped image space. The new aROI was used for Phase 1 training and inference. Note that both -y and + y expansions were in the anatomical posterior direction since no significant amount of GTV were identified anterior to the mandible-anchor-point.

Direction	Distance (voxels)	Distance (mm)
-x (left)	75	73.3
+x (right)	75	73.3
-y (posterior)	143	139.7
+y (anterior)	−23	−22.5
-z (caudal)	72	108
+z (cranial)	52	78

After expansion from the mandible-anchor-point, this aROI was additionally bounded by the case's CT image dimensions to prevent over-expansion to full-sized image out-of-bound regions. Each case's FDG-PET and CT were cropped to this cropped volume, yielding a significantly smaller volume for subsequent processing. An illustration of this mandible-anchored aROI pipeline is provided in Fig. 1, which shows adequate coverage of the primary and nodal tumor regions while excluding unrelated anatomy. Importantly, during inference, we retained the original spatial coordinates of the aROI so that any segmentation outputs could later be placed back into the full image grid at the correct location. This geometry-preserving strategy avoids any misalignment when fusing the final GTVp and GTVn masks into the original coordinate system.

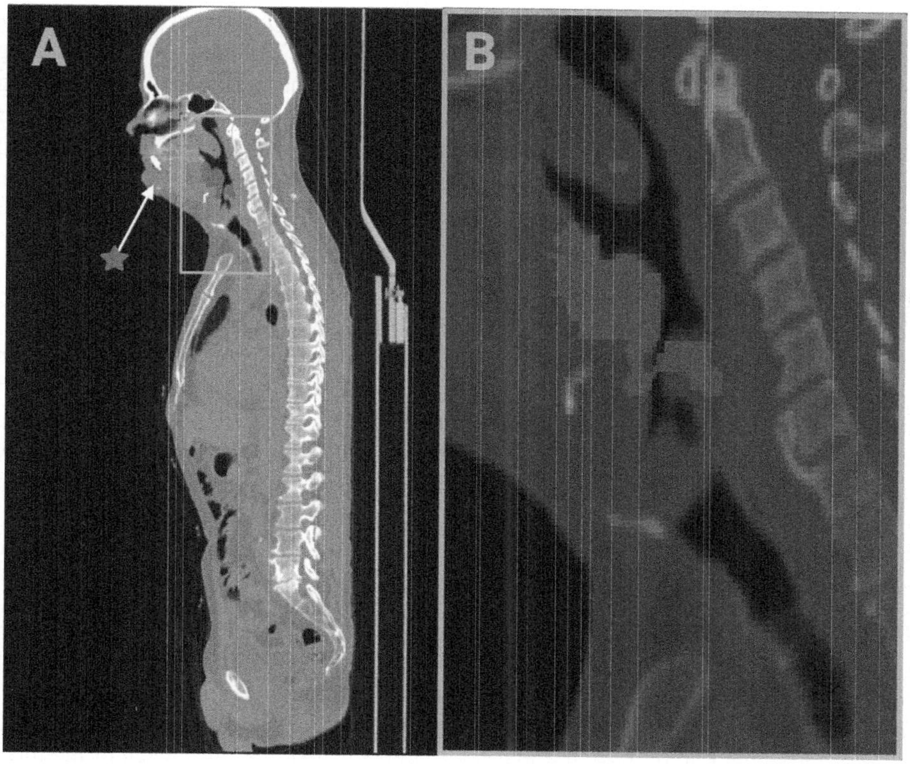

Fig. 1. Mandible-anchored field-of-view selection. (A) Whole-volume sagittal CT (512 × 512 × 568 voxels) resampled to 0.9766 × 0.9766 × 1.5 mm spacing, showing the mandible (purple) and the mandible anchor point (pink star) with expert annotated GTVp (Red) and the mandible-anchored aROI (light-blue box). (B) Corresponding cropped sagittal subvolume (151 × 121 × 125 voxels) centered on the anchor, used for Phase 1 inference.

2.3 Model Architecture, Training, and Inference

We implemented a four-phase Auto3DSeg pipeline using a 3D SegResNet backbone (18,19), that included segmentation of the mandible (Phase 0), coarse segmentation of GTVp and GTVn (Phase 1), and independent refinement stages for GTVp (Phase 2p) and GTVn (Phase 2n). Across all stages, the network used deep supervision with dsdepth of 4, an encoder-decoder with 1–2–2-4-4 convolutional blocks, Dice + Cross-Entropy loss, automatic mixed precision (AMP), AdamW optimization algorithm, and a batch size of 1. Data augmentation included random rotations in 3D, random intensity scaling and random intensity shifting to improve generalization. The CT image served as the canonical reference throughout the pipeline.

All training and inference ran on a single NVIDIA RTX 4090. Table 2 shows varying training parameters and metrics identified during each phase's training. We trained using cross-validation for each phase, and we evaluated performance on the held-out fold using Dice Similarity Coefficient (DSC) for both GTVp and GTVn. The number of folds used for each Phase was determined based on the amount of estimated available training and inference time due to real-world time constraints. Grand-Challenge only allows 10 min for inference for each case using an NVIDIA T4 GPU with 16 GB of available VRAM, of which 8 GB is shared amongst multiple processes [15].

Phase 0: Mandible (One Fold; CT-Only). For the mandible model, we trained a single-fold SegResNet on CT volumes resampled to 3 mm isotropic resolution, using the synthetic reference standard mandible labels. Training used an input tensor spatial dimension region-of-interest (ROI) size of 192 × 192 × 64 voxels for 19 epochs, and with a learning rate of 4e-4. This larger 3 mm resampling was selected due to the ease of mandible segmentation owing to its larger anatomical size and high contrast relative to nearby anatomy. Because the structure served only as an approximate guide for subsequent Phase window placement, no additional training beyond 19 epochs was performed. At inference, the mandible is predicted from the full RAS-canonical CT image, and the anterior mandible voxel is used as an anchor to compute the Phase 1 crop window.

Phase 1: Coarse GTVp + GTVn (3 Folds; CT + PET). For the coarse tumor model (joint GTVp and GTVn), we trained three folds using cross-validation on CT-PET pairs that are resampled to 0.9766 × 0.9766 × 1.5 mm and cropped using the mandible-anchored Phase 1 cropped subvolume, with training ROI size of 128 × 112 × 112 voxels, a learning rate of 4e-4, training for 137 epochs. At inference, each of the three folds is applied to the same RAS-canonical crop and fused with MultiLabel STAPLE to produce a consensus Phase 1 GTVp and GTVn label map in canonical space [21].

Phase 2p: Focused GTVp (15 Folds; CT + PET). For primary tumor refinement, we trained using a dataset including a tight GTVp cropped image by taking the Phase 1 GTVp bounding box and expanding it by 10 mm in x/y/z directions (Fig. 2). We used a ROI size of 48 × 48 × 48 voxels, resampled to 0.9766 × 0.9766 × 1.5 mm, used a learning rate to 2e-4, and trained for 137 epochs. We trained 15 folds using cross-validation, and at inference we ran all fold's models on the focused crop region and fused them with MultiLabel STAPLE; the fused GTVp then replaced the Stage 1 tumor prediction inside the focused region, with tumor label assignment prioritized over surrounding structures, before reintegration onto the full canonical grid.

For nodal refinement, we computed 26-connected components of Stage 1 GTVn, and for each instance GTVn lesion we expanded the bounding box by 10 mm in x/y/z directions (Fig. 3). We then repeated that process for all instance GTVn for each case. We used a ROI size of 48 × 48 × 48 voxels, resampled to 0.9766 × 0.9766 × 1.5 mm, used a learning rate to 2e-4, and trained for 137 epochs. We trained 7 folds using cross-validation, and, at inference, ensembled them with MultiLabel STAPLE per component; nodes were inserted without overriding tumor, and non-confirmed node voxels within the component's aROI were cleared before the result was fused back to the canonical grid.

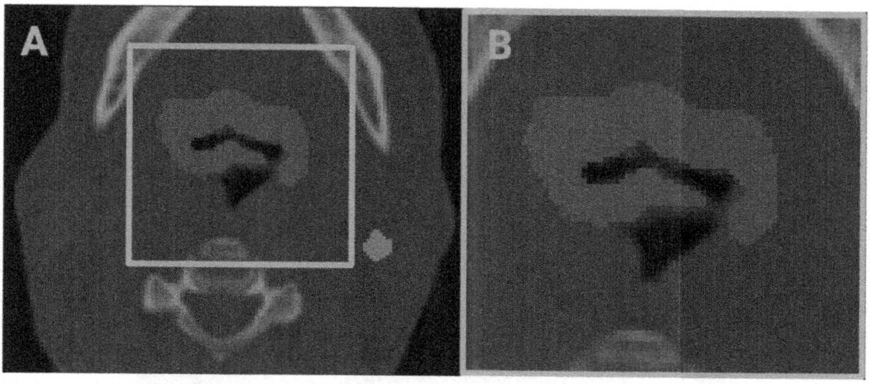

Fig. 2. GTVp-focused field-of-view refinement. Axial CT (A) from the Phase 1 mandible-anchored crop showing expert-annotated GTVp (red) and GTVn (green); the light-blue box denotes the Phase-2p, GTVp-centered aROI. Corresponding cropped axial subvolume (B) restricted to this aROI, generated by applying a 10 mm isotropic expansion to the GTVp bounding boxes, used for Phase 2p inference.

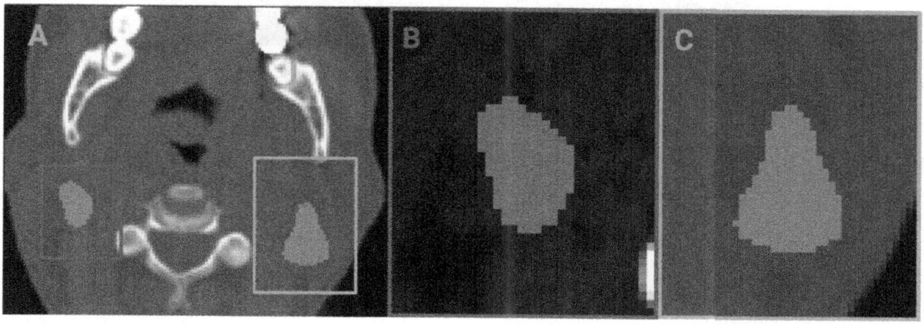

Fig. 3. GTVn-focused field-of-view refinement. Axial CT (A) from the Phase 1 mandible-anchored crop showing expert-annotated GTVn (green) with candidate nodal aROIs (pink and light-blue boxes). Corresponding instance-specific cropped axial subvolumes (B-C) centered on each node, generated by applying a 10 mm isotropic expansion to the instance GTVn bounding boxes, used for Phase 2n inference.

Finalization. After Phase 2 fusions, the canonical GTVp and GTVn label map were resampled back to the original input CT geometry (matching size, spacing, origin, and direction), small components ($<$ 150 voxels) of instance GTVp and instance GTVn lesions were removed, and a single CT-native label MetaImage Header File was saved per case to an output folder as seen in Fig. 4.

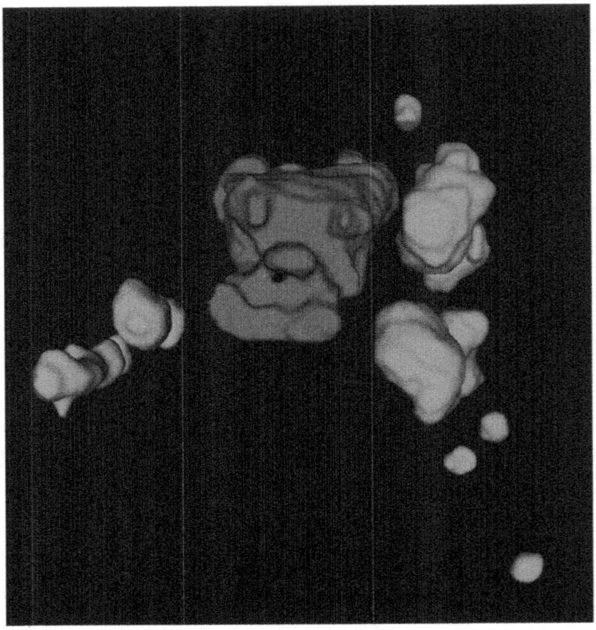

Fig. 4. 3D volume of final segmentation for GTVp (Red) and GTVn (Green).

Table 2. Summary of each phase's training ROI size, learning rate, observed VRAM used for training, and approximate training time per fold.

Stage	ROI (resampled voxels)	Initial Learning Rate	VRAM Used	Epochs per Fold	Training Time per Fold
Phase 0 (Mandible)	[192, 192, 64]	0.0004	$\approx$ 4 GB	19	5.8 h
Phase 1 (GTVp + GTVn)	[128, 112, 112]	0.0004	$\approx$ 12 GB	300	8.5 h
Phase 2p (GTVp focus)	[48, 48, 48]	0.0002	$\approx$ 4 GB	137	0.9 h
Phase 2n (GTVn focus)	[48, 48, 48]	0.0002	$\approx$ 4 GB	200	1.5 h

3 Results

3.1 Data

The training set included 682 co-registered CT and FDG-PET scans from patients with head and neck cancer, with expert contours for the GTVp and any GTVn if present. A subset of 73 cases also included the chest, abdomen, and pelvis.

3.2 Cross-Validation

We report the cross-validation results on the training sets for phases 0, 1, 2p, and 2n. The average cross-validation results are presented in Table 3, demonstrating consistent segmentation accuracy across folds. These results provided an estimate of generalization performance prior to final test submission.

Table 3. Cross-validation DSC results at the best performing epoch during training for GTVp and GTVn during each of the phases 0, 1, 2p, and 2n.

Phase	Number of Folds	Average ± Standard Deviation
0 (Mandible)	1	0.85 ± 0.0
1 (GTVp)	5	0.73 ± 0.014
1 (GTVn)	3	0.71 ± 0.014
2p (GTVp)	15	0.83 ± 0.010
2n (GTVn)	7	0.81 ± 0.005

3.3 Sanity Check Set and Testing Set Performance

Our final submitted algorithm was evaluated by the HECKTOR25 organizers on the held-out 2025 Sanity Check set and Testing set, comprising approximately 3 and 450 patients, respectively (15). The DLaBella29 team's method achieved a Sanity Check Phase inference average DSC of 0.87 for GTVp, an aggregate DSC of 0.75 for GTVn, and an Aggregate F1 of 0.67 for GTVn. This Sanity Check Phase inference utilized all 4 phases (0, 1, 2p, and 2n) as described in the methods section.

Because of shared VRAM constraints on the Grand-Challenge platform, inference on the 450 testing cases was limited to the coarse Phase 1 predictions, without refinement from Phase 2p or Phase 2n. Under these conditions, the testing set mean DSC was 0.5289 for GTVp, with an aggregate mean DSC of 0.6156 and aggregate F1 of 0.5561 for GTVn. By definition of the challenge, the GTVn aggregate DSC was computed by combining all nodal lesions per case into a single mask, such that the score reflected summed overlap between predicted and true nodal volumes. The F1-score evaluated lesion-level detection performance by balancing sensitivity and precision of nodal detection. An F1 of 0.5561 indicates that just over half of the nodal metastases were correctly identified with relatively few false positives, a reasonable result given the difficulty of detecting small nodes.

Qualitative internal review of inference of the public training cases suggested robust performance for large, FDG-avid primary tumors, often delineating them nearly as well as human experts. Performance on very small lymph nodes was more variable; some sub-centimeter nodes with low PET uptake were missed by the model, whereas others were detected but with slightly underestimated volume. Finally, mandible-anchored cropping significantly reduced inference time and did not exclude any tumors in the training cases, as all GTVs fell within the chosen aROI margins.

4 Discussion

We developed and evaluated a four-phase, anatomy-guided pipeline for automatic segmentation of oropharyngeal primary tumors and nodal disease on paired FDG-PET/CT. The key design choice was to anchor the coarse segmentation to the mandible (Phase 0) and to constrain learning and inference to anatomically plausible aROI through fixed, empirically chosen expansion margins around the mandible-anchor-point. This anatomically grounded cropping substantially reduced memory footprint and computation time, while maintaining coverage of all training tumors. Building on this, we used a coarse-to-fine progression: a joint GTVp and GTVn model for coarse localization (Phase 1), followed by focused refinements using tight, task-specific aROIs including GTVp centered crops (Phase 2p) and lesion-wise nodal crops derived from 26-connected components (Phase 2n). The phased design sought to improve performance over a single-phase model.

4.1 Cross-Validation Performance

The mandible model achieved a mean cross-validation DSC of 0.85 after only 19 training epochs, enabling robust and fast aROI definition for subsequent phases. Coarse tumor segmentation (Phase 1) produced mean cross-validation DSCs of 0.73 for GTVp and 0.71 for GTVn. Focused refinements improved both tasks: GTVp (Phase 2p) increased to 0.84 across 15 folds, and GTVn (Phase 2n) increased to 0.81 across 7 folds (Table 2). These improvements are consistent with the intended role of Phase 2 as a high-precision stage that fine-tunes instance detections by inferring on smaller cropped and anatomically informed aROIs, after Phase 1 has addressed full-image localization.

4.2 Held-out Evaluations

On the HECKTOR25 Sanity Check set, our full pipeline (all four phases) achieved an average DSC of 0.87 for GTVp and an aggregate DSC of 0.75 for GTVn, with an aggregate F1 of 0.67 for nodal presence/absence. In contrast, Testing set results were lower: 0.5289 DSC for GTVp, 0.6156 aggregate DSC for GTVn, and 0.5561 aggregate F1 for nodal detection. The principal driver of this generalization gap was a practical constraint: due to shared-GPU VRAM limits on the Grand-Challenge inference platform when processing the 450 case Testing set, we were required to run only the coarse model (Phase 1) during testing. As a result, none of the fine-tuning steps from Phase 2p and Phase 2n were applied at testing time, which is hypothetically consistent with the observed drop in performance. However, due to the smaller sample size of the Sanity Check set, a legitimate statistical comparison of the single-phase vs. four-phase algorithms cannot be made. Further testing should be considered to compare the performance of the single-phase algorithm compared to the four-phase algorithm.

4.3 Interpretation and Implications

The results support three practical conclusions. First, anatomy-anchored cropping is an effective and reproducible way to reduce search space and computation without sacrificing coverage; our fixed margins around a mandible-derived anchor included every training GTV and significantly reduced inference time. Second, a coarse-to-fine pipeline with lesion-wise refinement is important for head-and-neck disease, where the class imbalance and anatomical clutter make single-pass models particularly susceptible to false positives and false negatives in nodal basins and to boundary under-segmentation along mucosal surfaces. Third, inference configuration matters: disabling the refinement phases for operational reasons (here, platform VRAM) predictably degrades external performance, highlighting that system-level constraints can be as consequential as model choice when translating to large, real-world cohorts.

4.4 Strengths and Limitations

Strengths include (i) a transparent, modular design that cleanly separates localization and refinement; (ii) explicit lesion-wise handling of nodal disease using connected-component crops; (iii) efficiency compatible with a single RTX 4090 (with modest per-fold training times); and (iv) no dependence on external training datasets. Limitations include (i) reliance on accurate mandible segmentation for aROI definition; (ii) potential miss or truncation of very distant nodal disease if encountered in distributions different from the training set; and (iii) over-filtering risk from post-processing for tiny reference standard lesions. In addition, the Testing set constraint to Phase 1 only means the reported external numbers reflect our coarse model's ceiling rather than the whole four-phase algorithm's true capacity.

4.5 Future Directions

Several extensions are straightforward. The refinement phases could be made inference-robust under strict VRAM by reducing network size, inference optimization, and reducing the number of folds utilized so that Phases 2p and 2n can run even on shared VRAM hardware. Addition of test-time augmentation may stabilize boundaries and small-lesion recall. Exploring multi-anchor aROIs (e.g., mandible plus hyoid or soft-palate landmarks) could reduce the risk of missing atypically located disease. Finally, adding uncertainty quantification would alert clinicians when outputs are unreliable (e.g., out-of-distribution scans).

4.6 Clinical Perspective

In its intended multiphase configuration, our pipeline provides initial contours rapidly and with high DSC performance for typical, FDG-avid primaries and many nodal presentations, making it well-suited for draft-contouring workflows that incorporate expert verification. The coarse-only Testing set findings underscore that deployment details (hardware, memory budget, and batching strategy) are central to achieving clinically acceptable performance at scale. While challenges remain in perfecting automated head and neck tumor segmentation, our results show the potential to speed up and make more consistent radiotherapy contours, which could help enable adaptive treatment strategies in OPSCC.

5 Conclusion

In summary, we have demonstrated a multi-phase, mandible-anchored Auto3DSeg approach for automated GTV segmentation in oropharyngeal cancer PET/CT scans. By integrating anatomical knowledge with deep learning SegResNet networks, our algorithm effectively segmented primary and nodal tumors and achieved fair performance in the HECKTOR 2025 challenge. The approach emphasizes preserving geometric fidelity and leveraging multi-modal imaging. While challenges remain in perfecting automated head and neck tumor segmentation, our results show the potential to speed up and make more consistent radiotherapy contours, which could help enable adaptive treatment strategies in OPSCC. Continued improvements and validation on larger cohorts will be necessary, but automated segmentation is poised to become a valuable assistant in the radiation oncologist's toolkit, particularly as we move toward more personalized and adaptive therapy paradigms.

Data Availability Our code for all pre-processing, training, inference, and post -processing are available as open-source at **GitHub: dlabella29/HECKTOR25_Auto3DSeg**.

Acknowledgments. The authors thank the organizers of the HECKTOR 2025 challenge for providing the dataset and a collaborative platform. We also acknowledge MONAI and the Auto3DSeg developers for open-source tools that enabled this work.

Disclosures of Interests The authors have no competing interests to declare that are relevant to the content of this article.

References

1. Siegel, R.L., Giaquinto, A.N., Jemal, A.: Cancer statistics, 2024. CA Cancer J. Clin. **74**(1), 12–49 (2024)
2. Chajon, E., Lafond, C., Louvel, G., Castelli, J., Williaume, D., Henry, O., et al.: Salivary gland-sparing other than parotid-sparing in definitive head-and-neck intensity-modulated radiotherapy does not seem to jeopardize local control. Radiat. Oncol., 8, 132 (2013)

3. Petkar, I., Rooney, K., Roe, J.W.G., Patterson, J.M., Bernstein, D., Tyler, J.M., et al.: DARS: a phase III randomised multicentre study of dysphagia- optimised intensity- modulated radiotherapy (do-IMRT) versus standard intensity- modulated radiotherapy (S-IMRT) in head and neck cancer. BMC Cancer. **16**(1), 770 (2016)
4. Nutting, C.M., Morden, J.P., Harrington, K.J., Urbano, T.G., Bhide, S.A., Clark, C., et al.: Parotid-sparing intensity modulated versus conventional radiotherapy in head and neck cancer (PARSPORT): a phase 3 multicentre randomised controlled trial. Lancet Oncol. **12**(2), 127–136 (2011)
5. Castelli, J., Depeursinge, A., Ndoh, V., Prior, J.O., Ozsahin, M., Devillers, A., et al.: A PET-based nomogram for oropharyngeal cancers. Eur. J. Cancer. **75**, 222–230 (2017)
6. Mowery, Y.M., Vergalasova, I., Rushing, C.N., Choudhury, K.R., Niedzwiecki, D., Wu, Q., et al.: Early 18F-FDG-PET response during radiation therapy for HPV-related oropharyngeal cancer may predict disease recurrence. Int. J. Radiat. Oncol. Biol. Phys. **108**(4), 969–976 (2020)
7. Bogowicz, M., Leijenaar, R.T.H., Tanadini-Lang, S., Riesterer, O., Pruschy, M., Studer, G., et al.: Post-radiochemotherapy PET radiomics in head and neck cancer – the influence of radiomics implementation on the reproducibility of local control tumor models. Radiother. Oncol. **125**(3), 385–391 (2017)
8. Vallières, M., Kay-Rivest, E., Perrin, L.J., Liem, X., Furstoss, C., Aerts, H.J.W.L., et al.: Radiomics strategies for risk assessment of tumour failure in head-and-neck cancer. Sci. Rep. **7**(1), 10117 (2017)
9. Chen, A.M.: De-escalated radiation for human papillomavirus virus-related oropharyngeal cancer: evolving paradigms and future strategies. Front. Oncol., 13 (2023)
10. Regan, S.N., Rosen, B.S., Suresh, K., Cao, Y., Aryal, M.P., Allen, S.G., et al.: FDG-PET-based selective De-escalation of radiotherapy for HPV-related oropharynx cancer: results from a phase II trial. Int. J. Radiat. Oncol. Biol. Phys. **118**(5), e11 (2024)
11. Courtney, P.T., Santoso, L.M., Savjani, R.R., Reddy, K.V., Chai-Ho, W., Velez Velez, M.A., et al.: A phase II study of personalized ultrafractionated stereotactic adaptive radiotherapy for palliative head and neck cancer treatment (PULS-pal): a single-arm clinical trial protocol. BMC Cancer. **24**(1), 1564 (2024)
12. Atienza, C., Shepard, A., Uzomah, U., Rajan, S.K., Anderson, C.M., Katzer, J., et al.: Preliminary experience using MR-guided adaptive radiotherapy in head and neck cancer. Front. Oncol. **14**, 1474115 (2024)
13. Avkshtol, V., Meng, B., Shen, C., Choi, B.S., Okoroafor, C., Moon, D., et al.: Early experience of online adaptive radiation therapy for definitive radiation of patients with head and neck cancer. Adv. Radiat. Oncol. **8**(5), 101256 (2023)
14. Heukelom, J., Fuller, C.D.: Head and neck cancer adaptive radiation therapy (ART): conceptual considerations for the informed clinician. Semin. Radiat. Oncol. **29**(3), 258–273 (2019)
15. HECKTOR25 [Internet]: cited 2025 Sep 8]. hecktor25.grand-challenge.org
16. Saeed, N., Hassan, S., Hardan, S., Aly, A., Taratynova, D., Nawaz, U., et al.: A multimodal and multi-centric head and neck cancer dataset for segmentation. Diagn. Outcome Prediction. (2025)
17. Andrearczyk, V, Oreiller, V, Boughdad, S, Le Rest, CC, Elhalawani, H, Jreige, M, et al.: Overview of the HECKTOR Challenge at MICCAI 2021: Automatic Head and Neck Tumor Segmentation and Outcome Prediction in PET/CT Images (2022)
18. The MONAI Consortium: Project MONAI. Zenodo 2020. doi:https://doi.org/10.5281/zenodo.4323059.
19. Myronenko, A.: 3D MRI brain tumor segmentation using autoencoder regularization (2018). http://arxiv.org/abs/1810.11654

20. Wasserthal, J., Breit, H.C., Meyer, M.T., Pradella, M., Hinck, D., Sauter, A.W., et al.: TotalSegmentator: robust segmentation of 104 anatomic structures in CT images. Radiol. Artif. Intell. **5**(5), e230024 (2023)
21. Warfield, S.K., Zou, K.H., Wells, W.M.: Simultaneous truth and performance level estimation (STAPLE): an algorithm for the validation of image segmentation. IEEE Trans. Med. Imaging. **23**(7), 903–921 (2004)

Molecular-Information-Guided Framework for Head and Neck Tumor and Lymph Node Segmentation in PET/CT Images

Jee Yoon Jung[1], Min Jeong Cho[1,3,4], and Jae Sung Lee[1,2,3,4,5](✉)

[1] Department of Nuclear Medicine, Seoul National University College of Medicine, Seoul, South Korea
[2] Interdisciplinary Program in AI, Seoul National University, Seoul, South Korea
[3] Interdisciplinary Program in Bioengineering, Seoul National University, Seoul, South Korea
[4] Integrated Major in Innovative Medical Science, Seoul National University, Seoul, South Korea
[5] Brightonix Imaging Inc., Seoul, South Korea
jaes@snu.ac.kr

Abstract. Accurate segmentation of Head and Neck (H&N) tumor and lymph node in PET/CT images is essential for diagnosis and treatment planning. However, it remains challenging due to heterogeneous lesion morphology and variable physiological uptake. In this paper, we propose a 3D U-Net based architecture with a PET-guided Spatial Attention Module (PSAM). PSAM consumes the PET image to generate a spatial attention map that gates encoder skip features. Furthermore, we use Squeeze-and-Excitation (SE) Normalization, which dynamically recalibrates channel responses and improves multimodal fusion. Notably, we introduce a novel molecular-information-guided preprocessing pipeline, which reduces the input volume size. This design enables modality-aware modeling and aims for robust generalizable segmentation of both primary Gross Tumor Volume (GTVp) and nodal Gross Tumor Volume (GTVn) across multi-center PET/CT data. We obtain a mean Dice score of 0.6073 with class-wise Dice scores 0.7133 (GTVp) and 0.5013 (GTVn) on the validation set. On the official test set, our model achieved a Dice score of 0.3803 (GTVp) and 0.3733 (GTVn). Further studies are required to improve generalization performance across multi-center datasets.

Keywords: HECKTOR2025 · MICCAI2025 · Segmentation · Challenge · Deep Learning · 3D CT · 3D PET

1 Introduction

In recent years, H&N tumor segmentation has become a critical issue in cancer research, clinical diagnosis, and surgical planning. Medical images such as

N. Saeed et al. (Eds.): HECKTOR 2026, LNCS 16520, pp. 61–70, 2026.
https://doi.org/10.1007/978-3-032-25766-6_6

PET and CT play an important role in radiotherapy and treatment. However, traditional manual segmentation methods are time-consuming, labor-intensive, and subject to inter-expert variability. To overcome these challenges, significant progress has been made in automated segmentation methods, particularly those based on convolutional neural networks (CNNs).

One of the most successful models in this domain is U-Net [1,2]. Its encoder-decoder architecture with skip connections has demonstrated exceptional performance in medical image segmentation by effectively combining low-level and high-level features. However, U-Net faces limitations in extracting features for segmenting complex and diverse lesion morphologies. For instance, segmenting complex H&N tumor or subtle lymph nodes can be challenging with a single-scale feature approach. Furthermore, the performance of any model is highly dependent on the quality of its input data and the preprocessing methods used, which is amplified in HECKTOR challenges [3,4].

To address these limitations, we augment the U-Net architecture with a PET-guided spatial attention module. This attention module [5] allows the model to simultaneously consider PET features, enabling it to better recognize complex structures and subtle lesions within H&N tumor PET/CT images. We use Squeeze-and-Excitation Normalization [6] rather than Instance Normalization [7] which maximizes representational capacity by assigning dynamic weights to each channel of the feature maps. We propose a molecular-information-guided preprocessing pipeline that standardizes image geometry, localizes the field-of-view, and applies a novel cranial "PET-profile-guided brain peak cut" method to suppress non-relevant uptake. This pipeline reduces variability across centers and provides cleaner, more consistent inputs for robust model training.

2 Method

2.1 Dataset

The HECKTOR 2025 challenge provides 680 paired FDG-PET/CT patient cases from seven centers, with no bounding boxes supplied. Each case includes one 3D PET and one 3D CT image, together with a label delineating Gross Tumor Volume (GTVp) and nodal Gross Tumor Volume (GTVn). We use 600 cases for training and 80 cases for validation. The center-wise distribution is summarized in Table 1. These multi-center PET/CT images are based on the recently released HECKTOR dataset described in [8].

The dataset spans seven institutions with unequal per-center case counts and heterogeneous axial coverage—ranging from head-only to whole-body acquisitions—leading to center-specific differences in field-of-view and uptake patterns (Fig. 1). To ensure generalization across institutions, we constructed the validation split in a *center-proportional* manner.

Table 1. Number of patients for train/validation/total in seven centers

Center	Patients (train/val/total)	Center	Patients (train/val/total)
CHUM	44/12/56	HMR	14/4/18
CHUP	64/8/72	MDA	364/32/396
CHUS	60/12/72	USZ	7/4/11
HGJ	47/8/55	Total	600/80/680

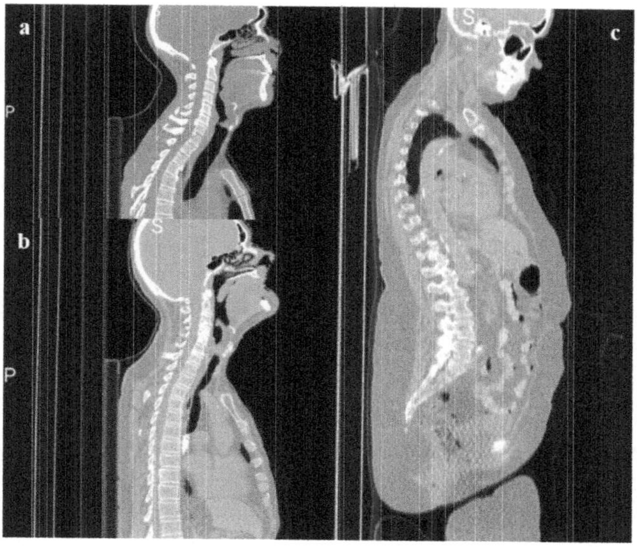

Fig. 1. Variation of data size across seven centers: (a) head only; (b) head and upper body; (c) whole body

2.2 Data Preprocessing

All PET/CT images were co-registered. We introduce a molecular-information-guided pipeline consisting of geometric resampling, cropping, PET-based localization, brain peak cut, normalization, and restoration. The network input is a two-channel volume (PET, CT) of fixed size $256 \times 256 \times 112$ (x–y–z).

Geometric Resampling and Voxelwise Alignment. CT volumes were resampled to $\varDelta = (1.0, 1.0, 3.0)$ mm using B-spline interpolation; PET volumes were resampled linearly and then regridded onto the CT lattice so that spacing, size, origin, and direction match exactly (voxelwise alignment).

Image Cropping. We evaluated several fixed crop sizes and applied a pass/fail criterion for target coverage—**Satisfied** (✔) if both targets (GTVp=1,

GTVn=2) were fully contained for all cases, and **Not satisfied** (✖) otherwise. Based on this criterion, we selected the smallest size, $\mathbf{256 \times 256 \times 112}$; the detailed pass/fail outcomes for all candidates are summarized in Table 2.

Table 2. Crop size test with a pass/fail criterion for target coverage.

Crop size (H×W×D)	Satisfied
192×192×112	✖
208×208×112	✖
224×224×112	✖
256×256×64	✖
256×256×96	✖
256×256×112	✓
128×128×128	✖

For each candidate crop size, the **"Satisfied/Not satisfied"** label in Table 2 was determined strictly on a per-case basis. No exceptions were allowed.

Molecular-Information-Guided Localization. Let $P \in \mathbb{R}^{X \times Y \times Z}$ denote the resampled PET. All z-axis operations below are performed along an anatomical inferior-to-superior index direction. We detect the superior cranial boundary by scanning from the top slice for suprathreshold uptake with $\tau = 0.5$:

$$z_{\text{top}} = \max\left\{ z \in \{0, \ldots, Z-1\} \;\middle|\; \max_{x,y} P[x, y, z] > \tau \right\}. \tag{1}$$

From the 20-slice slab immediately inferior to z_{top},

$$\mathcal{S} = \{\max(0, z_{\text{top}} - 19), \ldots, z_{\text{top}}\}. \tag{2}$$

We compute the activity centroid over the suprathreshold set

$$\Omega = \{(x, y, z) \in \{0, \ldots, X-1\} \times \{0, \ldots, Y-1\} \times \mathcal{S} \mid P[x, y, z] > \tau\}, \tag{3}$$

$$\bar{x} = \frac{1}{|\Omega|} \sum_{(x,y,z)\in\Omega} x, \qquad \bar{y} = \frac{1}{|\Omega|} \sum_{(x,y,z)\in\Omega} y. \tag{4}$$

We then crop a 256×256 in-plane window centered at $(\bar{x}, \bar{y})$. Defining half-widths $r_x = r_y = 128$, the coordinates are

$$x_1 = \min\big(\max(\lfloor \bar{x} \rfloor - r_x, 0), \max(0, X - 2r_x)\big), \quad x_2 = x_1 + 2r_x, \tag{5}$$

$$y_1 = \min\big(\max(\lfloor \bar{y} \rfloor - r_y, 0), \max(0, Y - 2r_y)\big), \quad y_2 = y_1 + 2r_y. \tag{6}$$

Boundary clamping and zero padding were applied if $X < 256$ or $Y < 256$.

PET Profile-Guided Brain Peak Cut. Within the in-plane crop, we compute the PET z-profile:

$$s(z) = \sum_{x=x_1}^{x_2-1} \sum_{y=y_1}^{y_2-1} P[x, y, z]. \tag{7}$$

Its peak index is

$$z_{\text{peak}} = \arg\max_{z} s(z). \tag{8}$$

We anchor the z-window to the top if strong uptake persists on the most superior slice or the peak is shallow:

$$\text{mean}\big(P[:, :, Z-1]\big) > 0.1 \quad \text{or} \quad z_{\text{peak}} \leq 50. \tag{9}$$

In both cases we extract a contiguous z-axis depth of 112 slices:

$$[z_1, z_2) = \begin{cases} [\max(0,\ z_{\text{top}} - 112),\ z_{\text{top}}), & \text{(top-anchored)}, \\ [\max(0,\ z_{\text{peak}} - 111),\ z_{\text{peak}} + 1), & \text{(peak-anchored)}. \end{cases} \tag{10}$$

If fewer than 112 slices are available, all available slices are kept and padding is applied inferiorly. For top-anchored scenario, the window is extracted from the 112 most superior slices, meaning the superior end is aligned to z_{top}. For peak-anchored scenario, Fig. 2 illustrates results in the cranial brain peak cut.

Although the z-window selection through PET-profile is heuristic and could require dataset-specific tuning in principle, the cranial PET uptake profile in HECKTOR was remarkably stable across institutions and scanners.

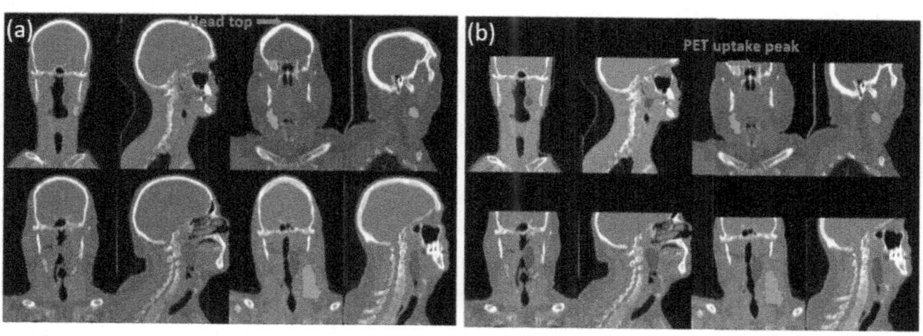

Fig. 2. Brain peak cut. (a) CT volumes before applying the cranial brain peak cut, showing strong cranial uptake; (b) cropped volumes after applying the proposed brain peak cut along the z-axis (peak-anchored).

Final Preprocessed Volume. The final PET/CT volume is cropped to a fixed field-of-view of

$$256 \times 256 \times 112,$$

centered in-plane at $(\bar{x}, \bar{y})$ and along z according to Eq. 10. The fixed field-of-view of $256 \times 256 \times 112$ was chosen after confirming that, across all HECKTOR training and validation cases from multiple centers. Both GTVp and GTVn consistently fell within this depth range after PET-guided localization. This empirically verified coverage supports the robustness of the selected window size despite its heuristic construction.

Intensity Normalization and Padding. We applied modality-specific normalization to account for the different dynamic ranges of CT and PET. Let $\sigma(\cdot)$ denote the logistic sigmoid.

For CT, intensities were clipped to the range of $[-1000, 1000]$ Hounsfield units (HU), linearly scaled to $[0, 1]$, and then passed through a sigmoid:

$$I_{\text{CT}}^{\text{norm}} = \sigma\left(\frac{\text{clip}(I_{\text{CT}}, -1000, 1000) + 1000}{2000}\right). \tag{11}$$

For PET, standardized uptake value (SUV) was normalized by global z-score within the cropped volume and subsequently squashed:

$$I_{\text{PET}}^{\text{norm}} = \sigma\left(\frac{I_{\text{PET}} - \mu_{\text{PET}}}{\sigma_{\text{PET}}}\right), \tag{12}$$

where $\mu_{\text{PET}}, \sigma_{\text{PET}}$ denote the mean and standard deviation of PET intensities.

To avoid saturating lesion contrast at high SUV, we empirically verified that hot lesions fall within the approximately linear region of the sigmoid input after z-scoring. Finally, the two normalized volumes were stacked as input channels, yielding a tensor of shape (C, Z, Y, X) with $C = 2$.

Provenance Logging and Restoration to Native Space. For each case we store a JSON sidecar with crop coordinates $(x_1, x_2, y_1, y_2, z_1, z_2)$, resampled geometry (size, spacing, origin, direction), and the original CT geometry. After inference, the predicted mask $\hat{M}$ on the cropped, resampled grid is pasted into a zero-initialized canvas of the resampled CT size at indices $[x_1{:}x_2,\ y_1{:}y_2,\ z_1{:}z_2]$, then resampled with nearest-neighbor interpolation onto the original CT grid to produce $\hat{M}_{\text{orig}}$ with native spacing, orientation, and dimensions.

2.3 Network Architecture

The proposed network adopts a 3D U-Net backbone and is organized around two key modules: a *PET-guided Spatial Attention Module* (PSAM), and *Squeeze-and-Excitation Normalization* (SE Norm). Co-registered PET and CT images are concatenated along the channel axis and passed to the backbone, while the PET volume alone is processed by PSAM to produce a spatial attention map that modulates encoder features and guides decoding. SE Norm is used as the normalization within backbone blocks.

PET-Guided Spatial Attention Module (PSAM). Motivated by the higher lesion conspicuity on PET, PSAM takes the PET volume $\mathbf{P} \in \mathbb{R}^{1\times D\times H\times W}$ and generates a single-channel attention map passed through a *sigmoid*. PSAM is a lightweight U-Net-style subnetwork producing a full-resolution map $\mathbf{A}$; multi-scale maps $\{\mathbf{A}^{(s)}\}$ for skip levels are obtained by average pooling with factors $\{1, 2, 4\}$. At each encoder stage s, the encoder feature $\mathbf{F}^{(s)}$ is gated by the corresponding PSAM map before it is concatenated into the decoder:

$$\tilde{\mathbf{F}}^{(s)} = \mathbf{F}^{(s)} \odot \mathbf{A}^{(s)}, \tag{13}$$

where $\odot$ denotes element-wise multiplication. Thus PSAM influences the network only via the skip pathway, suppressing physiologic uptake from outside lesions (e.g., salivary glands, brain, bladder) and highlighting metabolically active tumor regions that are fused with the anatomical context from CT.

Squeeze-and-Excitation Normalization (SE Norm). To counter residual false-positives from PET-only cues and to strengthen PET/CT fusion, we replace Instance Normalization (IN) with SE Norm in the convolutional blocks. Given an input feature $\mathbf{x}$, we first compute instance-normalized features $\mathbf{x}' = \mathrm{IN}(\mathbf{x})$. Global channel descriptors are then passed through a SE operator f_{SE} to produce per-channel affine parameters $(\boldsymbol{\gamma}, \boldsymbol{\beta})$:

$$(\boldsymbol{\gamma}, \boldsymbol{\beta}) = f_{\mathrm{SE}}\big(\mathrm{GAP}(\mathbf{x}')\big), \qquad \mathbf{y}_c = \gamma_c \mathbf{x}'_c + \beta_c,\ \forall c. \tag{14}$$

This modulation performs context-aware reweighting of channels, enabling the network to down-scale channels dominated by physiological PET uptake while up-scaling channels aligned with tumor morphology on CT. Practically, SE Norm stabilizes optimization and introduces data-dependent channel calibration, yielding cleaner skip fusion and more reliable decoding.

Loss Function. Given the substantial class imbalance inherent to PET/CT tumor delineation, we optimize the *Soft Dice* objective function. For prediction $\hat{\mathbf{y}}$ and reference $\mathbf{y}$:

$$\mathcal{L}_{\mathrm{Dice}}(\hat{\mathbf{y}}, \mathbf{y}) = 1 - \frac{2\sum_i \hat{y}_i y_i + \epsilon}{\sum_i \hat{y}_i^2 + \sum_i y_i^2 + \epsilon}, \tag{15}$$

where the sum runs over voxels (and classes for multi-class outputs) and ϵ is a small constant for numerical stability. The entire model is trained end-to-end using this objective without auxiliary constraints.

2.4 Training Details

All models are trained from scratch on the center-proportional split using the AdamW optimizer (learning rate 1×10^{-3}, weight decay 1×10^{-5}). A cosine–annealing schedule with warm restarts (T_0=25, $\eta_{\min}$=1×10^{-5}) is used, and training runs for 200 epochs with a batch size of 1. The Soft Dice loss (Eq. 15) is optimized, and the checkpoint with the highest mean validation Dice score over GTVp and GTVn is selected.

To ensure fair comparison, all baselines (U-Net, UNETR, U-Mamba) are trained with the same preprocessing, data split, optimizer, scheduler, and loss. No additional geometric augmentations are applied.

3 Results

We evaluate on the center-proportional validation split of HECKTOR 2025 (600 train/80 validation cases). We report the Dice score for the primary tumor (GTVp) and lymph node (GTVn), together with their average. All metrics are computed per case and then averaged over the set. We compare against U-Net [1], UNETR [9] and U-Mamba [10].

For a fair comparison, all baseline models were trained using exactly the same preprocessed PET/CT volumes. As summarized in Table 3, our method attains a Dice score of **0.7133** (GTVp) and **0.5013** (GTVn), yielding a mean of **0.6073**. This improves the mean Dice score over U-Net (0.5949), UNETR (0.5802) and U-Mamba (0.5932). The higher Dice score suggests that PET-guided skip gating helps sharpen boundaries in metabolically active primaries. Although our method achieved the best score among compared approaches, the absolute Dice score of GTVn remains lower than GTVp, reflecting the inherent difficulty of segmenting small, low-contrast lymph nodes.

Table 3. Quantitative comparison of baseline methods and the proposed method

Method	GTVp	GTVn	Mean (GTVp/GTVn)
Ours	**0.7133**	**0.5013**	**0.6073**
UNETR	0.6940	0.4664	0.5802
U-Net	0.7070	0.4828	0.5949
U-Mamba	0.7053	0.4811	0.5932

Test-Set Results. On the official HECKTOR 2025 test set, our method achieved a Dice score of **0.3803** (GTVp) and **0.3733** (GTVn), and an aggregate GTVn F1-score of **0.1982**. These scores were obtained through the challenge evaluation server after submitting our final model checkpoint.

The performance drop compared to the validation split is expected in a multi-center test environment, where differences in scanner types, reconstruction protocols, and annotation styles typically reduce absolute Dice scores. This behavior has been consistently observed in previous HECKTOR challenges. Despite this variance, our model maintained stable segmentation performance across centers without requiring external domain-specific tuning, supporting the practical robustness of the proposed PET-guided preprocessing and lightweight fusion design in real deployment scenarios.

4 Conclusion

We presented a PET-guided 3D U-Net framework for H&N tumor and lymph-node segmentation that (i) gates encoder skip features via PSAM, (ii) employs SE Norm for stronger channel-wise fusion of PET and CT, and (iii) standardizes inputs with a PET-guided brain-peak cut pipeline. On the HECKTOR 2025 validation split, the method achieves a mean Dice score of 0.6073 without external data or test-time augmentation. Further studies are necessary to strengthen generalization capability across diverse center datasets. Future work will explore tighter PET/CT coupling (e.g., cross-modal attention in the encoder), uncertainty-aware post-processing, and automated hyperparameter selection for center-aware generalization.

Acknowledgments. This work was supported by the Basic Research Project (No. RS-2024-00354123) of the National Research Foundation of Korea (NRF) funded by the Ministry of Science and ICT (MSIT), and the Institute of Information & Communications Technology Planning & Evaluation (IITP) grant (No. RS-2021-II211343) funded by the Korean government (MSIT) under the Artificial Intelligence Graduate School Program (Seoul National University).

Disclosure of Interests. The authors have no competing interests to declare that are relevant to the content of this article.

References

1. Ronneberger, O., Fischer, P., Brox, T.: U-Net: convolutional networks for biomedical image segmentation. In: Navab, N., Hornegger, J., Wells, W.M., Frangi, A.F. (eds.) MICCAI 2015. LNCS, vol. 9351, pp. 234–241. Springer, Cham (2015). https://doi.org/10.1007/978-3-319-24574-4_28
2. Çiçek, Ö., Abdulkadir, A., Lienkamp, S.S., Brox, T., Ronneberger, O.: 3D U-Net: learning dense volumetric segmentation from sparse annotation. In: Ourselin, S., Joskowicz, L., Sabuncu, M.R., Unal, G., Wells, W. (eds.) MICCAI 2016. LNCS, vol. 9901, pp. 424–432. Springer, Cham (2016). https://doi.org/10.1007/978-3-319-46723-8_49
3. Oreiller, V., Andrearczyk, V., Jreige, M., et al.: Head and neck tumor segmentation in PET/CT: the HECKTOR challenge. Med. Image Anal. **77**, 102336 (2022). https://doi.org/10.1016/j.media.2021.102336
4. Andrearczyk, V., Oreiller, V., Hatt, M., Depeursinge, A.: Overview of the HECKTOR challenge at MICCAI 2022: automatic head and neck tumor segmentation and outcome prediction in PET/In: Andrearczyk, V., Oreiller, V., Hatt, M., Depeursinge, A. (eds.) HECKTOR 2022. LNCS, vol. 13626. Springer, Cham(2023). https://doi.org/10.1007/978-3-031-27420-6_1
5. Oktay, O., Schlemper, J., Le Folgoc, L.: Attention U-Net: Learning Where to Look for the Pancreas arXiv:1804.03999 (2018)
6. Hu, J., Shen, L., Sun, G.: Squeeze-and-Excitation Networks. In: CVPR, pp. 7132–7141 (2018). https://doi.org/10.1109/CVPR.2018.00745
7. Ulyanov, D., Vedaldi, A., Lempitsky, V.: Instance Normalization: The Missing Ingredient for Fast Stylization (2016). arXiv:1607.08022

8. Saeed, N., Hassan, S., Hardan, S., Aly, A., Taratynova, D., Nawaz, U.: A Multi-modal and Multi-centric Head and Neck Cancer Dataset for Segmentation, Diagnosis, and Outcome Prediction arXiv:2509.00367 (2025)
9. Hatamizadeh, A., Tang, Y., Nath, V.: UNETR: transformers for 3D Medical Image Segmentation. In: WACV, pp. 1748–1758 (2022). https://doi.org/10.1109/WACV51458.2022.00181
10. Ma, J., Li, Z., Xie, Y.: U-Mamba: Enhancing Long-range Dependency for Biomedical Image Segmentation arXiv:2401.04722 (2024)
11. Cho, M.J., Hwang, D., Yie, S.Y., Lee, J.S.: Multi-modal co-learning with attention mechanism for head and neck tumor segmentation on ^{18}F-FDG PET-CT. EJNMMI Phys. **11**, 67 (2024). https://doi.org/10.1186/s40658-024-00670-y

A Two-Stage Coarse-to-Fine Ensembling Segmentation Framework with Multi-channel CT Enhancement for Head and Neck Tumor and Lymph Segmentation in PET and CT Image

Chuanyi Huang and Lisheng Wang(✉)

School of Automation and Intelligent Sensing, Shanghai Jiao Tong University, Shanghai 20024, China
lswang@sjtu.edu.cn

Abstract. Head and neck (H&N) cancer segmentation from PET/CT is challenging due to heterogeneous imaging protocols across centers and the small proportion of tumor and lymph node volumes relative to the full field-of-view. We propose a two-stage coarse-to-fine framework for automatic segmentation of primary tumors (GTVp) and metastatic lymph nodes (GTVn) in the HECKTOR 2025 challenge. The framework first applies a head localization stage using an nnUNet to extract a coarse region-of-interest (ROI). In the fine segmentation stage, we integrate predictions from two complementary backbones: nnUNetResEncUNetLarge and MONAI-based SegResNet, both trained with five-fold cross-validation. To further enhance tumor delineation, especially on CT modality and across centers, we introduce multi-channel CT representations by concatenating raw CT, its squared intensity, cubic-root intensity, and PET as four input channels for nnUNetResEncUNetLarge. This design improves sensitivity to tumor intensity patterns and robustness against inter-center heterogeneity. The framework was evaluated quantitatively on the official test set of task 1 for the HECKTOR2025 challenge, achieving a GTVp DSC of 0.7341, a GTVn aggregated DSC of 0.7312, and a GTVn aggregated F1 score of 0.7260 as team SJTU_lab426.

Keywords: Head an Neck Cancer Automatic segmentation · Coarse-to-Fine Segmentation · Multi-Channel CT Enhancement · nnUNet · SegResNet

1 Introduction

Head and Neck (H&N) cancer ranks among the top five most prevalent cancer types globally [1]. Accurate segmentation of the primary gross tumor volume (GTVp) and involved lymph nodes (GTVn) is critical for radiotherapy treatment planning and outcome prediction [2,3]. Traditionally, tumor delineation is

N. Saeed et al. (Eds.): HECKTOR 2026, LNCS 16520, pp. 71–82, 2026.
https://doi.org/10.1007/978-3-032-25766-6_7

performed manually by clinicians, which is labor-intensive, time-consuming, and prone to variability.

With the availability of 3D multimodal imaging modalities such as CT and PET, automatic segmentation using deep learning has become a promising approach. PET highlights metabolic activity but at relatively low resolution, whereas CT provides high-resolution anatomical details. Leveraging both modalities has shown improved performance in H&N tumor delineation.

The HEad and neCK TumOR (HECKTOR) challenge, organized in three editions in conjunction with MICCAI, serves as a benchmark for automated head and neck (H&N) cancer analysis using multimodal PET/CT imaging. In the latest edition, HECKTOR 2025, the evaluation protocol now emphasizes not only Dice similarity coefficient (DSC) but also lymph detection performance and cross-center robustness.

Previous editions, such as HECKTOR 2022, highlighted the difficulty of accurate segmentation under heterogeneous imaging conditions. The winning entry [4] (Myronenko et al.) employed an ensemble of MONAI-based SegResNet [5] models trained with five-fold cross-validation, achieving an aggregated DSC of 0.788. The runner-up solution leveraged nnUNet [6] with coarse-to-fine processing and multi-model ensembling, demonstrating the effectiveness of localization strategies and strong baselines. These top solutions reveal two essential insights: (1) accurate ROI extraction and model ensembling are key to achieving strong performance; (2) although PET provides reliable localization, its tumor boundaries are often indistinct. In contrast, CT offers richer boundary information but suffers from limited contrast between lesions and surrounding tissues, as well as inter-center intensity variations that reduce generalization. Therefore, enhancing CT-based representations is crucial to fully exploit its structural advantages while mitigating these limitations.

Motivated by these observations, our method adopts a two-stage coarse-to-fine strategy with nnUNet for robust head localization, followed by an ensemble of nnUNetResEncUNetLarge and MONAI SegResNet for fine segmentation. To strengthen CT-driven delineation and improve robustness across heterogeneous multi-center data, we introduce CT enhancement by augmenting the raw CT with squared and cubic-root intensity transforms, concatenated with PET as four-channel input. This design explicitly enriches CT representation, facilitating sharper lesion boundary detection and stronger cross-center generalization. [7]

2 Method

2.1 Dataset

The HECKTOR 2025 challenge [8] provides an extended multimodal dataset [9] for head and neck (H&N) tumor lesion segmentation and diagnosis which contains 680 cases from 7 centers.

Each case comprises a co-registered 3D PET/CT pair and a voxel-wise binary mask delineating the primary tumor and any metastatic lymph nodes. Scanning coverage differs across centers, as shown in Fig. 1: some studies are restricted to the head-and-neck region, others extend to the thorax or upper abdomen, and a subset provides whole-body acquisitions, introducing substantial anatomical-coverage heterogeneity.

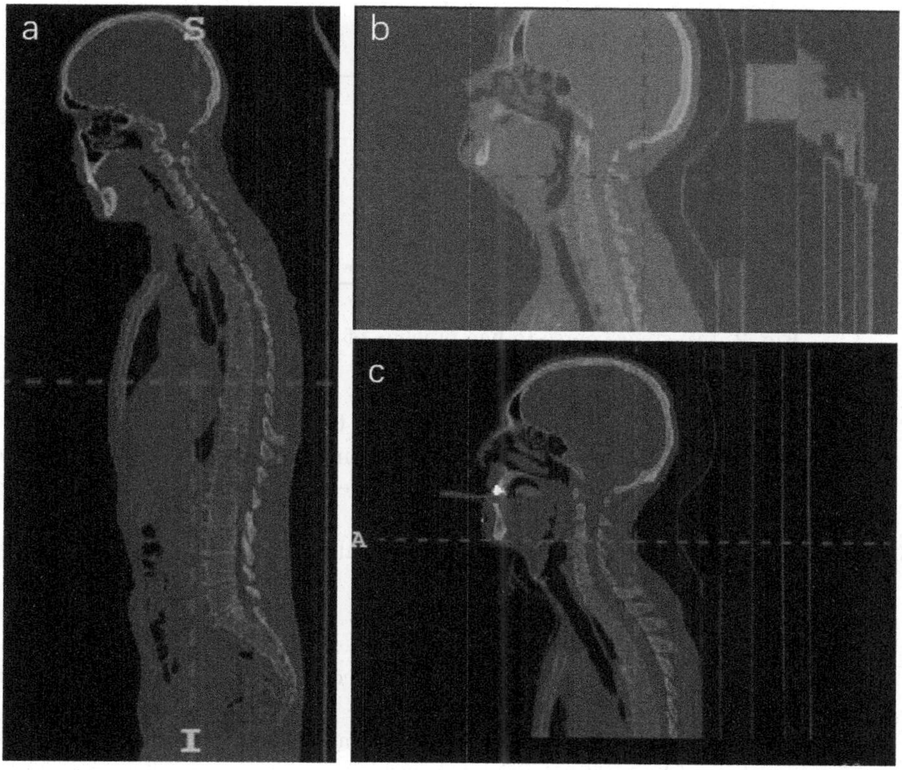

Fig. 1. Variation of image size from 7 centers. (a) whole upper body. (b) only head region. (c) head and upper body.

2.2 Overview of the Proposed Framework

Our method follows a two-stage coarse-to-fine pipeline designed to efficiently localize the head-and-neck (H&N) region and perform accurate tumor and segmentation. The overall workflow can be seen in Fig. 2 and can be summarized as follows:

1. **Head Localization (Coarse Stage):** An nnUNet model is trained to detect the H&N region from the full-body CT scan. A bounding box is generated to crop the relevant region-of-interest (ROI), thereby reducing input size and eliminating irrelevant anatomy.

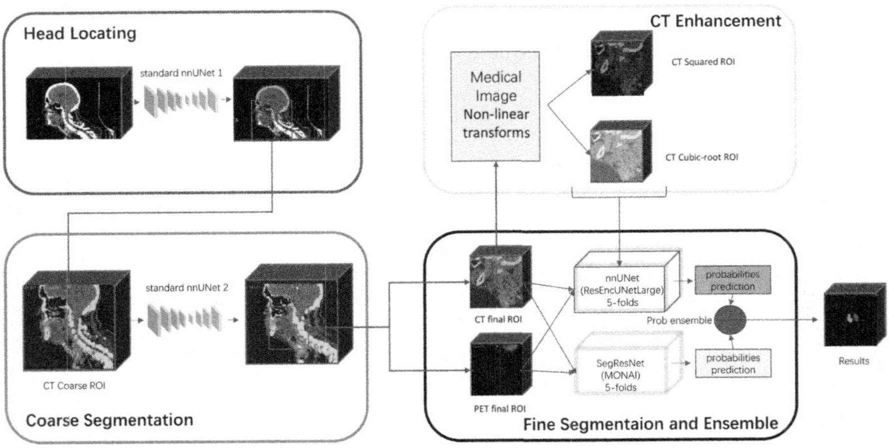

Fig. 2. two-stage coarse-to-fine pipeline of the whole framework

2. **Coarse Segmentation Stage:** We define the coarse ROI as the entire head-and-neck volume within which tumors and metastatic lymph nodes are expected to reside, and we obtain this initial region using a standard nnUNet model trained for coarse segmentation.
3. **Fine Segmentation Stage:** Within the localized ROI, two complementary segmentation backbones are applied:
   - *nnUNetResEncUNetLarge* – a residual encoder-decoder variant of nnUNet.
   - *MONAI SegResNet* – a widely adopted encoder-decoder architecture with deep supervision.

   Both models are trained with five-fold cross-validation. Their predictions are ensembled to produce robust final outputs.
4. **Multi-Channel CT Enhancement:** To strengthen CT-driven lesion delineation and improve robustness across heterogeneous multi-center datasets, we augment the CT modality by generating squared (x^2) and cubic-root ($x^{1/3}$) intensity channels in addition to the raw CT (x). Together with PET (y), these form a four-channel input $[x, x^2, x^{1/3}, y]$. Then we used it as multi-channel inputs for nnUNetResEncUNetLarge.
5. **Inference and Post-processing:** During inference, predictions from the ensemble are averaged. Small isolated false positives are removed via connected-component analysis.

2.3 Network Architecture and Details

Head Localization Model. To cope with the large variability along the z-axis (ranging from a few dozen to several hundred slices) while the transverse plane remains 512 × 512, we first isolated a dedicated head-and-neck ROI. Because heads always appear near the top but may be left- or right-shifted (due to different acquisition centers), an automatically defined bounding box is unreliable.

We therefore adopted a coarse-to-fine strategy: the initial step simply localizes the approximate head region rather than producing an exact segmentation. For this localization task we trained a standard nnUNet using CT images only. Each volume is resampled—starting from the top of the original scan—to a uniform grid of 256 × 256 × 128 voxels at 2 × 2 × 3 mm spacing, employing B-spline interpolation. Forty CT scans were randomly selected from the training set and manually labeled for the head region in just a few hours. Prior to training, all intensities were clipped to [-110, 190] HU and normalized to [-1, 1].

Although isotropic spacing is often recommended, we followed nnU-Net's default preprocessing strategy, which determines anisotropic voxel spacing based on the median physical resolution of the dataset. This choice preserves the native resolution characteristics of head-and-neck scans and avoids unnecessary resampling artifacts.

The detailed parameters of the head-locating model are listed in the Table 1 below.

Table 1. nnU-Net 3D Full Resolution Configuration for Head Localization Model

Property	Configuration
Preprocessor	DefaultPreprocessor
Batch Size	2
Patch Size	96 × 160 × 160
Median Image Size	128 × 256 × 256
Spacing	(3.0, 2.0, 2.0) mm
Normalization	Z-Score normalization (no mask)
Resampling	B-spline (order = 3, data), Nearest-neighbor (order = 1, segmentation)
Network Class	PlainConvUNet (3D)
Number of Stages	6
Features per Stage	[32, 64, 128, 256, 320, 320]
Kernel Sizes	3 × 3 × 3 (all stages)
Strides	{(1,1,1), (2,2,2), (2,2,2), (2,2,2), (2,2,2), (1,2,2)}
Convolutions per Stage (Encoder)	[2, 2, 2, 2, 2, 2]
Convolutions per Stage (Decoder)	[2, 2, 2, 2, 2]
Convolution Bias	True
Normalization Layer	InstanceNorm3d ($\epsilon = 10^{-5}$, affine=True)
Nonlinearity	LeakyReLU (inplace = True)
Dropout	None
Loss Function	Cross-entropy + Dice (batch Dice = False)

Coarse Segmentation Model. To define the coarse region that encompasses both primary tumors and metastatic lymph nodes within the head-and-neck area, we employ a straightforward nnU-Net model. CT and PET volumes are first cropped according to this coarse ROI. Intensities inside the CT crop are clipped to [–110, 190] HU and then linearly scaled to [–1, 1], whereas PET values are simply normalized to [0, 1] at the same coarse level. Once the coarse ROI is available, we derive the subsequent fine ROI from the union of all tumor and lymph-node labels. The bounding box of the fine ROI is centered on the centroid of these labels (blue square in Fig. 3). This cube is resampled to 144 × 144 × 144 voxels at 1 × 1 × 1 mm spacing via B-spline interpolation—identical to last year's setup—yielding a 144 mm isotropic volume comfortably larger than an average neck or chin diameter and thus sufficient to enclose every target. The specific parameters of the coarse-segmentation model are provided in the Table 2 below.

Table 2. nnU-Net 3D Full Resolution Configuration for Coarse Segmentation Model

Property	textbfConfiguration
Preprocessor	DefaultPreprocessor
Batch Size	2
Patch Size	128 × 128 × 128
Median Image Size	144 × 144 × 144
Spacing	(2.0, 2.0, 2.0) mm
Normalization	Z-Score normalization (2 channels, no mask)
Resampling	B-spline (order =,3, data), Nearest-neighbor (order,=,1, segmentation)
Network Class	PlainConvUNet (3D)
Number of Stages	6
Features per Stage	[32, 64, 128, 256, 320, 320]
Kernel Sizes	3 × 3 × 3 (all stages)
Strides	{(1,1,1), (2,2,2), (2,2,2), (2,2,2), (2,2,2), (2,2,2)}
Convolutions per Stage (Encoder)	[2, 2, 2, 2, 2, 2]
Convolutions per Stage (Decoder)	[2, 2, 2, 2, 2]
Convolution Bias	True
Normalization Layer	InstanceNorm3d ($\epsilon = 10^{-5}$, affine=True)
Nonlinearity	LeakyReLU (inplace,=,True)
Dropout	None
Loss Function	Cross-entropy + Dice (batch Dice = False)

Fine Segmentation Models. The fine ROI tightly encloses tumors and metastatic lymph nodes. CT and PET volumes are resampled from the original study using this ROI; CT intensities are clipped to $[-110, 190]$ HU and linearly scaled to $[-1, 1]$, whereas PET values are normalized to $[0, 1]$.

Fine segmentation proceeds in two stages: distributed training followed by simple probability averaging.

The specific parameters of the coarse-segmentation model are provided in Table 3 and Table 4

Table 3. nnU-Net ResUNet 3D Full Resolution Configuration for Fine Segmentation Models

Property	Configuration
Preprocessor	DefaultPreprocessor
Batch Size	4
Patch Size	$160 \times 160 \times 160$
Median Image Size	$144 \times 144 \times 144$
Spacing	(1.0, 1.0, 1.0) mm
Normalization	CT Normalization + Z-Score (2 channels, no mask)
Resampling	B-spline (order,=,3, data), Nearest-neighbor (order,=,1, segmentation)
Network Class	ResidualEncoderUNet (3D)
Number of Stages	6
Features per Stage	[32, 64, 128, 256, 320, 320]
Kernel Sizes	$3 \times 3 \times 3$ (all stages)
Strides	{(1,1,1), (2,2,2), (2,2,2), (2,2,2), (2,2,2), (2,2,2)}
Residual Blocks per Stage	[1, 3, 4, 6, 6, 6]
Convolutions per Stage (Decoder)	[1, 1, 1, 1, 1]
Convolution Bias	True
Normalization Layer	InstanceNorm3d ($\epsilon = 10^{-5}$, affine=True)
Nonlinearity	LeakyReLU (inplace,=,True)
Dropout	None
Loss Function	Cross-entropy + Dice (batch Dice,=,False)

1. **Distributed training.** Two architectures are trained with 5-fold cross-validation each, producing 10 models in total:
   (1)nnUNet Large ResUNet: 4-channel input
   $$[x,\ x^2,\ x^{1/3},\ y],$$
   where x denotes CT and y denotes PET. The additional x^2 and $x^{1/3}$ channels strengthen CT-driven lesion delineation and improve robustness across heterogeneous multi-center data.

(2)MONAI SegResNet: 2-channel input [CT, PET]. Every model outputs two independent binary probability maps (tumor foreground and lymph-node foreground).

2. **Probability averaging.** The 20 resulting probability maps (2 classes $\times$ 10 models) are averaged class-wise; the two averaged volumes are then thresholded to obtain the final binary labels.

Table 4. AutoSeg3D (SegResNetDS) Configuration for Fine Segmentation

Property	Configuration
Input Modality	CT (2 channels, plus optional PET)
Output Classes	3 (tumor, lymph_node, background)
ROI Size	$144 \times 144 \times 144$
Spacing (Median/Lower/Upper)	(1.0, 1.0, 1.0) mm
Normalization	Range normalization, crop foreground
Batch Size	1
Optimizer	AdamW (weight decay 1e−5)
Loss Function	Dice + Cross-Entropy Loss (include background, squared pred, softmax)
AMP	True
Network Architecture	SegResNetDS
Initial Filters	32
Downsampling Blocks	[1, 2, 2, 4, 4]
Residual Depth	4
Normalization	Instance Normalization (INSTANCE_NVFUSER)
Input Channels	2
Output Channels	3
Nonlinearity	LeakyReLU (in MONAI default)
Channels Last	True
Data Augmentation	Random crop, crop foreground, auto scale ROI/filter allowed
Resampling	Disabled (native resolution 1mm^3)
Intensity Bounds	[0.3204, 0.6318]

2.4 Training Details

All models were trained on two NVIDIA RTX 3090 GPUs with 24 GB memory each. The training configurations in terms of number of epochs and loss functions are summarized below:

- **Head locating nnU-Net:** 500 epochs, using Dice + Cross-Entropy loss.
- **Coarse segmentation nnU-Net:** 1000 epochs, using Dice + Cross-Entropy loss.
- **Fine segmentation nnU-Net (Residual Encoder UNet):** 1000 epochs, using Dice + Cross-Entropy loss.
- **Fine segmentation SegResNet:** 300 epochs, using Dice + Cross-Entropy loss.

The loss functions are defined as follows:

Dice Loss. For a single class c, the Dice coefficient is

$$\text{Dice}_c = \frac{2\sum_i p_{i,c} g_{i,c}}{\sum_i p_{i,c}^2 + \sum_i g_{i,c}^2},$$

where $p_{i,c}$ is the predicted probability for voxel i and class c, $g_{i,c}$ is the ground truth (one-hot), and i sums over all voxels. The Dice loss is then

$$\mathcal{L}_{Dice} = 1 - \frac{1}{C}\sum_{c=1}^{C} \text{Dice}_c.$$

Cross-Entropy Loss

$$\mathcal{L}_{CE} = -\frac{1}{N}\sum_{i=1}^{N}\sum_{c=1}^{C} g_{i,c} \log p_{i,c},$$

where N is the total number of voxels and C is the number of classes.

The loss formulation used in AutoSeg3D is mathematically identical to that of nnU-Net, both combining Dice and Cross-Entropy losses in equal proportion. AutoSeg3D adopts the same Dice + CE structure through MONAI's implementation, which serves as a unified loss interface across multiple sub-models. Therefore, while AutoSeg3D provides a framework-level wrapper for ensemble training and logging, it does not alter the underlying loss definition or weighting scheme.

3 Results and Discussion

Sanity-check Leaderboard

Table 5 summarizes our four preliminary submissions on the public sanity-check set (Task 1). Models are listed in the order they were uploaded; the ranking therefore reflects earlier rather than final performance.

Validation Leaderboard

Table 6 reports our two submissions on the hidden validation set (Task 1). The first row employs the full pipeline (nnUNet Large ResUNet + MONAI SegResNet + CT enhancement), while the second row uses the same two backbones without the additional CT channels.

Table 5. Sanity-check results (Task 1). The column *GTVp Dice* denotes primary-tumor Dice; *GTVn Aggr. Dice / F1* denote lymph-node metrics. Abbreviations: **nL-RU** = nnUNet Large ResUNet, **SRN** = SegResNet (MONAI), **CTE** = CT Enhancement. The first row corresponds to the full ensemble and enhancement pipeline, subsequent rows progressively ablate components.

Model	GTVp Dice	GTVn Aggr. Dice	GTVn Aggr. F1
nL-RU + SRN + CTE	0.8851	0.7973	0.8000
SRN + CTE	0.8778	0.7755	0.8000
nL-RU + CTE	0.8727	0.7503	0.8000
nL-RU (baseline)	0.8718	0.7222	0.7500

Table 6. Validation results (Task 1). Metrics are computed on the hidden validation set. Abbreviations: **nL-RU** = nnUNet Large ResUNet, **SRN** = SegResNet (MONAI), **CTE** = CT Enhancement.

Model	GTVp Dice	GTVn Aggr. Dice	GTVn Aggr. F1
nL-RU + SRN + CTE	0.7547	0.7743	0.6235
nL-RU + SRN	0.7217	0.7820	0.5975

Test Leaderboard

Table 7 reports our official submission on the hidden test set (Task 1). The results are for the full pipeline (nnUNet Large ResUNet + MONAI SegResNet + CT Enhancement).

Table 7. Test set results (Task 1). Metrics are computed on the official hidden test set. Abbreviations: **nL-RU** = nnUNet Large ResUNet, **SRN** = SegResNet (MONAI), **CTE** = CT Enhancement.

Model	GTVp Dice	GTVn Aggr. Dice	GTVn Aggr. F1
nL-RU + SRN + CTE	0.7341	0.7312	0.7260

Discussion

The experimental results highlight several important findings. First, the coarse-to-fine design proves effective: the initial head-localization and coarse segmentation stages substantially reduce irrelevant anatomy, simplifying the fine segmentation task. This strategy not only accelerates training and inference but also mitigates false positives in distant regions. Second, integrating complementary backbones (nnU-Net Large ResUNet and MONAI SegResNet) consistently improves robustness. The sanity-check leaderboard (Table 5) shows that the ensemble with CT enhancement achieves the best Dice scores for both GTVp and GTVn, confirming the benefit of multi-model fusion. Importantly, this ensemble-based strategy was used throughout all final submissions, ensuring consistency between model description and reported results.

Another key observation lies in the role of CT enhancement. By concatenating squared and cubic-root intensity transforms with raw CT, the model becomes more sensitive to subtle tumor-intensity variations while remaining robust to inter-center heterogeneity. This robustness is further supported by the model's stable validation performance across institutions included in the official split, suggesting improved generalization to varying scanner characteristics and acquisition protocols.

Nevertheless, the effect of CT enhancement differs between tasks. As shown in Tables 5 and 6, the enhanced CT input yields higher GTVp Dice but slightly lower GTVn Dice. This discrepancy can be attributed to the intrinsic contrast differences between primary tumors and metastatic lymph nodes. While intensity-based transformations enhance tumor boundaries, they may amplify CT noise or intensity bias near small lymph nodes, which exhibit lower contrast and greater inter-center variability. Consequently, CT enhancement tends to favor GTVp delineation but may compromise the consistency of GTVn predictions. Future work could address this trade-off via adaptive channel selection or loss reweighting between tumor and lymph-node classes.

Our approach ranked 5th overall on the HECKTOR2025 test set and demonstrated exceptional performance in metastatic lymph-node detection—the clinically critical task of identifying GTVn lesions. Specifically, our method achieved the highest GTVn Aggregated F1 score (0.7260), surpassing the next best result by 9.4% (0.7260 vs 0.6638). This significant improvement in detection F1—which jointly reflects precision and recall—suggests that our multi-model ensemble combined with CT enhancement provides superior sensitivity for localizing small metastatic lesions in heterogeneous PET/CT data.

Despite these gains, several limitations remain. First, although the ensemble improves stability, it increases computational cost during training and inference. Second, the reliance on intensity-based CT transformations may limit generalization to unseen imaging protocols. More sophisticated methods, such as self-supervised pretraining or radiomics-inspired feature augmentation, could further strengthen cross-center robustness. Finally, our current post-processing is limited to connected-component filtering; incorporating uncertainty estimation or anatomical priors could more effectively reduce false positives.

Overall, the results demonstrate that combining coarse-to-fine localization, backbone ensembling, and CT enhancement provides a robust and generalizable solution for multi-center head-and-neck cancer segmentation. Future work will focus on improving lymph-node delineation and reducing the computational burden of ensemble inference.

References

1. Parkin, D.M., Bray, F., Ferlay, J., Pisani, P.: Global cancer statistics, 2002. CA: Cancer J. Clin. **55**(2), 74–108 (2005)
2. Vallieres, M., et al.: Radiomics strategies for risk assessment of tumour failure in head-and-neck cancer. Sci. Rep. **7**(1), 10117 (2017)
3. Bogowicz, M., et al.: Comparison of pet and CT radiomics for prediction of local tumor control in head and neck squamous cell carcinoma. Acta Oncol. **56**(11), 1531–1536 (2017)
4. Myronenko, A., Siddiquee, M.M.R., Yang, D., He, Y., Xu, D.: Automated head and neck tumor segmentation from 3d pet/ct hecktor 2022 challenge report. In: 3D Head and Neck Tumor Segmentation in PET/CT Challenge, pp. 31–37. Springer, Heidelberg (2022). https://doi.org/10.1007/978-3-031-27420-6_2
5. Myronenko, A.: 3D MRI brain tumor segmentation using autoencoder regularization. In: Crimi, A., Bakas, S., Kuijf, H., Keyvan, F., Reyes, M., van Walsum, T. (eds.) BrainLes 2018. LNCS, vol. 11384, pp. 311–320. Springer, Cham (2019). https://doi.org/10.1007/978-3-030-11726-9_28
6. Isensee, F., Jaeger, P.F., Kohl, S.A., Petersen, J., Maier-Hein, K.H.: nnu-net: a self-configuring method for deep learning-based biomedical image segmentation. Nat. Methods **18**(2), 203–211 (2021)
7. Chang, Q., et al.: Mining multi-center heterogeneous medical data with distributed synthetic learning. Nat. Commun. **14**(1), 5510 (2023)
8. Saeed, N., et al.: A multimodal and multi-centric head and neck cancer dataset for segmentation, diagnosis and outcome prediction. arXiv preprint (2025)
9. Saeed, N., et al.: A multimodal and multi-centric head and neck cancer dataset for segmentation, diagnosis, and outcome prediction. https://arxiv.org/abs/2509.00367 (2025)

Joint Learning: Segmentation with Prognosis and/or HPV Prediction

Less is More: Efficient PET/CT Segmentation and Multimodal Prediction of Recurrence-Free Survival and HPV Status in Head and Neck Cancer

Lishan Cai[1,2(✉)], XingLong Liang[2,3], Tianyu Zhang[2,3], Jiaju Huang[4], Tao Tan[2,4], and Yunchao Yin[1]

[1] Department of Radiation Oncology, Amsterdam University Medical Center, De Boelelaan 1117, 1081 HV Amsterdam, The Netherlands

[2] Department of Radiology, The Netherlands Cancer Institute, Plesmanlaan 121, 1066 CX Amsterdam, The Netherlands

l.cai@amsterdamumc.nl

[3] Department of Radiology and Nuclear Medicine, Radboud University Medical Centre, Geert Grooteplein 10, 6525 GA Nijmegen, The Netherlands

[4] Faculty of Applied Sciences, Macao Polytechnic University, Macau 999078, Macao Special Administrative Region of China, China

Abstract. Accurate delineation of primary head and neck tumors and metastatic lymph nodes on PET/CT is critical for radiotherapy planning and prognostic assessment. Building on this clinical need, the HECKTOR 2025 challenge uses a large multi-centric dataset to provide a comprehensive benchmark for multimodal methods that integrate imaging and clinical information across three key tasks: segmentation of the primary tumor and involved lymph nodes, recurrence-free survival prediction, and HPV status classification. In this study, we (Team MEDAI) present our solutions for all three challenge tasks. For automated tumor segmentation, we employed an ensemble of ten lightweight STU-Net (small) models, achieving efficient and precise delineation of both primary tumors and metastatic lymph nodes. For recurrence-free survival prediction and HPV status classification, we developed a multimodal framework that integrates volumetric PET/CT imaging, lesion masks derived from the segmentation models, and structured clinical variables. Code is available at https://github.com/Liiiii2101/HECKTOR2025-MEDAI. Team: MEDAI.

Keywords: Medical Image Analysis · HECKTOR challenge · Deep Learning · Segmentation · Recurrence-Free Survival · HPV Status

1 Introduction

Head and neck cancer (HNC), one of the most common malignancy worldwide, arises from the anatomical sites of the upper aerodigestive tract [6,12]. Positron

L. Cai and X. Liang—Contributed equally.

N. Saeed et al. (Eds.): HECKTOR 2026, LNCS 16520, pp. 85–96, 2026.
https://doi.org/10.1007/978-3-032-25766-6_8

emission tomography /computed tomography (PET/CT), which provide complementary and synergistic information for HNC lesion segmentation and tumor characterization by highlighting metabolic and morphological tissue properties, is recommended for staging HNC, with additional roles in prognostication, treatment planning, and identifying unknown primary tumors [7]. Currently, radiotherapy is integral to the therapeutic management of HNC [2]. Precise tumor contouring is essential to ensure adequate dose delivery to the targeted tumor while sparing neighboring normal tissues. Manual segmentation of head and neck tumors and involved lymph nodes is time-consuming, labor-intensive, and prone to inter-observer variability. Accurate and automated segmentation of primary gross tumors and involved lymph nodes can support and streamline clinical workflows. Furthermore, when combined with clinical features, automated segmentation masks can be used to predict recurrence-free survival (RFS), offering valuable prognostic insight for HNC. Accurate RFS prediction helps identify patients at elevated risk of early recurrence, those who may benefit from treatment intensification, closer surveillance, or early referral for supportive interventions, while also supporting more individualized follow-up strategies for lower-risk patients. Additionally, accurate assessment of biomarkers such as human papillomavirus (HPV) status from PET/CT and clinical data can improve risk stratification and diagnostic accuracy.

In the past decade, deep learning (DL) has shown promising results in medical image analysis [1,4]. Notably, DL models have demonstrated strong performance in HNC tumor segmentation using PET/CT in previous HEad and neCK TumOR Lesion Segmentation, Diagnosis and Prognosis (HECKTOR) challenge 2022 [3]. HECKTOR 2025 [14] provides a platform for developing 3D algorithms to segment primary HNC tumors (GTVp) and nodal metastases tumors (GTVn) on PET/CT, as well as for recurrence survival prediction and HPV status classification using multimodal and multi-centric dataset.

In this article, we present our approaches for all three tasks: automatic segmentation of primary tumors and involved lymph nodes on FDG-PET/CT, prediction of recurrence-free survival using PET/CT and clinical data, and classification of HPV status based on PET/CT and clinical information.

2 Dataset

2.1 Overview

For HECKTOR 2025, the dataset comprises a large-scale, multi-centric collection of multimodal PET/CT scans and detailed clinical data from 1,123 patients with histologically confirmed HNC. The publicly available training set comprises approximately 700 cases collected from eight different centers. The hidden leaderboard validation set contains approximately 50 unseen cases, whereas the hidden final leaderboard test set comprises around 450 cases from three centers.

2.2 Preprocessing

Resampling and Cropping. The data preprocessing is inspired by the first-place solution of HECKTOR 2022 by Myronenko et al. [13]. All images were resampled to isotropic voxel spacing of $1 \times 1 \times 1\,\text{mm}^3$ using B-spline interpolation for CT/PET and nearest-neighbor interpolation for lesion masks. Overlapping bounding boxes between CT and PET volumes were computed to ensure spatial alignment and remove excess background to focus on the relevant anatomical region. A region-of-interest (ROI) was automatically determined using PET intensities. The top portion of the PET was analyzed to identify the largest high-intensity region. The crop center was defined as the centroid of this region. A fixed-size crop ($200 \times 200 \times 310$) around this center was extracted for CT, PET, and segmentation masks if available. This resampling and cropping were applied across all three tasks to reduce input image size, significantly accelerating training and minimizing network workload on irrelevant regions.

Normalization for Segmentation. nnU-Net [10] CT normalization scheme was applied to all cropped CT images. Intensity values from all foreground classes (excluding background) across the training set were collected to compute the mean, standard deviation, and 0.5/99.5 percentiles. Values were clipped to these percentiles, normalized by subtracting the mean, and scaled by the standard deviation. For PET, Z-Score normalization was applied by subtracting the mean and dividing by the standard deviation.

RFS Prediction and HPV Status Classification. Structured clinical variables $\mathbf{x}_{\text{clin}} \in \mathbb{R}^p$ included demographic and treatment-related information (age, sex, tobacco and alcohol use, performance status, M stage, treatment regimen), as well as quantitative imaging-derived biomarkers. The latter comprised conventional parameters such as MTV (primary tumor volume), NTV (positive lymph node volume), T-SUV (primary tumor SUV_{max}), N-SUV (nodal SUV_{max}), TLG (total lesion glycolysis), and NLG (nodal lesion glycolysis). For each patient, a $96 \times 96 \times 96$ 3D patch was extracted around the lesion centroid (computed from lesion masks; if absent, the geometric center was used). CT values were clipped to $[-1000, 3000]$ Hounsfield units and linearly normalized to $[0, 1]$. The final input tensor was stacked as $[\text{CT}, \text{PET}, \text{Mask}] \in \mathbb{R}^{3 \times D \times H \times W}$, where mask labels $\{0, 1, 2\}$ corresponded to background, primary tumor, and nodal disease, respectively. The mask channel was converted to one-hot and the $\{1, 2\}$ channels were used as explicit lesion guidance. Continuous variables were median-imputed for missing values and standardized using Z-Score normalization, while categorical variables were imputed with "Unknown" and one-hot encoded.

3 Method

3.1 GTVp and GTVn Segmentation

Architecture. For GTVp and GTVn segmentation on CT/PET, the Scalable and Transferable U-Net (STU-Net) [9] was employed. STU-Net, an extension of the nnU-Net framework known for its strong performance, incorporates refined convolutional blocks to enhance scalability, see Fig. 1. Specifically, the basic nnU-Net convolutional blocks were augmented with residual connections [8] to facilitate scaling of model depth. Inspired by Liang et al. [11], the STU-Net small (STU-Net-S) configuration was adopted, with a depth of (1, 1, 1, 1, 1, 1) and width of (16, 32, 64, 128, 256, 256), making it considerably lighter and smaller than the other variants. The preprocessed images (CT/PET) were concatenated as a two-channel input, and the model was trained to simultaneously segment both GTVp and GTVn.

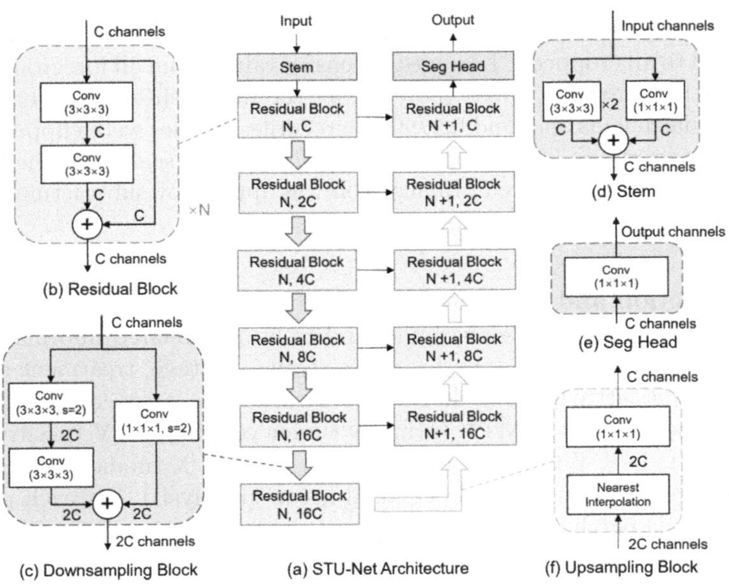

Fig. 1. STU-Net illustration by Huang et al. [9]. (a) architecture overview; (b) residual blocks for large-scale modeling; (c) downsampling in encoder stages; (d–e) stem and segmentation head for channel conversion; (f) weight-free interpolation for task-adaptive upsampling.

Loss. The loss function is the combination of cross-entropy and Dice loss.

$$\mathcal{L} = \lambda_{CE}\left(-\frac{1}{N}\sum_{i=1}^{N}\sum_{c=0}^{2} y_{i,c}\log(p_{i,c})\right) + \lambda_{Dice}\left(-\frac{1}{3}\sum_{c=0}^{2}\frac{2\sum_{i=1}^{N} p_{i,c}y_{i,c}}{\sum_{i=1}^{N} p_{i,c}^2 + \sum_{i=1}^{N} y_{i,c}^2 + \epsilon}\right).$$

$p_{i,c}$ is the predicted probability (softmax) that voxel i belongs to class c; $y_{i,c}$ is ground truth (1 if voxel i is class c, else 0). GTVp and GTVn were trained together. We empirically set $\lambda_{\text{CE}} = \lambda_{\text{Dice}} = 1$.

Data Split. STU-Net-S was trained with 5-fold cross-validation on all training cases, and a separate 10-fold cross-validation was also trained on the same data.

Optimization. Built on nnU-Net, STU-Net automatically configured all hyper-parameters. Training for each fold used a batch size of 2, a patch size of (192, 112, 112), and 1,000 epochs on an NVIDIA RTX A6000 GPU. During training, diverse real-time augmentation strategies are utilized, such as geometric transformations (rotation and scaling), intensity adjustments (brightness, contrast, and gamma correction), noise and blur perturbations, low-resolution simulation, and image mirroring.

3.2 RFS Predication

We developed a multimodal survival prediction network that integrates volumetric PET/CT imaging, lesion masks, and structured clinical features, see Fig. 2.

Image Encoder with Explicit Lesion Guidance. The image backbone was a 3D ResNet-18 [8], which processed the CT and PET channels. In parallel, a lightweight *Lesion-Guidance Module (LGM)* encoded the two lesion channels (GTVp and GTVn ground truth masks) into feature maps matching the backbone's first stage output. After the backbone's initial feature extraction layer, which captures low-level visual patterns, the two streams were fused by element-wise addition to incorporate explicit lesion guidance at the earliest stage.

$$\mathbf{f}_{\text{fuse}} = \phi_{\text{conv1}}([\text{CT}, \text{PET}]) + \text{LGM}(\text{Mask}),$$

which was subsequently propagated through the residual blocks, global average pooling, and flattened into an image-level representation $\mathbf{f}_{\text{img}} \in \mathbb{R}^d$.

Clinical Feature Processing. Structured clinical variables $\mathbf{x}_{\text{clin}} \in \mathbb{R}^p$ included continuous features (age, MTV, NTV, SUV, TLG, NLG) and categorical factors (sex, tobacco/alcohol use, performance status, M stage, treatment). Continuous features were median-imputed and Z-Scored, while categorical features were imputed with "Unknown" and one-hot encoded. A single-layer MLP produced a clinical embedding:

$$\mathbf{f}_{\text{clin}} = \text{MLP}(\mathbf{x}_{\text{clin}}) \in \mathbb{R}^{256}.$$

Multimodal Fusion and Survival Head. The final representation was obtained by concatenating image and clinical embeddings,

$$\mathbf{f} = [\mathbf{f}_{\text{img}}; \mathbf{f}_{\text{clin}}],$$

followed by dropout and an MLP head to output logits $\mathbf{z} \in \mathbb{R}^K$ for K discrete time intervals (here $K = 4$; cut points at 769, 1357, and 2626 days). The cut points were chosen based on the empirical distributions of RFS times and ensuring sufficient samples per intervals for stable optimization.

Discrete-Time Survival Modeling. We adopted a discrete-time hazard parameterization [15]:

$$h_k = \sigma(z_k), \quad k = 1, \ldots, K,$$

$$S_k = \prod_{j=1}^{k} (1 - h_j), \quad S_0 = 1$$

where h_k is the hazard in interval k, and S_k the survival probability up to interval k. Given observed interval index $y \in \{0, \ldots, K-1\}$ and censoring indicator $c \in \{0, 1\}$, the negative log-likelihood was

$$\ell_{\text{base}} = -(1 - c)\big[\log S_{y-1} + \log h_y\big] - c \log S_y.$$

We further applied a convex combination with the uncensored component (weight $\alpha = 0.5$) to stabilize optimization:

$$\mathcal{L} = \sum_i \Big((1 - \alpha)\,\ell_{\text{base},i} + \alpha\,\ell_{\text{uncens},i}\Big).$$

The patient-level risk score was defined as

$$r = -\sum_{k=1}^{K} S_k,$$

which is monotonically associated with recurrence risk.

Data Split. A 5-fold cross-validation was performed on all training cases.

Optimization. Optimization used AdamW (weight decay 10^{-2}) with learning rates 1×10^{-4} for the image (ResNet-18+LGM) and clinical+classifier branches (5×10^{-4}). Models were trained for 20 epochs with batch size 16 on an NVIDIA RTX A6000 GPU. Early stopping was guided by validation concordance index (C-index), computed in a Harrell-style fashion from comparable event pairs. The best model per fold was selected by maximal internal validation C-index.

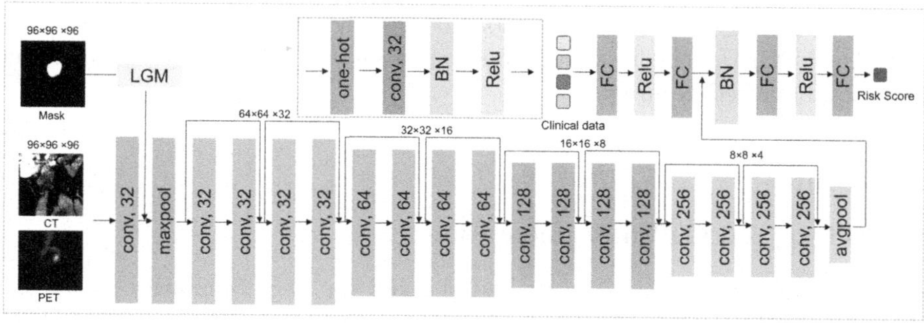

Fig. 2. The illustration of the proposed multimodal survival prediction network. PET/CT images and lesion masks are processed in parallel and fused through an early convolutional layer, while clinical variables are encoded through fully connected layers. The lesion mask is processed by a lesion-guidance module (LGM, grey dashed box, indicated by the grey arrow), which transforms the three-class mask (representing tumor, lymph nodes, and background) into a one-hot representation. This transformed mask is passed through convolution, batch normalization, and ReLU layers to generate lesion-aware feature maps, which enhance the focus on regions of interest. Image features and clinical features are then concatenated and passed through joint classifiers to predict the risk score. (Color figure online)

3.3 HPV Status Classification Task

The HPV classification task employed the same multimodal network and preprocessing pipeline as described for survival prediction—combining volumetric PET/CT imaging, lesion masks via the *LGM*, and structured clinical features. The only architectural difference was the prediction head, which produced a single logit $z \in \mathbb{R}$ corresponding to HPV status ($y \in \{0, 1\}$), with probability $p = \sigma(z)$.

Loss Function and Calibration. To address class imbalance, training optimized a per-sample weighted binary cross-entropy loss,

$$\mathcal{L}_{\text{BCE-w}} = -\,w(y)\,[\,y \log p + (1-y)\log(1-p)\,],$$

where $w(y) = w_{\text{pos}}$ if $y = 1$ and $w(y) = w_{\text{neg}}$ if $y = 0$. Unless otherwise specified, we set $w_{\text{pos}} = 1$ and $w_{\text{neg}} = \frac{n_{\text{pos}}}{\max(n_{\text{neg}},1)}$ according to training-set class counts. Balanced accuracy at a reference threshold of 0.5 was additionally logged during training and testing.

Data Split. A 5-fold cross-validation was performed on all training cases.

Optimization. Optimization used AdamW (weight decay 10^{-2}) with learning rates 1×10^{-4} for the image (ResNet-18+LGM) and clinical+classifier branches

(5×10^{-4}). Models were trained for 30 epochs with batch size 16 on an NVIDIA RTX A6000 GPU. The best checkpoint per fold is selected by the maximal validation balanced accuracy.

4 Result

4.1 GTVp and GTVn Segmentation

Segmentation performance was evaluated using the Dice Similarity Coefficient (Dice) for GTVp and GTVn, and the F1 score computed from IoU ($\geq$30%). Segmentation results were first evaluated in cross-validation (Table 1, 2), after which our algorithms were submitted to the validation leaderboard (Table 3) and final test leaderboard. On average, 10-fold cross-validation did not outperform 5-fold cross-validation; however, applying the 10-fold ensemble strategy yielded improvements on the validation leaderboard set (around 50 unseen cases), particularly for the F1 score of GTVn. Interestingly, although STU-Net-S (both 5-fold and 10-fold) achieved better GTVp segmentation in cross-validation, it showed stronger performance (Dice) on GTVn than GTVp in the leaderboard validation and final leaderboard test. Other STU-Net variants, including STU-Net Base (STU-Net-B), were also trained using 5-fold cross-validation. The cross-validation results showed no significant performance improvement (see Appendix). However, STU-Net-B has a larger number of trainable parameters, higher GPU memory requirements, and requires approximately twice the training time compared to STU-Net-S (see Table 4).

Table 1. Segmentation Performance Using 5-Fold Cross-validation (STU-Net-S)

Metrics	Fold 1	Fold 2	Fold 3	Fold 4	Fold 5	Average
Dice (GTVp)	0.7307	0.6761	0.6921	0.6934	0.6790	0.6943
Dice (GTVn)	0.6399	0.6621	0.6862	0.6595	0.6632	0.6622
F1 (GTVn)	0.5942	0.6590	0.6768	0.6581	0.6269	0.6430

Table 2. Segmentation Performance Using 10-Fold Cross-validation (STU-Net-S)

Metrics	Fold 1	Fold 2	Fold 3	Fold 4	Fold 5	Fold 6	Fold 7	Fold 8	Fold 9	Fold 10	Average
Dice (GTVp)	0.6891	0.7295	0.6586	0.7384	0.6710	0.6813	0.6551	0.6292	0.7027	0.6777	0.6833
Dice (GTVn)	0.6523	0.6290	0.6713	0.6170	0.5558	0.6528	0.6532	0.6423	0.6617	0.6232	0.6359
F1 (GTVn)	0.6165	0.6085	0.6748	0.5371	0.5573	0.5990	0.6096	0.6466	0.6078	0.5495	0.6007

Table 3. Leaderboard External Validation of Segmentation Performance

Metrics	Ensemble (5-Fold)	Ensemble (10-Fold)	Final (10-Fold)
Dice (GTVp)	0.7626	0.7653	0.7418
Dice (GTVn)	0.7931	0.7932	0.7640
F1 (GTVn)	0.6385	0.6641	0.6472

Both Emsemble (5-Fold and 10-Fold) were validated using around 50 unseen cases

Final refers to the Final leaderboard test results, based on around 450 unseen cases.

Table 4. Computational Expenses

Network	Param (M)	FLOPs (T)	VRAM (G)	Train (s)	Infer (s)	Depth	Width
STU-Net-S	14.55	0.66	4.4	41	5	(1,1,1,1,1,1)	(16,32,64,128,256,256)
STU-Net-B	58.16	2.62	7.9	78	15	(1,1,1,1,1,1)	(32,64,128,256,512,512)

The comparison of computational cost of STU-Net-S and STU-Net-B

Train: averaged training time per epoch

Infer: averaged inference time per case

4.2 RFS Prediction

The C-index was used to evaluate RFS prediction. The leaderboard validation results were obtained from an ensemble of our 5-fold cross-validation models, showing similar C-index values to those observed in the 5-fold cross-validation. However, a substantial drop in performance was observed on the final leaderboard test set, with the C-index decreasing to 0.5281. see Table 5.

Table 5. RFS Prediction Results

Metric	Fold 1	Fold 2	Fold 3	Fold 4	Fold 5	Average	Validation	Final
C-Index	0.7073	0.6383	0.7009	0.7160	0.7715	0.7068	0.7060	0.5281

Validation refers to the leaderboard validation results, based on around 50 unseen cases.

Final refers to the Final leaderboard test results, based on around 450 unseen cases.

4.3 HPV Status Classification

Balanced accuracy and specificity were used to evaluate HPV status classification. The leaderboard validation results, obtained from an ensemble of our 5-fold cross-validation models, revealed a notable performance gap: balanced accuracy was substantially lower on the leaderboard compared to cross-validation. This trend persisted on the final leaderboard test set, where the balanced accuracy further dropped to 0.5085, highlighting a discrepancy between cross-validation and unseen test performance. See Table 6.

Table 6. HPV Status Classification Results

Fold	Balanced Accuracy	Specificity
Fold 1	0.8532	1.0000
Fold 2	0.8183	0.6667
Fold 3	0.9361	0.9000
Fold 4	0.7837	0.6154
Fold 5	0.9541	1.0000
Average	0.8691	0.8364
Validation	0.6076	0.9048
Final	0.5085	–

Validation refers to the leaderboard validation results, based on around 50 unseen cases.

Final refers to the final leaderboard test results, based on around 450 unseen cases. Consist of 80% HPV-positive cases and 20% HPV-negative cases.

5 Discussion and Conclusion

In this study, we employed the small variant of STU-Net to efficiently perform simultaneous segmentation of GTVp and GTVn. Across the leaderboard validation, the 10-fold ensemble outperformed the 5-fold ensemble across all three metrics, with a notable 3% increase in the GTVn F1 score. Consequently, the 10-fold ensemble was selected for the final leaderboard test, where it achieved first place overall in the segmentation task. GTVn are smaller and more variable in shapes and locations. The 10-fold ensemble, benefiting from increased model diversity and reduced prediction variance, effectively detects and localizes GTVn. We also evaluated other STU-Net variants, including STU-Net Base (STU-Net-B). Cross-validation results showed no significant performance improvement despite the substantially higher computational cost. Due to submission constraints, evaluation of STU-Net-B on the leaderboard was not conducted at this stage.

Using a 5-fold ensemble of the multimodal survival prediction network, which integrates imaging, predicted lesion masks, and structured clinical features, the C-index on the leaderboard validation was comparable to cross-validation. However, a substantial performance gap was observed on the final leaderboard test, indicating limited model generalization. It is worth noting that RT-Dose and CT-planning scans were not included in our model, and their incorporation could potentially further enhance the performance of RFS prediction. The same multimodal framework was applied to the HPV status classification task. However, substantial overfitting was observed, with leaderboard validation and final leaderboard test metrics—particularly balanced accuracy—considerably worse than cross-validation, likely due to high model complexity and class imbalance. Future work could explore strategies to address class imbalance, such as advanced sampling techniques and to reduce model complexity through architecture simplification or regularization. The study by Celgla et al. [5] has shown that primary tumor features—SUVmax, TotalSUV, MTV, TLG, TLRmax, and TLRTLG—are informative for predicting HPV status, particularly for identifying HPV-negative tumors. Future work could further explore these features to develop more accurate models for HPV classification.

In this study, we present our solutions for the three tasks of the HECKTOR 2025 challenge. A 10-fold ensemble of STU-Net-S achieved strong segmentation performance. Using the predicted lesion masks, we developed a multimodal network that integrates the original images with clinical features to predict recurrence-free survival (RFS) and classify HPV status. Future work will focus on improving the generalizability of the RFS prediction and HPV classification models.

Appendix

Segmentation Performance Using 5-Fold Cross-validation (STU-Net-B).

Metris	Fold 1	Fold 2	Fold 3	Fold 4	Fold 5	Average
Dice (GTVp)	0.7254	0.6744	0.6899	0.6974	0.6693	0.6913
Dice (GTVn)	0.6323	0.6885	0.6870	0.6831	0.6464	0.6675
F1 (GTVn)	0.5843	0.6751	0.6789	0.6481	0.6258	0.6424

The experiment setup is the same as 5-fold cross validation using STU-Net-S.

References

1. Altaf, F., Islam, S.M., Akhtar, N., Janjua, N.K.: Going deep in medical image analysis: concepts, methods, challenges, and future directions. IEEE Access **7**, 99540–99572 (2019)
2. Anderson, G., Ebadi, M., Vo, K., Novak, J., Govindarajan, A., Amini, A.: An updated review on head and neck cancer treatment with radiation therapy. Cancers **13**(19), 4912 (2021)
3. Andrearczyk, V., et al.: Overview of the hecktor challenge at miccai 2022: automatic head and neck tumor segmentation and outcome prediction in pet/ct. In: 3D Head and Neck Tumor Segmentation in PET/CT Challenge, pp. 1–30. Springer, Heidelberg (2022). https://doi.org/10.1007/978-3-031-27420-6_1
4. Cai, L., et al.: Improving rectal tumor segmentation with anomaly fusion derived from anatomical inpainting: a multicenter study. Sci. Rep. **16**(1), 1545 (2026)
5. Cegla, P., et al.: [18f] fdg pet/ct imaging and hematological parameters can help predict hpv status in head and neck cancer. Nuklearmedizin-NuclearMedicine **64**(01), 22–31 (2025)
6. Dm, P.: Global cancer statistics, 2002. CA Cancer J. Clin. **55**, 74–108 (2005)

7. Escott, E.J.: Role of positron emission tomography/computed tomography (pet/ct) in head and neck cancer. Radiol. Clin. **51**(5), 881–893 (2013)
8. He, K., Zhang, X., Ren, S., Sun, J.: Deep residual learning for image recognition. In: Proceedings of the IEEE Conference on Computer Vision and Pattern Recognition, pp. 770–778 (2016)
9. Huang, Z., et al.: Stu-net: scalable and transferable medical image segmentation models empowered by large-scale supervised pre-training. arXiv preprint arXiv:2304.06716 (2023)
10. Isensee, F., Jaeger, P.F., Kohl, S.A., Petersen, J., Maier-Hein, K.H.: nnu-net: a self-configuring method for deep learning-based biomedical image segmentation. Nat. Methods **18**(2), 203–211 (2021)
11. Liang, X., et al.: Dpdnet: an dual-prompt-driven network for universal pet-ct segmentation. arXiv preprint (2025)
12. Mody, M.D., Rocco, J.W., Yom, S.S., Haddad, R.I., Saba, N.F.: Head and neck cancer. Lancet **398**(10318), 2289–2299 (2021)
13. Myronenko, A., Siddiquee, M.M.R., Yang, D., He, Y., Xu, D.: Automated head and neck tumor segmentation from 3d pet/ct hecktor 2022 challenge report. In: 3D Head and Neck Tumor Segmentation in PET/CT Challenge, pp. 31–37. Springer, Heidelberg (2022). https://doi.org/10.1007/978-3-031-27420-6_2
14. Saeed, N., et al.: A multimodal and multi-centric head and neck cancer dataset for segmentation, diagnosis, and outcome prediction (2025). https://arxiv.org/abs/2509.00367
15. Zhang, Y., Xu, Y., Chen, J., Xie, F., Chen, H.: Prototypical information bottlenecking and disentangling for multimodal cancer survival prediction. arXiv preprint arXiv:2401.01646 (2024)

Multi-stage Multimodal Progressive Learning for Coordinated Segmentation, Diagnosis, and Prognosis in Head and Neck Cancer

Yue Lin[1], Shenghai Wu[1], Hao Wang[2], Lei Bi[2], and Mingyuan Meng[2](✉)

[1] Research Institute, Newland Digital Technology, Fuzhou, China
[2] School of Computer Science, The University of Sydney, Sydney, Australia
mingyuan.meng@sydney.edu.au

Abstract. Head and Neck (H&N) cancer is among the most common cancers worldwide, and its related clinical decision-making constitutes a systematic process that requires the integration of multimodal clinical data and the coordination of diverse tasks in the clinical workflow. However, how to effectively coordinate the interrelated clinical tasks to maximize their synergistic potential is still an open question. In this study, we propose a Multi-stage Multimodal Progressive Learning (named MMPL) framework for coordinated modeling of segmentation, diagnosis, and prognosis tasks, in the context of *HECKTOR 2025* challenge at *MICCAI 2025*. Our MMPL progressively learns three clinical tasks that collectively facilitate personalized treatment planning: (i) tumor segmentation, (ii) HPV status classification, and (iii) survival prediction. Specifically, we establish a unified network backbone, consisting of a triple-stream encoder with adaptive PET/CT information fusion and an attention-gated decoder that can be applied to all three tasks. This backbone is successively trained for segmentation, classification, and survival prediction at three learning stages, where the knowledge is progressively learned with the guidance of prior knowledge accumulating from former stages. Further, the intermediate outputs (e.g., segmentation masks, HPV status) are leveraged as guidance on radiomics analysis or as supplementary indicators for the final prediction. In the final testing phase, our team *InterStellar* achieved top-tier performance across all three tasks, ranking first in HPV status classification and fourth in other two tasks.

Keywords: Multi-stage Progressive Learning · Multimodal Learning · Segmentation · Diagnosis · Prognosis

1 Introduction

With over 900,000 cases diagnosed annually worldwide, Head and Neck (H&N) cancer poses a significant and persistent challenge to global public health [1].

N. Saeed et al. (Eds.): HECKTOR 2026, LNCS 16520, pp. 97–107, 2026.
https://doi.org/10.1007/978-3-032-25766-6_9

Clinical decision-making for H&N cancer patients often integrates heterogeneous multimodal clinical data, such as medical imaging (e.g., MRI, PET/CT) and clinical indicators (e.g., demographics, TNM stage), for comprehensive assessment of disease severity and progression risk [2–5]. This assessment process typically involves the coordination of three interrelated tasks. First, the precise segmentation of the primary tumor (GTVp) and metastatic lymph nodes (GTVn) establishes the lesion localization and spatial context. Second, the diagnostic determination of crucial clinical characteristics (e.g., HPV status) identifies key etiologic and biological factors that carry significant prognostic implications and inform the interpretation of cancer stage and treatment intensity. Third, the prognostic assessment of the patients' outcomes synthesizes these upstream findings to estimate disease progression risk, which directly facilitates personalized treatment planning in accordance with clinical guidelines [2]. The above clinical workflow reflects a systematic process that requires the integration of multimodal data and the coordination of three tasks: *segmentation* → *diagnosis* → *prognosis.*

Most related methods are optimized for individual tasks, leaving cross-task synergies underexploited. For example, segmentation-target methods focus on automated delineation of H&N tumors in PET/CT [6–9], while imaging-based diagnosis/prognosis are typically treated as standalone problems that are developed independently using radiomics or deep-learning models [10–15]. Some recent works have explored the joint modeling of segmentation and survival prediction via joint multi-task learning [16–18], indicating that transferring knowledge from tumor segmentation can significantly benefit survival prediction [19,20]. However, diagnostic phenotyping is still kept outside the loop, and systems aligned with the clinical workflow of *segmentation* → *diagnosis* → *prognosis* remain scarce, underscoring the need for a unified framework that can effectively coordinate these tasks to leverage their cross-task synergies.

Since MICCAI 2020, the HECKTOR challenge has provided a multi-center, multimodal PET/CT benchmark and has completed three editions by 2022 with broad community engagement [21,22]. In 2025, building on prior focus on segmentation and survival outcome prediction, the HECKTOR 2025 challenge extends to include HPV status classification as a third task, aligning with the clinical workflow of segmentation, diagnosis, and prognosis [23]. Specifically, the 2025 edition (HECKTOR 2025) comprises three tasks: Task 1—automatic detection and segmentation of H&N primary tumor and lymph nodes in FDG-PET/CT images; Task 2—prediction of recurrence-free survival (RFS) from FDG-PET/CT images together with available clinical information and radiotherapy planning dose maps; and Task 3—diagnosis of HPV status from FDG-PET/CT images together with available clinical information [23].

In the context of HECKTOR 2025, we introduce a Multi-stage Multimodal Progressive Learning (MMPL) framework that mirrors the clinical workflow to leverage cross-task synergies among segmentation, diagnosis, and prognosis. Specifically, our MMPL adopts a unified network backbone shared across the three tasks, comprising a triple-stream encoder for PET/CT with adaptive cross-modal fusion and an attention-gated decoder together with task-specific prediction heads for (i) primary tumor and lymph node segmentation, (ii) HPV status classification, and (iii) RFS prediction. Learning proceeds in three successive stages that follow the clinical workflow, beginning with segmentation to learn robust representations of anatomy and disease extent, continuing with diagnosis that uses tumor-anchored features together with PET/CT information and relevant clinical indicators (e.g., demographics, TNM stage, performance status) to classify HPV status, and eventually concluding with RFS prediction that builds on all the prior knowledge from the earlier stages. Intermediate outputs are explicitly reused downstream: segmentation provides lesion localization and enables radiomics extraction from PET/CT within GTVp/GTVn, while HPV predictions serve as a complementary predictive indicator for survival estimation. This progressive, clinically aligned learning paradigm allows knowledge to flow from *segmentation* to *diagnosis* and then to *prognosis*, thereby leveraging both task dependencies and PET/CT complementarity.

2 Methods

2.1 Overview

We propose a Multi-stage Multimodal Progressive Learning (MMPL) framework that is aligned with the clinical workflow of *segmentation* → *diagnosis* → *prognosis*. MMPL proceeds through three successive learning stages: (S1) primary tumor and lymph node segmentation, (S2) HPV status classification, and (S3) RFS prediction, using a unified network backbone shared across all stages. The backbone follows the encoder–decoder design validated in the prior work [20]: It uses a *triple-stream encoder* with separate PET and CT streams and an adaptive fusion stream that mixes information across pyramid levels, followed by an *attention-gated decoder* that aggregates multi-scale features via gated skip connections, and produces a task-agnostic representation reused across all three stages. Three *task-specific heads* are individually attached to this shared representation for task-specific prediction, as illustrated in Fig. 1.

Our MMPL is built on a *prior-guided progressive learning strategy* that coordinates stages at two complementary levels while remaining faithful to clinical practice. At the parameter level, the shared backbone undergoes knowledge transfer and refinement: weights learned during segmentation are propagated and further optimized for diagnosis and then for prognosis, allowing prior knowledge to accumulate and be reused across tasks. At the output level, intermediate results serve as explicit guidance: the GTVp/GTVn masks (predicted in S1) provide lesion localization for mask-guided radiomics extraction reused by S2 and S3, and the HPV probability (predicted in S2) is incorporated as a supplementary indicator for S3. Clinical indicators are incorporated in the stage-specific statistical models, being concatenated with image-derived features for HPV status classification and used as covariates in the survival model. This progressive, clinically aligned learning paradigm enables knowledge to flow from *tumor/nodal segmentation* to *diagnosis* and then to *prognosis*, leveraging cross-task synergies while preserving interpretability.

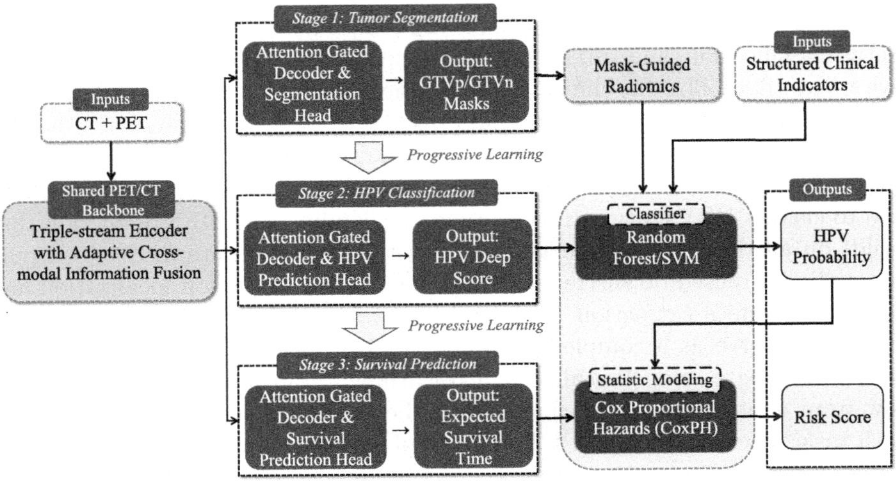

Fig. 1. Overview of our MMPL framework.

2.2 Data Preprocessing

Image Preprocessing. All PET/CT images undergo a consistent preprocessing procedure for both training and inference to prevent distribution shift. First, the co-registered PET and CT scans are resampled to an isotropic 1.0 mm spacing using B-spline interpolation over a common grid defined by their physical intersection. Subsequently, a Region of Interest (ROI) is automatically localized via a PET-guided strategy. This involves selecting the cranial-most 25% of the image volume along the z-axis, within which PET intensities are z-score normalized. A binary mask is then created by thresholding voxels with z-score greater than 1.0. The centroid of the largest 3D connected component in this mask is designated as the ROI center, where a $200 \times 200 \times 310$ voxel patch is extracted from both PET and CT. The CT intensities are clipped to the $[-1024, 1024]$ HU range and then scaled to $[-1, 1]$, while PET intensities are standardized using a z-score normalization across all non-zero voxels. For model training, random 128^3 sub-patches are cropped from the ROI. The corresponding segmentation labels are resampled using nearest-neighbor interpolation and processed into two separate binary masks for GTVp and GTVn.

Clinical Data Preprocessing. The provided structured clinical indicators are processed with the following procedure: categorical variables (e.g., sex, smoking status, alcohol status, performance status) are one-hot encoded; continuous variables are standardized via z-score normalization, using statistics fitted on the training split only to prevent information leakage. Missing values are imputed by the median of the training data for continuous variables. All preprocessing settings fitted on the training data are frozen and reused for inference.

2.3 Stage 1: Tumor Segmentation

The segmentation head is a 3D convolutional layer attached to the shared backbone. As described in [20], the attention-gated decoder performs four successive upsampling stages from the coarsest features, and the resulting features from the last decoder stage are projected by the segmentation head into two channels to produce voxel-wise probability maps for GTVp and GTVn.

Overlap–Detection–Aware (ODA) Loss. To reflect clinical priorities of precise GTVp boundaries and high sensitivity to small GTVn lesions, we use a composite objective coupling Dice with a focal Tversky term [24,25]. For $c \in \{T, N\}$ with binary labels y_c and predictions $\hat{y}_c$,

$$\mathcal{L}_{\text{seg}} = \sum_{c\in\{T,N\}} \left[\mathcal{L}_{\text{Dice}}(y_c, \hat{y}_c) + \left(1 - \text{TI}(y_c, \hat{y}_c; \alpha_c, \beta_c)\right)^{\gamma_c}\right] + \mathcal{L}_{\text{stab}}, \tag{1}$$

where $\mathcal{L}_{\text{Dice}}(y, \hat{y}) = 1 - \dfrac{2\langle y, \hat{y}\rangle + \varepsilon}{\|y\|_1 + \|\hat{y}\|_1 + \varepsilon}$ and

$$\text{TI}(y, \hat{y}; \alpha, \beta) = \frac{\text{TP} + \varepsilon}{\text{TP} + \alpha\,\text{FP} + \beta\,\text{FN} + \varepsilon}, \tag{2}$$

with $\text{TP} = \langle y, \hat{y}\rangle$, $\text{FP} = \langle 1 - y, \hat{y}\rangle$, and $\text{FN} = \langle y, 1 - \hat{y}\rangle$. We use near-symmetric parameters for GTVp $(\alpha_T, \beta_T, \gamma_T) = (0.5, 0.5, 1.33)$ and recall-biased parameters for GTVn $(\alpha_N, \beta_N, \gamma_N) = (0.3, 0.7, 1.50)$. A stabilization term improves optimization on empty or low-signal crops:

$$\mathcal{L}_{\text{stab}} = \sum_{c\in\{T,N\}} \Big(\mathcal{L}_{\text{BCE}}(y_c, \hat{y}_c) + \mathcal{L}_{\text{Dice}}(1 - y_c, 1 - \hat{y}_c)\Big) \tag{3}$$

Inference Procedure. We compute the PET-guided 1.0 mm ROI (as described in Sect. 2.2) and run overlapping sliding-window inference; window-wise probabilities are averaged across overlaps. Class-specific thresholds are applied, labels are composed with tumor-first priority, and the result is mapped back to the native CT grid. Post-processing consists of 3D hole filling and removal of connected components smaller than 50 voxels per class.

Mask-Guided Radiomics. Using the predicted masks of GTVp and GTVn, we extract radiomics features from both PET and CT to provide structured, interpretable descriptors to later stages. In particular, features cover morphology/shape, first-order statistics, and texture families (e.g., GLCM, GLRLM, GLSZM) computed on the original images as well as on standard filtered images (e.g., LoG, wavelet sub-bands), with fixed-bin discretization and filter settings as specified in [17]. Subsequently, features are standardized by z-score normalization using statistics fitted on the training data to prevent information leakage.

2.4 Stage 2: HPV Status Classification

The HPV prediction head is a shallow MLP head attached to the attention-gated decoder at four scales (1/8, 1/4, 1/2, full resolution). At each scale, the output of the last convolutional layer is fed into a global average pooling layer to form a scale-wise vector. The four vectors are concatenated and fed into the HPV prediction head, yielding a scalar logit whose sigmoid is supervised with a class-balanced binary cross-entropy. The logit is used as the deep score for downstream integration with clinical indicators and radiomics features.

Supervised Classifier. In line with clinical diagnosis practice, we aggregate three evidence sources: (i) the deep score from the HPV prediction head; (ii) the pre-extracted, *mask-guided* PET/CT radiomics from Stage 1, and (iii) structured clinical indicators as encoded and standardized as in Sect. 2.2. The concatenated vector is fed into a supervised ensemble classifier (random forest [26], scikit-learn) to output the HPV probability p_{HPV}. To enhance robustness, class imbalance is handled with SMOTE within each training fold [27]. Hyperparameters (e.g., number of trees, depth, minimum samples per leaf) are selected on validation folds to maximize balanced accuracy.

2.5 Stage 3: Survival Prediction

The survival prediction head is also a shallow MLP head that uses the same multi-scale features as Stage 2. Unlike Stage 2, the prediction head maps the four vectors to a K-dimensional vector of conditional survival probabilities over consecutive time intervals and is trained with a censoring-aware discrete-time negative log-likelihood [28]. Given a fixed setting of time intervals, the expected survival time is $\widehat{T} = \sum_{i=1}^{K} S_i \, \Delta t_i$, where S_i denotes the cumulative survival probability up to interval i, and Δt_i is the duration of interval i.

Cox Proportional Hazards (CoxPH) Integration. For the final risk score prediction, we integrate (i) the predicted survival time, (ii) the pre-extracted, *mask-guided* PET/CT radiomics from Stage 1, (iii) the final HPV probability from Stage 2, and (iv) structured clinical indicators (as encoded and standardized as in Sect. 2.2) via a CoxPH model [29]. Feature selection is performed within each training fold to avoid information leakage: Univariate Cox analysis retains clinical indicators with $p<0.05$, while Least Absolute Shrinkage and Selection Operator (LASSO) regression is applied to select radiomics features.

3 Experimental Setup

Dataset Overview. HECKTOR 2025 uses a multi-center, multimodal head-and-neck cancer dataset [23]. The corpus contains 1,123 pretreatment FDG-PET/CT studies from ten institutions. Major contributors are MD Anderson (444 cases; 39.6%), CHUB (216 cases; 19.2%), and University Hospital Zurich

(101 cases; 9.0%). Harmonized clinical data include RFS time and censoring indicator, HPV status, demographics, and staging. Across the full cohort, RFS information is available for 1,052 patients: 843 censored and 209 events; HPV status is available for 873 patients: 587 positive and 286 negative [23]. Our method was developed with the organizer-released training subset, including 726 patients from seven centers for all three tasks, while the remaining data was retained by the organizers for online validation and testing.

Training Subset. All internal validation, model selection, and ablations were conducted on the organizer-released training subset available to us. The effective label availability in the training data is as follows:

- Tumor Segmentation (Task 1): 680 cases with valid GTVp/GTVn masks.
- Survival Prediction (Task 2): 678 cases with RFS labels (542 censored and 136 non-censored).
- HPV status classification (Task 3): 588 cases with HPV labels (58 HPV-negative and 530 HPV-positive).

Data Splits. We used two complementary validation schemes on the organizer-released training subset. (i) *Five-fold patient-level cross-validation:* patients were randomly partitioned into five disjoint folds at the *patient* level. Task-specific folds were induced by intersecting the global split with each task's label-available subset (segmentation, HPV, RFS). (ii) *Five-fold center-out validation:* the seven centers were grouped into five folds by holding out one large center or a pair of smaller centers per fold to balance validation size; all patients from held-out centers form the validation set for that fold, ensuring that the validation distribution is center-disjoint from training.

Challenge Protocol. We followed the official HECKTOR 2025 rules: Our method was developed merely on the released training subset, and the performance on the held-out data was assessed by the organizers. The testing labels are not public, and no external data was used.

4 Results

All quantitative results reported below are the mean across five-fold patient-level cross-validation on the released training data, which guided our model selection during development. For the final challenge submission, we additionally trained five models using five-fold center-out validation. The final results ensemble the output of ten models. The organizers evaluated our final submission on the held-out test set of HECKTOR 2025; according to the official leaderboard, our team *InterStellar* ranked 4th, 4th, and 1st on Tasks 1–3, respectively. Since the test labels and full per-case metrics are not publicly available, we restrict detailed quantitative analyses in this paper to the organizer-released training subset and summarize the official test-set performance separately.

4.1 Performance of Tumor Segmentation (Task 1)

The evaluation metrics follow the official HECKTOR protocol: GTVp is tracked by mean Dice, whereas GTVn emphasizes both volumetric overlap and lesion detectability. Accordingly, we report Dice results for GTVp and GTVn, whereas for GTVn, the aggregated F1 score is reported to evaluate detection performance.

Table 1 presents the five-fold cross-validation results on the training data, which demonstrates that compared to using Dice loss alone (Dice-only), ODA improves GTVn detectability and overlap (higher lesion F1 and GTVn Dice) and also raises GTVp Dice.

Table 1. Five-fold cross-validation results for Task 1.

Method	Dice(GTVp)	Dice(GTVn)	F1(GTVn)
Dice-only	0.7643	0.6616	0.7164
ODA (Dice+Focal Tversky+stabilizers)	0.8161	0.8206	0.8391

4.2 Performance of HPV Status Classification (Task 3)

During development, model selection within each fold was based on AUC. After selecting the model, we chose a decision threshold on the corresponding validation split to maximize balanced accuracy, and then reported sensitivity and specificity at that threshold.

Table 2 presents the five-fold cross-validation results for the deep learning model (Deep-only) and the additional integration with radiomics features and clinical indicators (Deep+Rad+Clin). Compared to the deep-only baseline, adding radiomics features and clinical indicators yields a higher AUC and substantially improves specificity with only a minor degrade in sensitivity, thereby increasing balanced accuracy at the selected thresholds.

Table 2. Five-fold cross-validation results for Task 3. AUC is used for model selection within each fold. Sensitivity and specificity are computed at the validation threshold that maximizes balanced accuracy.

Method	AUC	Sensitivity	Specificity
Deep-only	0.9535	0.9863	0.5338
Deep+Rad+Clin	0.9601	0.9795	0.7667

4.3 Performance of Survival Prediction (Task2)

Following the official HECKTOR protocol, the survival prediction performance is evaluated with C-index [30]. **Table** 3 presents the five-fold cross-validation results for the deep learning model (Deep-only) and the CoxPH integration model, which demonstrates that the integration of radiomics features, clinical indicators, and HPV probability yields a higher C-index.

Table 3. Five-fold cross-validation results for Task 2.

Method	C-index
Deep-only	0.6974
CoxPH Integration	0.7107

4.4 Official Test-Set Performance

In addition to the internal cross-validation results reported above, we also report the official HECKTOR 2025 test-set performance of our final submission, as evaluated by the organizers on the held-out test set. As summarized in Table 4, our team *InterStellar* ranked first in HPV status classification and fourth in other two tasks.

Table 4. Test-set performance of team *InterStellar* on the held-out HECKTOR 2025 test set.

Task	Metric	Score
Task 1: Segmentation	GTVp DSC	0.7301
	GTVn Agg DSC	0.7406
	GTVn Agg F1	0.6638
Task 2: Survival	C-index	0.5873
Task 3: HPV status	Balanced accuracy	0.5583

5 Conclusion and Limitations

In the study, we have outlined MMPL, a Multi-stage Multimodal Progressive Learning framework that mirrors the clinical workflow of *segmentation* → *diagnosis* → *prognosis*. Built on a unified PET/CT backbone with task-specific heads, MMPL links the stages through a *prior-guided progressive learning strategy* at both the parameter and the output levels. This clinically aligned learning paradigm enables knowledge to flow from segmentation to diagnosis and then to prognosis, promoting cross-task synergy. As demonstrated in the five-fold cross-validation, MMPL improved lymph node detectability and overall segmentation quality with the proposed ODA objective, increased HPV specificity at comparable sensitivity when combining deep score with mask-guided radiomics and clinical indicators, and raised the survival prediction via CoxPH integration. Our final submission ensembles ten models trained with both patient-level and center-out cross-validation and achieved top-tier performance on the official HECKTOR 2025 leaderboard, ranking first in HPV status classification and fourth in other two tasks.

Although the challenge provides radiotherapy dose maps for outcome modeling, our current implementation does not incorporate dose information because only a very small number of cases in the available training subset included usable dose maps. Future work will integrate dose maps and examine their interaction with PET/CT images and clinical indicators.

References

1. Sung, H., Ferlay, J., Siegel, R.L.: Global Cancer Statistics 2020: GLOBOCAN estimates of incidence and mortality worldwide for 36 cancers in 185 countries. CA Cancer J. Clin. **71**(3), 209–249 (2021)
2. Colevas, A.D., Cmelak, A.J., Pfister, D.G.: NCCN guidelines® insights: head and neck cancers, version 2.2025. J. Natl. Compr. Canc. Netw. **23**(2) (2025)
3. Ang, K.K., Harris, J., Wheeler, R., et al.: Human papillomavirus and survival of patients with oropharyngeal cancer. N. Engl. J. Med. **363**(1), 24–35 (2010)
4. Amin, M.B., Edge, S., Greene, F., et al. (eds.): AJCC Cancer Staging Manual, 8th edn. Springer, New York (2017)
5. Meng, M., Bi, L., Fulham, M., Feng, D., Kim, J.: Merging-diverging hybrid transformer networks for survival prediction in head and neck cancer. In: MICCAI 2023. LNCS, vol. 14225, pp. 400–410 (2023)
6. Murugesan, G.K.: Head and neck primary tumor segmentation using deep learning (nnU-Net framework). In: HECKTOR 2021. LNCS, vol. 13209, pp. 224–235. (2022)
7. Oreiller, V., Andrearczyk, V., Jreige, M., Castelli, J., Prior, J.O., Vallières, M., Visvikis, D., Hatt, M., Depeursinge, A.: Head and neck tumor segmentation in PET/CT: the HECKTOR challenge. Med. Image Anal. **77**, 102336 (2022)
8. Andrearczyk, V., Oreiller, V., Boughdad, S.: Automatic head and neck tumor segmentation and outcome prediction relying on FDG-PET/CT images: findings from the second edition of the HECKTOR challenge. Med. Image Anal. **90**, 102972 (2023)
9. Li, G.Y., Chen, J., Jang, S.-I., Gong, K., Li, Q.: SwinCross: cross-modal swin transformer for head-and-neck tumor segmentation in PET/CT images. arXiv:2302.03861 (2023)
10. Jo, K.H., et al.: 18F-FDG PET/CT parameters enhance MRI radiomics for predicting HPV status in OPSCC. Yonsei Med. J. **64**(12), 992–1002 (2023)
11. Woo, C., et al.: Development and testing of a machine-learning model for HPV status using ^{18}F-FDG PET/CT-derived parameters in OPSCC. Korean J. Radiol. **24**(1), 1–12 (2023)

12. Fanizzi, A., et al.: Explainable CNN-based prediction of HPV status in OPSCC. Sci. Rep. **14**, 16134 (2024)
13. Vallières, M., Kay-Rivest, E., Perrin, L.J., et al.: Radiomics strategies for risk assessment of tumour failure in head-and-neck cancer. Sci. Rep. **7**, 10117 (2017)
14. Huynh, B.N., Groendahl, A.R., Tomic, O.: Head and neck cancer treatment outcome prediction: conventional radiomics vs. deep-learning radiomics on pre-treatment PET/CT. Front. Med. **10**, 1217037 (2023)
15. Gu, B., et al.: Prediction of 5-year progression-free survival in advanced nasopharyngeal carcinoma with pretreatment PET/CT using multi-modality deep learning-based radiomics. Front. Oncol. **12**, 899351 (2022)
16. Meng, M., Peng, Y., Bi, L., Kim, J.: Multi-task deep learning for joint tumor segmentation and outcome prediction in head and neck cancer. In: HECKTOR 2021. LNCS, vol. 13209, pp. 160–167. (2022)
17. Meng, M., Bi, L., Feng, D.D., Kim, J.: Radiomics-enhanced deep multi-task learning for outcome prediction in head and neck cancer. In: HECKTOR 2022. LNCS, vol. 13626, pp. 135–143 (2023)
18. Meng, M., Gu, B., Bi, L., Song, S., Feng, D.D., Kim, J.: DeepMTS: deep multi-task learning for survival prediction in patients with advanced nasopharyngeal carcinoma using pretreatment PET/CT. IEEE J. Biomed. Health Inform. **26**(9), 4497–4507 (2022)
19. Gu, B., et al.: Multi-task deep learning-based radiomic nomogram for prognostic prediction in locoregionally advanced nasopharyngeal carcinoma. Eur. J. Nucl. Med. Mol. Imaging **50**(13), 3996–4009 (2023)
20. Meng, M., Gu, B., Kim, J.: Adaptive segmentation-to-survival learning for survival prediction from multi-modality medical images. NPJ Precision Oncology **8**, 63 (2024)
21. Andrearczyk, V., Oreiller, V., Boughdad, S.: Overview of the HECKTOR challenge at MICCAI 2020: automatic head and neck tumor segmentation in PET/CT. In: HECKTOR 2020. LNCS, vol. 12603, pp. 1–21. (2021)
22. Andrearczyk, V., Oreiller, V., Abobakr, M.: Overview of the HECKTOR challenge at MICCAI 2022: automatic head and neck tumor segmentation and outcome prediction in PET/CT. In: HECKTOR 2022. LNCS, vol. 13626, pp. 1–30 (2023)
23. Saeed, N., Hassan, S., Hardan, S.: A Multimodal and Multi-centric Head and Neck Cancer Dataset for Segmentation, Diagnosis, and Outcome Prediction (2025). arXiv:2509.00367
24. Salehi, S.S.M., Erdogmus, D., Gholipour, A.: Tversky loss function for image segmentation. In: MLMI, MICCAI Workshops, pp. 379–387 (2017)
25. Abraham, N., Khan, N.: A novel focal Tversky loss function with improved Attention U-Net for lesion segmentation. In: ISBI Workshops, pp. 1–4 (2019)
26. Breiman, L.: Random forests. Mach. Learn. **45**, 5–32 (2001)
27. Chawla, N.V., Bowyer, K.W., Hall, L.O., et al.: SMOTE: synthetic minority over-sampling technique. J. Artif. Intell. Res. **16**, 321–357 (2002)
28. Kvamme, H., Borgan, Ø.: Continuous and discrete-time survival prediction with neural networks. Lifetime Data Anal. **27**, 710–736 (2021)
29. Cox, D.R.: Regression models and life-tables. J. Roy. Stat. Soc.: Ser. B (Methodol.) **34**(2), 187–202 (1972)
30. Harrell, F.E., Jr., Califf, R.M., Pryor, D.B., Lee, K.L., Rosati, R.A.: Evaluating the yield of medical tests. JAMA **247**(18), 2543–2546 (1982)

Enhancing Survival Outcomes in Head and Neck Cancer Through Joint HPV Classification and Tumor Segmentation

Dalal Chamseddine[1,2(✉)], Shamimeh Ahrari[1], Mira Rizkallah[2], Thomas Carlier[1,3], and Diana Mateus[2]

[1] Nuclear Medicine Department, University Hospital, Nantes, France
{shamimeh.ahrari,thomas.carlier}@chu-nantes.fr
[2] Nantes Université, Centrale Nantes, CNRS, LS2N, UMR, 6004, Nantes, France
{dalal.chamseddine,mira.rizkallah,diana.mateus}@ec-nantes.fr
[3] Nantes Université, Inserm, CNRS, Université d'Angers, CRCI2NA, Nantes, France

Abstract. Head and Neck Cancer (HNC) is a broad term for cancers that develop in the head and neck region. Accurate survival prediction is critical for guiding patient management and treatment planning. Traditional survival models, such as Kaplan–Meier curves and Cox Proportional Hazards models, are limited by their dependence on linearity and proportional hazards assumptions. Recently, deep learning–based survival models have demonstrated promising results for risk prediction. However, current approaches still struggle to fully integrate multimodal data and to capture region-specific features effectively. In this work, we employed a Multitask Learning framework that simultaneously performs Human Papillomavirus (HPV) classification, tumor segmentation, and survival prediction based on Positron Emission Tomography, Computed Tomography imaging, and clinical features. Integrating these three tasks into a unified model enables the use of shared feature representations. The segmentation module facilitates the extraction of tumor-specific features, while the classification branch incorporates HPV status prediction as a critical prognostic factor in HNC.

This approach was developed and evaluated as part of our participation in the MICCAI 2025 HEad and neCK TumOR segmentation and outcome prediction challenge as the SIMS-LIFE team.

Keywords: Multitask learning · Survival prediction · PET/CT · Head and neck cancer

1 Introduction

Head and Neck Cancer (HNC) is the seventh most common cancer worldwide. It typically arises from squamous cells covering the mucosal surfaces of the lip, oral cavity, pharynx, larynx, and paranasal sinuses. The prognosis for HNC varies

D. Chamseddine and S. Ahrari—Contributed equally to this work.

N. Saeed et al. (Eds.): HECKTOR 2026, LNCS 16520, pp. 108–118, 2026.
https://doi.org/10.1007/978-3-032-25766-6_10

greatly, with an overall 5-year survival rate of 50–60% [11]. The global incidence of HNC continues to rise, with 946,456 new cases and 482,001 deaths reported worldwide in 2025 [2], emphasizing the importance of accurately and promptly diagnosing high-risk patients. In this context, survival analysis is a powerful tool for estimating risk, guiding early prognosis, and personalizing treatment plans.

^{18}F-FluoroDeoxyGlucose Positron Emission Tomography (PET) and Computed Tomography (CT) imaging play a crucial role in tumor characterization at both initial staging and follow-up of HNC, thanks to the complementary nature of both anatomical and functional information these medical images provide [10]. Traditional survival prediction methods are usually based on clinical and tabular information collected by clinicians or handcrafted radiomics features [7] extracted from PET/CT images, which are then modeled using statistical survival models such as the Cox Proportional Hazards (CoxPH) [5]. In this regard, several studies investigating the impact of radiomics features in patients with HNC have shown promising results in improving survival predictions. For example, Haidar et al. [8] demonstrated that such features can provide complementary prognostic information, enabling more accurate outcome estimations. Other studies have further shown that choices within the radiomics pipeline, such as harmonization strategies, sub-volume feature extraction, and segmentation methods, can significantly influence survival predictions for HNC, thereby improving the performance of the CoxPH models in risk stratification [23].

More recently, deep survival models [6,13,15] based on deep learning have been introduced to overcome the limitations of traditional approaches, which often assume linear effects and proportional risks. Deep survival models are designed to capture non-linear feature interactions and integrate heterogeneous data sources. In HNC, such approaches have shown promise in more accurately predicting patient outcomes [19] and have the potential to outperform traditional survival models [1]. Moreover, other studies have leveraged graph-convolutional networks to build survival prediction models [18].

Building on deep models, Multitask Learning (MTL) has been explored to further improve survival prediction. MTL lies in learning shared representations across related tasks, which reduces the prediction error and improves event occurrence estimation within specific time intervals [16]. Leveraging the multiple ground-truth tasks provided in the HEad and neCK TumOR (HECKTOR) Grand Challenge 2025, we incorporate two auxiliary tasks alongside our main task of survival prediction within a unified network to enhance risk estimation.

To this end, in this work, we employed a modified version of DeepMTS [20]. While the original framework focused on segmentation and survival analysis, our adaptation integrates both classification and segmentation with survival analysis to maximize the extraction of relevant features while preserving prognostic information. In particular, the classification branch predicts Human Papillomavirus (HPV) status, a key prognostic factor strongly associated with patient outcomes. Multimodal PET/CT data served as input, and deep features derived from both the classification and segmentation backbones were combined with clinical features to generate the final Recurrence-Free Survival (RFS) prediction. In addition, a strategy was adopted to address incomplete data, handling cases with missing labels and/or missing categorical clinical features. Experiments on the challenge dataset suggest that incorporating HPV classification can contribute to improved risk prediction performance.

2 Multitask Framework

This study focused on RFS prediction, defined as the time interval between the date of diagnosis and the date of disease recurrence. Using PET, CT, and clinical features as input, the model performed survival prediction as the primary task, with classification and segmentation serving as auxiliary tasks. Accordingly, the survival label, HPV status, and segmentation mask were used as ground-truth labels.

Figure 1 illustrates the overall model architecture, which is a modified version of DeepMTS [20]. Within this multitask framework, training was performed using a combined multitask loss (L_{Total}) defined as follows:

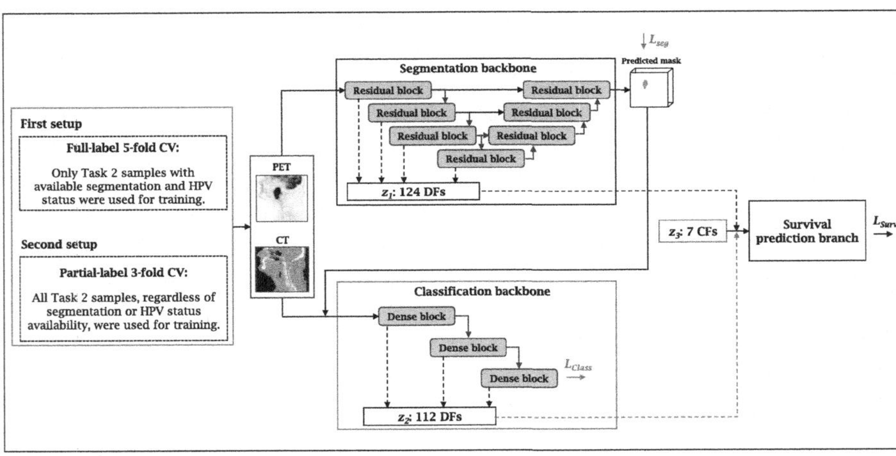

Fig. 1. Flowchart of the overall pipeline, with key modifications relative to the original DeepMTS highlighted in red. CV: Cross-Validation; PET: Positron Emission Tomography; CT: Computed Tomography; DF: Deep Feature; CF: Clinical Feature. (Color figure online)

$$L_{Total} = L_{Seg} + L_{Class} + L_{Surv} + 0.1L2_{Reg}, \tag{1}$$

Based on the original DeepMTS, the preprocessed PET and CT images were first concatenated on the channel axis and fed into the segmentation backbone, a modified version of 3D U-Net [4]. The predicted tumor probability map was compared with the ground-truth segmentation label using the sum of Dice [21] and Focal [17] losses (L_{Seg}), instead of only the Dice used in DeepMTS [20], to emphasize hard tumor pixels that would otherwise be overwhelmed by the large background regions. Next we describe the details of the loss functions:

$$L_{Seg} = L_{Dice} + L_{Focal}, \tag{2}$$

$$L_{Dice} = 1 - \frac{2\sum_i^N p_i y_i}{\sum_i^N p_i^2 + \sum_i^N y_i^2}, \tag{3}$$

$$L_{Focal} = \frac{1}{N}\sum_{i=1}^{N} FL(p_i, y_i), \tag{4}$$

where

$$FL(p, y) = \begin{cases} -\alpha(1-p)^\gamma log(p) & y = 1 \\ -(1-\alpha)p^\gamma log(1-p) & y = 0 \end{cases} \tag{5}$$

Here N is the total number of voxels, $p \in \{0, 1\}$ is the predicted tumor probability map, and $y \in \{0, 1\}$ is the ground-truth segmentation label. In Eq. 5, α is for the voxel weighting factor and γ is a focusing parameter were set to 0.25 and 2, respectively.

Subsequently, the tumor probability map and the preprocessed PET/CT images were concatenated and input into the HPV classification backbone, which is one of our main modifications. The classification branch was implemented as a cascaded network based on a modified 3D DenseNet [12], introducing it as a new branch added to the original DeepMTS [20]. The network parameters were optimized using a binary focal cross-entropy loss (L_{Class}) [17], which follows the same formulation as in Eq. 5, but this time comparing the predicted HPV status (p_c) of the whole image with the ground-truth classification labels (y_c).

Next, the clinical features (z_3) were concatenated with 124 deep features (z_1) derived from the encoder branch of the segmentation backbone and 112 deep features (z_2) extracted from the classification backbone, and fed into the survival branch, which consisted of three Fully Connected (FC) layers. As in the original DeepMTS, the predicted risk factor was compared with the ground-truth survival label using the Cox negative log partial likelihood loss (L_{Surv}) [13]:

$$L_{Surv} = -\frac{1}{N_{E=1}} \sum_{i:E_i=1} (h_i - \log \sum_{j \in R(T_i)} e^{h_j}) \tag{6}$$

where $N_{E=1}$ is the number of patients with disease recurrence, $E_i \in \{0, 1\}$ is the event indicator (1=event, 0=censored), h denotes the predicted risk scores, T is the ground-truth observed times, and $R(T_i)$ is the risk set defined as $\{j : T_j \geq T_i\}$, representing the set of patients j who have survived up to time T_i.

Additionally, an L2 regularization ($L2_{Reg}$) term with a coefficient of 0.1 was applied to all FC layers of the survival branch, consistent with the original framework.

Since HPV and/or segmentation labels were not present for all samples, but we aimed to utilize all available data, we adopted a simple strategy to handle missing labels. When a segmentation mask was available, the primary tumor and metastatic lymph node delineations were merged into a single ground-truth segmentation label; otherwise, a zero-valued image was generated. Missing HPV status and categorical clinical features were assigned to a separate category to account for incomplete data. We considered an approach inspired by tree-based algorithms, such as XGBoost with a linear booster, to handle missing values [3]. Accordingly, all missing values were coded as 0, and the remaining categories were shifted forward by one to preserve their distinction.

3 Experimental Settings

3.1 Dataset

In this study, we used a publicly available dataset from the HECKTOR 2025 challenge [22], which was designed for developing and benchmarking automatic methods for HNC segmentation and survival prediction. For each sample, the CT image was paired with the corresponding registered PET image. The challenge organizers precomputed the Standardized Uptake Value (SUV) for the PET images, and all PET/CT files were provided in NIfTI format. The considered clinical features consisted of age, gender, tobacco and alcohol consumption, treatment (radiotherapy only or combined with chemotherapy and/or surgery), performance status, and distant metastasis stage.

For our main task of RFS prediction (Task 2), a training set of 678 samples was collected from seven centers, including CHUM (n = 56), CHUP (n = 44), CHUS (n = 72), HGJ (n = 55), HMR (n = 18), MDA (n = 422), and USZ (n = 11). Six samples were excluded from the analysis, two due to negative SUV values and four due to significant extravasation at the injection area, which impairs the SUV computation. The HECKTOR challenge provided a validation set of 50 samples (HECKTOR validation set), while the test set contains 400 samples with withheld ground-truth labels. Further details of the dataset are available in [22].

3.2 Image Preprocessing

For early PET/CT fusion, we initially performed resampling onto a common voxel grid to address differences in voxel size between the two modalities. The CT images exhibited higher spatial resolution than the corresponding PET images, with CT voxel sizes ranging from $0.49 \times 0.49 \times 2\ mm^3$ to $2.73 \times 2.73 \times 3\ mm^3$, while PET voxel sizes ranged from $0.98 \times 0.98 \times 2.50\ mm^3$ to $5.47 \times 5.47 \times 3.27\ mm^3$. All images were resampled to isotropic voxels of $2 \times 2 \times 2\ mm^3$, using spline interpolation for the PET/CT images and nearest-neighbor interpolation for the corresponding segmentations. Subsequently, the images were cropped to $128 \times 128 \times 128$ voxels, centered on the tumor using PET intensity-based bounding boxes derived from SUV thresholding.

3.3 Metrics

Considering RFS prediction as the primary objective of this study, the following metrics were used to evaluate model performance for each task.

Concordance Index (C-Index). The C-index is an extension of the area under the curve that considers censored data. It refers to the model's ability to accurately produce a trustworthy ranking of survival durations according to the personal scores [9]. This metric is measured between 0 and 1, where any value less than 0.5 indicates random predictions. The equation for this metric is as follows:

$$C\text{-index} = \frac{\sum_{i,j} \mathbf{1}_{T_j<T_i} \cdot (\mathbf{1}_{r_j>r_i} + 0.5 \cdot \mathbf{1}_{r_j=r_i})}{\sum_{i,j} \mathbf{1}_{T_i<T_j} \cdot \delta_i} \tag{7}$$

Here T_i and T_j represent the time for a pair of patients, respectively, δ denotes the event indicator, and r represents the risk score.

Dice Coefficient. It is a similarity metric calculated between the ground-truth and the predicted segmentations. Its value is between 0 (no overlap) and 1 (perfect prediction). This metric is defined as:

$$\text{Dice}(y_{\text{true}}, y_{\text{pred}}) = \frac{2\sum(y_{\text{true}} \cdot y_{\text{pred}}) + \epsilon}{\sum y_{\text{true}} + \sum y_{\text{pred}} + \epsilon} \tag{8}$$

where y_{true} and y_{pred} indicate the ground-truth and the predicted segmentations, respectively, and ϵ represents a constant of $1e-8$.

Balanced Accuracy. It accounts for class imbalance by averaging the recall of each class and can be calculated according to the following equation:

$$Balanced\ \ Accuracy = \frac{1}{2} \cdot \left(\frac{TP}{P} + \frac{TN}{N}\right) \tag{9}$$

where TP represents true positives, TN indicates true negatives, P represents all positives, and N represents all negatives.

3.4 Implementation Details

The model implementation was performed using TensorFlow 1.x on a 16 GB NVIDIA Quadro RTX 5000 for the first setup and TensorFlow 2.x on a 20 GB NVIDIA RTX 4000 Ada Generation for the second setup (see the description of setups in Sect. 4.2). Both models were trained for 500 epochs with a batch size of 4. Early stopping was applied based on the validation set C-index. The Adam optimizer [14] was initialized with a learning rate of 1×10^{-4} and subsequently reduced to 5×10^{-5}, 1×10^{-5}, and 1×10^{-6} at epochs 100, 200, and thereafter. The code is publicly available at https://github.com/Dalalsh/HNC-Multi-task-Learning.

4 Experimental Validation and Results

4.1 Task Ablation

For the ablation study, three model configurations were evaluated prior to selecting the final model for submission. The first model (Seg+Surv) followed the original DeepMTS framework [20], incorporating the segmentation and survival branches. The second model consisted solely of the survival branch (Surv). The last model was the modified version of DeepMTS (Fig. 1) that integrated three tasks: classification, segmentation, and survival (Class+Seg+Surv). In the ablation study, experiments were conducted using a single train/validation/test split across all patients, with 60% of the samples allocated to the training, 30% to the validation, and 10% to the test set. All models were trained for 100 epochs to assess performance with and without the multitask configuration.

As shown in Fig. 2, the validation loss curve for the Surv model exhibited some instability, whereas the curves for Seg+Surv and Class+Seg+Surv demonstrated better convergence. Comparing the validation C-index across the three model configurations, the Class+Seg+Surv configuration tended to provide a better performance. As reported in Table 1, incorporating HPV status classification improved overall network performance, with the multitask Class+Seg+Surv model achieving the higher validation C-index values than both the Surv and Seg+Surv configurations. This indicates that incorporating clinically relevant classification tasks can enhance the discriminative power of the model and contribute positively to survival prediction.

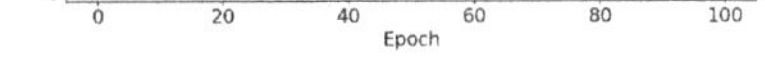

(a) Seg+Surv loss

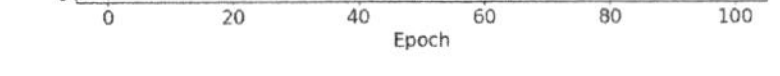

(b) Surv loss

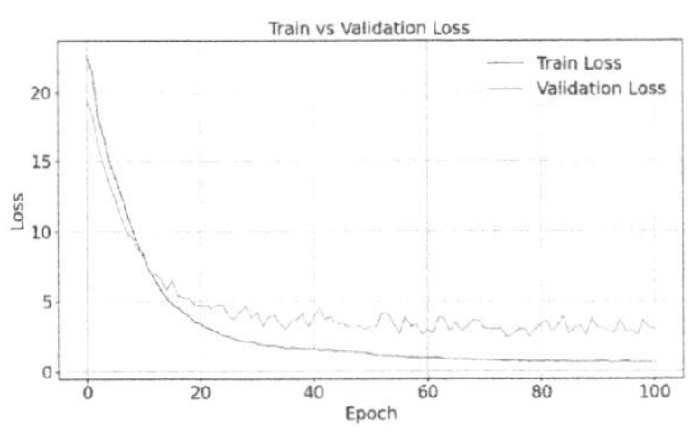

(c) Class+Seg+Surv loss

Fig. 2. Total loss over 100 epochs for the ablation study.

Table 1. Results of the ablation study. Higher C-index values across the validation set for each of the three model configurations at each epoch are highlighted in bold.

Epoch	Training C-index			Validation C-index		
	Seg+Surv	Surv	Class+Surv+Seg	Seg+Surv	Surv	Class+Surv+Seg
0	0.5445	0.4964	0.5265	0.4031	0.4687	**0.4901**
10	0.5018	0.5538	0.5603	0.4724	0.4444	**0.6070**
20	0.7216	0.7255	0.7717	0.5813	0.6604	**0.6939**
30	0.9217	0.8748	0.9322	0.6224	0.5999	**0.6580**
40	0.9323	0.9221	0.9338	0.6417	0.5442	**0.7206**
50	0.9625	0.9558	0.9406	0.5922	0.5791	**0.7986**
60	0.9772	0.9467	0.9634	0.5323	0.6065	**0.7899**
70	0.9769	0.9721	0.9658	0.6073	**0.7055**	0.6694
80	0.9772	0.9672	0.9835	0.6406	0.5520	**0.7198**
90	0.9818	0.9675	0.9679	0.5833	0.5480	**0.6326**
100	0.9823	0.9665	0.9778	0.5495	**0.6123**	0.5639

4.2 Final Submission

Based on observations from the ablation study (Table 1), the Class+Seg+Surv configuration was selected for our final multitask framework and applied Cross-Validation (CV) techniques to achieve a more generalized predictive model. Accordingly, two training and validation setups were evaluated (Fig. 1) using the Class+Seg+Surv model configuration.

Full-Label 5-Fold CV. In the first setup, a 5-fold CV was performed using only samples from the Hecktor challenge Task 2 that had labels available for both segmentation masks and HPV status (n = 518). Samples missing either label (n = 154) were systematically added to the validation set of each fold.

Partial-Label 3-Fold CV. The second setup employed a 3-fold CV that included all Task 2 samples in the training set (n = 672) regardless of segmentation mask or HPV status availability. In this setup, samples with missing labels contributed to model optimization solely through their image data and were excluded from the corresponding loss calculations (L_{Class} and L_{Seg}), aiming to leverage the full image distribution to enhance feature representation despite partial labels.

For the final submission, we considered the average of the best model from each fold to obtain the final predicted risk score on the shared validation set. This approach was intended to reduce the influence of any outliers in the training data on the final predictions and to make predictions based on an ensemble of models. Figure 3 shows the mean total loss across CV folds for both setups, with the networks exhibiting stable validation loss across the CV folds.

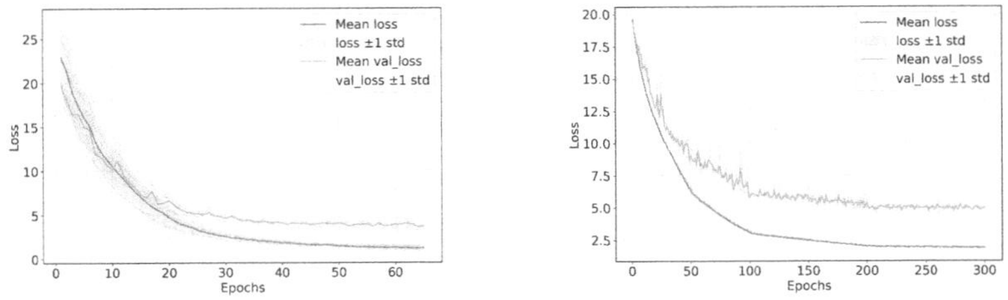

(a) Full-label 5-fold CV (b) Partial-label 3-fold CV

Fig. 3. Mean total loss across CV folds for the Class+Seg+Surv multitask configuration with early stopping.

Table 2 report the C-index values for the considered setups. For the local validation sets, the results are presented as mean C-index values across CV folds, followed by the 95% confidence intervals. The C-index values on the HECKTOR validation and test sets are also provided, where our team achieved first place on the HECKTOR test set (0.658), with a clear margin over the second-place score (0.602).

Table 2. C-index results on the local validation set (from our CV), the HECKTOR validation and test sets (provided by the challenge), based on the Class+Seg+Surv multitask configuration.

Setup	Local validation	HECKTOR	
		Validation set	Test set
Full-label5-fold CV	0.666 [0.632, 0.705]	0.566	0.658
Partial-label3-fold CV	0.682 [0.671, 0.703]	0.583	0.494

5 Conclusion and Limitation

This study focused on predicting survival outcomes using a multitask framework that simultaneously performs classification, segmentation, and survival prediction. A key observation was the critical role of incorporating HPV status as a clinical integration in survival prediction. However, implementing such a multimodal and multitask approach is challenging, as complete multimodal data are often not available for all samples. To address this, categorical features with missing values were assigned to a separate category. Additionally, to enable the model to learn image feature representations from all available samples, unlabeled data for classification and/or segmentation were included during training but excluded from loss computation. Finally, we considered an ensemble technique that uses a CV scheme to improve the generalizability of the model to unseen samples. Although the improvements in the C-index were moderate, they were consistent across our local validation set and the HECKTOR validation set.

This approach could potentially be extended by employing other losses beyond the survival loss to better handle these unlabeled samples. While the framework achieved promising performance, future work could explore more advanced survival prediction methods, such as DeepHit or attention-based networks, to strengthen the survival branch. In addition, refining training strategies for the classification branch and incorporating attention or uncertainty modeling can enhance interpretability in clinical settings.

Acknowledgments. This work has been partially funded by SIRIC ILIAD (INCa-DGOS-INSERM-ITMO Cancer 18011), the French "Program d'Investissement d'Avenir" (ANR-16-IDEX-0007), the region "Pays de la Loire" through their support to I-Site NExT, as well as by Siemens Healthineers, the industrial partner of the NExT research industrial chair IMRAM.

Disclosure of Interests. The authors have no competing interests to declare that are relevant to the content of this article.

References

1. Afshar, P., et al.: From handcrafted to deep-learning-based cancer radiomics: challenges and opportunities. IEEE Signal Process. Mag. **36**(4), 132–160 (2019)
2. El-Bayoumy, K., et al.: Current challenges and potential opportunities for interception and prevention of head and neck cancer. In: Carcinogenesis 46.2 (2025), bgaf025
3. Chen, T., Guestrin, C.: Xgboost: a scalable tree boosting system. In: Proceedings of the 22nd ACM SIGKDD International Conference on Knowledge Discovery and Data Mining, pp. 785–794 (2016)
4. Çiçek, Ö., et al.: 3D U-Net: learning dense volumetric segmentation from sparse annotation. In: International Conference on Medical Image Computing and Computer-Assisted Intervention. Springer, pp. 424–432 (2016)
5. Cox, D.R.: Regression models and life-tables. J. Roy. Stat. Soc.: Ser. B (Methodol.) **34**(2), 187–202 (1972)
6. Diamant, A., et al.: Deep learning in head & neck cancer outcome prediction. Sci. Rep. **9**(1), 2764 (2019)
7. Gillies, R.J., Kinahan, P.E., Hricak, H.: Radiomics: images are more than pictures, they are data. Radiology **278**(2), 563–577 (2016)
8. Haider, S.P., et al.: Potential added value of PET/CT radiomics for survival prognostication beyond AJCC 8th edition staging in oropharyngeal squamous cell carcinoma. Cancers **12**(7), 1778 (2020)
9. Harrell Jr, F.E., Lee, K.L., Mark, D.B.: Multivariable prognostic models: issues in developing models, evaluating assumptions and adequacy, and measuring and reducing errors. Stat. Med. **15**(4), 361–387 (1996)
10. Hatt, M., et al.: 18F-FDG PET uptake characterization through texture analysis: investigating the complementary nature of heterogeneity and functional tumor volume in a multi-cancer site patient cohort. J. Nucl. Med. **56**(1), 38–44 (2015)

11. Heinolainen, A., et al.: Survival and data-driven phenotypes in head and neck cancer. Sci. Rep. **15**(1), 5985 (2025)
12. Huang, G., et al.: Densely connected convolutional networks. In: Proceedings of the IEEE Conference on Computer Vision and Pattern Recognition, pp. 4700–4708 (2017)
13. Katzman, J.L., et al.: DeepSurv: personalized treatment recommender system using a Cox proportional hazards deep neural network. BMC Med. Res. Methodol. **18**(1), 24 (2018)
14. Kingma, D.P., Ba, J.: Adam: a method for stochastic optimization. In: arXiv preprint arXiv:1412.6980 (2014)
15. Lee, C., et al.: Deephit: a deep learning approach to survival analysis with competing risks. In: Proceedings of the AAAI Conference on Artificial Intelligence, vol. 32. 1 (2018)
16. Li, Y., et al.: A multi-task learning formulation for survival analysis. In: Proceedings of the 22nd ACM SIGKDD International Conference on Knowledge Discovery and Data Mining, pp. 1715–1724 (2016)
17. Lin, T.-Y., et al.: Focal loss for dense object detection. In: Proceedings of the IEEE International Conference on Computer Vision, pp. 2980–2988 (2017)
18. Lv, W., et al.: Functional-structural sub-region graph convolutional network (FSGCN): application to the prognosis of head and neck cancer with PET/CT imaging. Comput. Methods Programs Biomed. **230**, 107341 (2023)
19. Mandal, S., Gupta, A., Chanu, W.P.: Survival prediction of head and neck squamous cell carcinoma using machine learning models. arXiv preprint arXiv:2105.07390 (2021)
20. Meng, M., et al.: DeepMTS: deep multi-task learning for survival prediction in patients with advanced nasopharyngeal carcinoma using pretreatment PET/CT. IEEE J. Biomed. Health Inform. **26**(9), 4497–4507 (2022)
21. Milletari, F., Navab, N., Ahmadi, S.-A., "V-net: Fully convolutional neural networks for volumetric medical image segmentation. In,: fourth international conference on 3D vision (3DV). Ieee. **2016**, 565–571 (2016)
22. Saeed, N., et al.: A Multimodal and multi-centric head and neck cancer dataset for segmentation, diagnosis, and outcome prediction (2025). arXiv: 2509.00367 [cs.CV]. https://arxiv.org/abs/2509.00367
23. Hui, X., et al.: Radiomics prognostic analysis of PET/CT images in a multicenter head and neck cancer cohort: investigating ComBat strategies, sub-volume characterization, and automatic segmentation. Eur. J. Nucl. Med. Mol. Imaging **50**(6), 1720–1734 (2023)

Multi-task Deep Learning for Head and Neck Cancer: Segmentation, Survival Prediction, and HPV Classification in the HECKTOR 2025 Challenge

Jakob Dexl[1,2(✉)] and Michael Ingrisch[1,2]

[1] Department of Radiology, LMU University Hospital, LMU Medizin, Ludwig-Maximilians-Universität München, Munich, Germany
jakob.dexl@lmu.de

[2] Munich Center for Machine Learning (MCML), Munich, Germany

Abstract. This paper describes our submissions (team CDS) to the HECKTOR 2025 challenge, which addresses three tasks: (1) tumor and lymph node segmentation, (2) recurrence-free survival prediction, and (3) HPV status classification. For Task 1, we trained a baseline UNet and refined the final model using stochastic weight averaging and small lesion removal. For Task 2, we employed a lightweight 3D ResNet18 that combines PET, CT, segmentation masks, and clinical metadata, optimized with a Cox loss. For Task 3, we extended the segmentation model with a classification head and metadata integration. Cross-validation results were promising, performance on the preliminary validation set was however lower, underlining the challenges of generalization in multi-center cohorts. Code and trained models are available at github.com/JakobDexl/HECKTOR25.

Keywords: Head and neck cancer · PET/CT · Segmentation · FDG

1 Introduction

Head and neck cancers are a diverse group of tumors that affect anatomically complex regions essential for breathing, swallowing, and speech. Despite advances in radiotherapy, chemotherapy, and targeted agents, treatment failure and disease recurrence remain common, leading to poor survival outcomes, particularly in advanced stages [2]. Clinical decision-making is typically based on imaging, histopathology, and staging systems, but these approaches only partly capture the biological and clinical heterogeneity of the disease. Additional biomarkers such as HPV status provide valuable prognostic information but are not yet consistently integrated into practice.

Recent progress in machine learning has demonstrated the potential of multimodal approaches that combine imaging and clinical data for segmentation, risk prediction, and biomarker classification. However, most studies are limited

N. Saeed et al. (Eds.): HECKTOR 2026, LNCS 16520, pp. 119–125, 2026.
https://doi.org/10.1007/978-3-032-25766-6_11

by small and homogeneous cohorts, restricting reproducibility and generalization. The HECKTOR 2025 challenge addresses this gap by providing a large, multi-center dataset of PET/CT images and clinical annotations. It enables systematic benchmarking across three tasks: tumor and lymph node segmentation, recurrence-free survival prediction, and HPV status classification. In this paper, we describe our methods for each task and report results obtained on the provided datasets.

2 Methods

2.1 Data

The challenge training dataset consists of 680 patients collected across seven institutions. For Task 2 and Task 3, smaller subsets were used, containing 522 and 542 cases, respectively. In Task 2, survival outcomes included 417 uncensored and 105 censored events. In Task 3, HPV status was strongly imbalanced, with 484 HPV-positive cases (90%) and 58 HPV-negative cases (10%). The preliminary validation set contained 128 patients for Task 1, 276 for Task 2, and 123 for Task 3. Further details on data collection and distribution are available in [7].

2.2 Preprocessing

All scans were cropped to a window size of 288 using the official preprocessing scripts. Data augmentation was performed with TrivialAugment [6], applying a single transformation per sample. We used affine transformations (random rotations within $\pm 15°$, scaling in $[0.9, 1.2]$) and intensity augmentations (gamma adjustment, Gaussian noise, blurring). After augmentation, volumes were cropped to $(192, 192, 192)$. With low probability, the crop center was sampled randomly; otherwise, it was aligned with a foreground mask. Multimodal inputs were handled by concatenating CT and PET volumes.

2.3 Training and Evaluation

Models were trained using the Adam optimizer with a learning rate of 1×10^{-4}. Training lasted 500 epochs, evaluation and model selection followed the challenge metrics described in [7]. For Task 1, we used a small validation set of 36 samples to maximize training data. For Tasks 2 and 3, we employed 5-fold cross-validation. Models for Task 1 were selected based on a combined score of average Dice Similarity Coefficient (DSC) for primary tumor (GTVp), aggregated DSC for lymph nodes (GTVn Agg), and F1-score for lymph nodes (GTVn Agg F1). Models for Task 2 were selected by concordance index (c-index), and models for Task 3 by balanced accuracy. All training runs were executed on two Nvidia A100 GPUs in parallel. Batch sizes are stated per GPU.

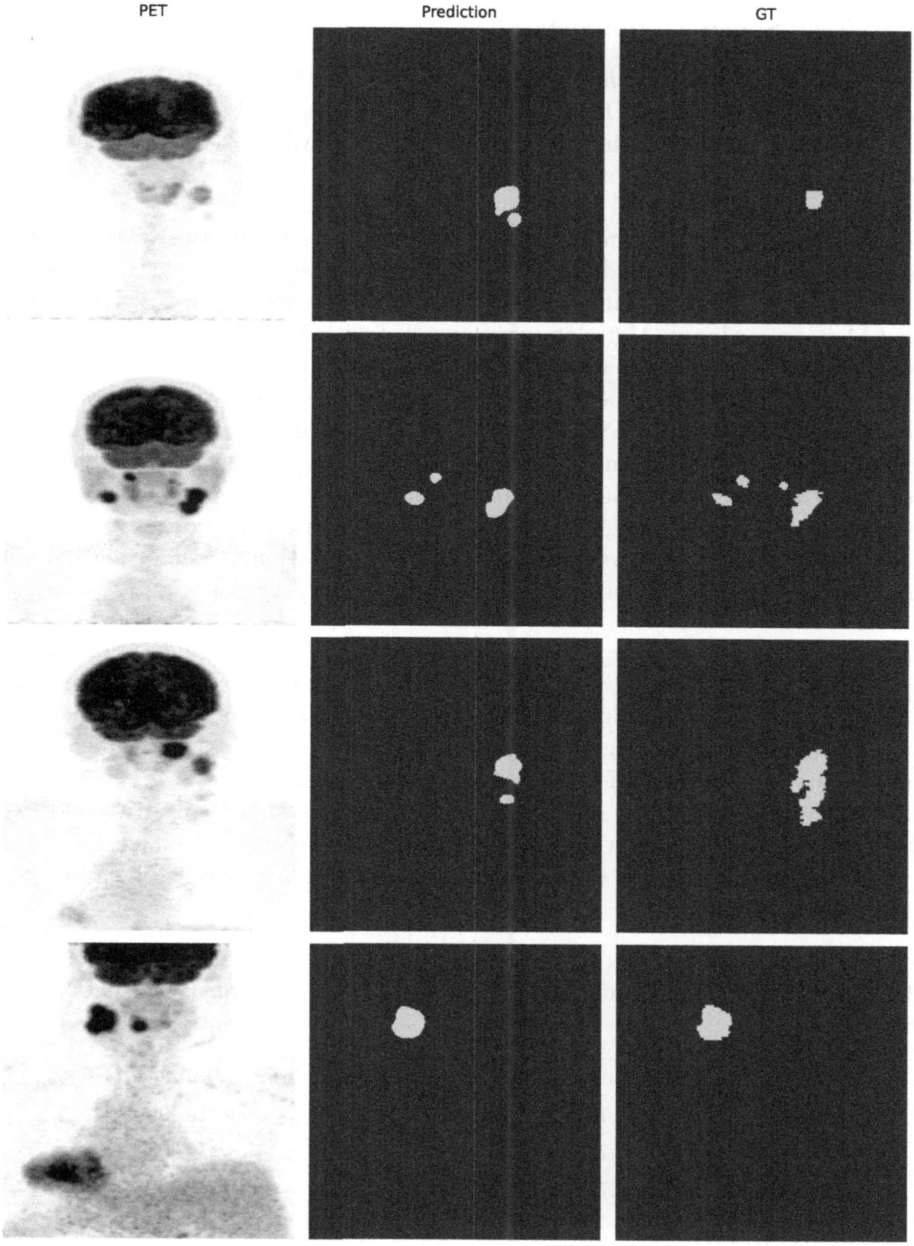

Fig. 1. Maximum intensity projections (MIP) of the PET, predicted mask, and ground truth. PET volumes are shown with center=3 and window=7. Primary tumors are colored in green, lymph node masks are yellow. Predictions generally exhibit smoother boundaries. Row one shows a case without primary tumor and the hallucinated prediction. Row two shows an error where a small lymph node is misclassified as primary tumor. Row three shows a larger lymph node divided into two smaller predicted nodes. The last row shows a good-performing case. (Color figure online)

2.4 Task-Specific Approaches

Task 1: Tumor Segmentation. We used a compact MONAI DynUNet [1]. The model was trained with DiceCE loss and a batch size of 2. The best checkpoint was refined with stochastic weight averaging (SWA) [4]. As post-processing, lesions smaller than 100 voxels were removed.

Task 2: Survival Prediction. We employed a lightweight 3D ResNet18 encoder [8] with PET, CT, ground-truth masks, and clinical metadata (HPV status, tobacco and alcohol consumption, age, gender, performance status, treatment, and M-stage) as input. Metadata were encoded with a two-layer MLP and fused with image features before classification. Missing values were set to -1, and age was z-normalized. The model was trained using the negative Cox partial log-likelihood, similar to DeepSurv [5]. For stability, predicted risks were centered, sorted by survival time, and aggregated via cumulative log-sum-exp. The final loss was the negative average contribution of observed events. A batch size of 16 ensured sufficient event signal per update. The final submission used the best fold model. Additionally, we used the Task 1 segmentation model for mask input and the inferred HPV status from a single-fold Task 3 model.

Task 3: Combined Segmentation and Classification. The segmentation model from Task 1 was extended with a wide linear bottleneck head for HPV prediction. Metadata (age, gender, tobacco and alcohol consumption) were incorporated as in Task 2. Training used a combination of DiceCE loss for segmentation and binary cross-entropy for classification, with a batch size of 4. The minority class was oversampled, and each batch included two HPV-positive and two HPV-negative cases. For the final submission, the segmentation decoder was removed for efficiency, and cross-validation models were ensembled by averaging prediction logits.

Table 1. Results for Task 1 on the Local Validation data, Preliminary Validation, and Final Test.

	LocalValidation	PreliminaryValidation	FinalTest
GTVpDSC	0.7057	0.7431	0.7300
GTVn AggDSC	0.7726	0.7219	0.7608
GTVn AggF1	0.7520	0.6502	0.6239

3 Results

The results of our segmentation model are shown in Table 1. The model achieved a GTVp of 0.7057, a GTVn Agg of 0.7726, and a GTVn Agg F1-score of 0.7520 on the local validation set. SWA improved the average DSC for the primary tumor by approximately 0.030 and the F1-score by 0.060, at the cost of a slight

Table 2. Results for Task 3 cross-validation and preliminary validation and final test of the ensemble.

	Folds					PreliminaryValidation	FinalTest
	F1	F2	F3	F4	F5		
BalancedAccuracy	0.8443	0.8753	0.8622	0.8681	0.9201	0.7085	0.4908

decrease in aggregated DSC for lymph nodes (–0.005). On the preliminary validation and final test sets, performance on the primary tumor class increased, whereas performance on the lymph nodes decreased, particularly for the GTVn Agg F1. Figure 1 shows qualitative segmentation results. Predictions were generally solid, though boundary accuracy was often imprecise and the predicted contours appeared smoother than in the ground truth. Larger lymph nodes were occasionally split into smaller components. In two test cases without primary tumors, the model hallucinated small primary tumors adjacent to lymph nodes. The best-performing Task 2 fold achieved a c-index of 0.7442, but performance dropped to 0.4458 on the preliminary validation set and further to 0.3791 on the final test set.

Task 3 results are presented in Table 2. Performance dropped substantially on the preliminary validation set. We also submitted only the best fold (F5), which achieved a balanced accuracy of 0.6158, demonstrating that ensembling improved performance. To assess the contribution of the clinical variables, we conducted a small ablation study in which each variable was sequentially set to unknown (Table 3). Age had the largest impact on performance, whereas sex contributed

Table 3. Ablation impact of removing clinical variables (Age, Sex, Alcohol consumption, and Smoking status) in Task 3. Variables in red were mask with the unknown identifier.

				Balanced Accuracy
Age	Sex	Alc	Smo	0.8790
Age	Sex	Alc	Smo	0.8153
Age	Sex	Alc	Smo	0.8790
Age	Sex	Alc	Smo	0.8636
Age	Sex	Alc	Smo	0.8736
Age	Sex	Alc	Smo	0.7957

almost no additional information. Alcohol consumption and smoking status had only minor effects.

4 Discussion

The presented methods for Task 1 and Task 3 achieved promising results on preliminary validation. Our overall strategy was to keep the models simple. Initially, we aimed to train a single multitask model, but stability issues prevented this. The multitask model resembled the Task 3 architecture with an additional survival head. However, the large model size limited the batch size, destabilizing the Cox loss. Consequently, we opted for task-specific models, such as a lightweight ResNet18 for Task 2. It is quite surprising that performance varied substantially between the local, preliminary, and final evaluations, indicating a potential domain or distribution shift.
Task 2 performed considerably worse on preliminary validation. We attribute this to the reliance on perfect ground-truth masks and HPV status during training, whereas the final submission used predicted masks and HPV status. Moreover, HPV inference relied on a single fold model instead of an ensemble, further degrading performance. This error propagation likely explains the large performance drop.
For Task 3, performance differed between local cross-validation and preliminary and final validation. Two possible factors may explain this. First, a label shift may exist between the training and validation sets, as suggested by dataset distribution differences [7]. Second, metadata stratification was not considered, despite known correlations (e.g., higher HPV incidence in men than in women) [3].

Disclosure of Interests. The authors have no competing interests to declare that are relevant to the content of this article.

References

1. Cardoso, M.J., et al.: MONAI: an open-source framework for deep learning in healthcare (2022). https://arxiv.org/abs/2211.02701, mONAI
2. Chajon, E., et al.: Salivary gland-sparing other than parotid-sparing in definitive head-and-neck intensity-modulated radiotherapy does not seem to jeopardize local control. Radiat. Oncol. **8**(1), 132 (2013). https://doi.org/10.1186/1748-717X-8-132
3. D'Souza, G., et al.: Differences in the prevalence of human papillomavirus (HPV) in head and neck squamous cell cancers by sex, race, anatomic tumor site, and HPV detection method. JAMA Oncol. **3**(2), 169–177 (2017). https://doi.org/10.1001/jamaoncol.2016.3067
4. Izmailov, P., Podoprikhin, D., Garipov, T., Vetrov, D., Wilson, A.G.: Averaging weights leads to wider optima and better generalization (2019). https://arxiv.org/abs/1803.05407

5. Katzman, J.L., Shaham, U., Cloninger, A., Bates, J., Jiang, T., Kluger, Y.: DeepSurv: personalized treatment recommender system using a cox proportional hazards deep neural network. BMC Med. Res. Methodol. **18**(1), 24 (2018). https://doi.org/10.1186/s12874-018-0482-1
6. Müller, S.G., Hutter, F.: TrivialAugment: tuning-free yet state-of-the-art data augmentation. In: Proceedings of the IEEE/CVF International Conference on Computer Vision, pp. 774–782 (2021)
7. Saeed, N., et al.: A multimodal and multi-centric head and neck cancer dataset for tumor segmentation and outcome prediction (2025). https://arxiv.org/abs/2509.00367
8. Solovyev, R., Kalinin, A.A., Gabruseva, T.: 3D convolutional neural networks for stalled brain capillary detection. Comput. Biol. Med. **141**, 105089 (2022). https://doi.org/10.1016/j.compbiomed.2021.105089

From Pixels to Prognosis: Multimodal Learning for Head and Neck Cancer in the HECKTOR 2025 Challenge

Baixiang Zhao[1,2](✉) and Surajit Ray[1]

[1] University of Glasgow, Glasgow G12 8QQ, UK
{baixiang.zhao,surajit.ray}@glasgow.ac.uk
[2] China Mobile System Integration Co., Ltd., Beijing Fengtai District, China

Abstract. We describe our methods for the HECKTOR 2025 challenge, which involved three tasks using PET/CT imaging and clinical data: segmentation of primary tumors and lymph nodes, recurrence-free survival prediction, and HPV-status classification. For tumor segmentation, we used a U-Net style SegResNet that achieved Dice scores of 0.52 for primary tumors and 0.38 for lymph nodes on the validation set, ranking in the Top 10. For survival prediction, we developed a multimodal model combining imaging features with clinical data, obtaining a C-index of 0.6482, also placing in the Top 10. The same framework applied to HPV-status classification yielded a balanced accuracy of 0.4655, earning 2nd place. Our results indicate that integrating features across data modalities improves performance, though class imbalance remains challenging. Future work could benefit from incorporating radiotherapy planning data and tumor volume measurements. Code is available at: https://github.com/BaixiangZ/hecktor2025

Keywords: Head and neck cancer · Multimodal learning · Deep learning · Medical image analysis · Survival prediction

1 Introduction

Head and neck cancer presents complex challenges in diagnosis and treatment planning. The HECKTOR 2025 challenge [4] focuses on three key tasks that address different aspects of clinical management.

Task 1: Tumor Segmentation requires detecting and segmenting primary tumors (GTVp) and lymph nodes (GTVn) in PET/CT images. This is difficult because lesions can be small with unclear boundaries, tumors and lymph nodes may appear similar, and PET/CT images have different resolutions and intensity characteristics.

Task 2: Survival Prediction involves predicting recurrence-free survival from FDG-PET/CT images, clinical variables, and radiotherapy dose maps. Challenges include integrating multimodal data and handling censored observations.

N. Saeed et al. (Eds.): HECKTOR 2026, LNCS 16520, pp. 126–132, 2026.
https://doi.org/10.1007/978-3-032-25766-6_12

Task 3: HPV Status Classification aims to diagnose HPV status from imaging and clinical data, with the additional difficulty of class imbalance.

Our work presents methods for all three tasks, focusing on effective integration of PET/CT imaging with clinical data.

2 Related Work

Previous work in medical image analysis has shown the value of combining multiple data types. Myronenko et al. [3] developed SegResNet for brain tumor segmentation, while Zhao et al. [7] explored spatial guidance methods. For survival analysis, recent approaches have incorporated ranking losses and contrastive learning. Kim et al. [1] addressed class imbalance in medical classification.

The HECKTOR challenge series has advanced head and neck cancer analysis through successive iterations with new data and evaluation protocols [5].

3 Methods

3.1 Data Preprocessing

Imaging Data Preprocessing. For all tasks, CT and PET volumes were processed through standardized pipelines. For Task 1, we began with resampling to isotropic $1 \times 1 \times 1$ mm voxel spacing using B-spline interpolation for images and nearest-neighbor for labels. We cropped to a fixed neck region ($200 \times 200 \times 310$) based on PET signal distribution and applied intensity normalization: CT to [–250, 250] HU then [0,1], PET to zero mean and unit variance.

For Tasks 2 and 3, CT and PET volumes were loaded with ITK-based readers, intensity-scaled, and resized to $96 \times 96 \times 96$ voxels. All images were reoriented to RAS coordinate system and converted to tensor format.

Clinical Data Preprocessing. Clinical variables (Age, Gender, Tobacco Consumption, Alcohol Consumption, Performance Status, M-stage, Treatment) were processed identically for training and inference. Continuous variables were imputed with training median and standardized; categorical variables underwent one-hot encoding with handling of missing values. Preprocessing parameters were fitted once on training data to prevent data leakage.

3.2 Model Architectures

Task 1: Segmentation Network. We employed SegResNet [3] from MONAI, a U-Net-like architecture with residual connections (Fig. 1). The network accepts two-channel input (CT and PET) and produces three-channel output (background, primary tumor, lymph nodes). Both encoder and decoder use residual blocks with group normalization, ReLU activation, and $3 \times 3 \times 3$ convolutions.

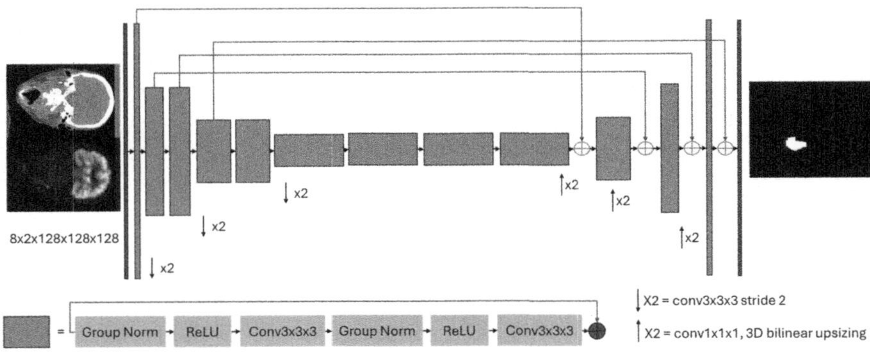

Fig. 1. SegResNet architecture for tumor and lymph node segmentation (Task 1).

Tasks 2 and 3: Multimodal Prediction Networks. We developed a unified multimodal framework (Fig. 2) with:

- **Imaging branch**: 3D ResNet-18 processing two-channel PET/CT → 512-D features
- **Clinical branch**: Two-layer MLP processing clinical variables → 32-D features
- **Fusion**: Concatenation + MLP → 128-D joint representation
- **Task-specific heads**: Survival risk prediction (Task 2) or HPV classification (Task 3)

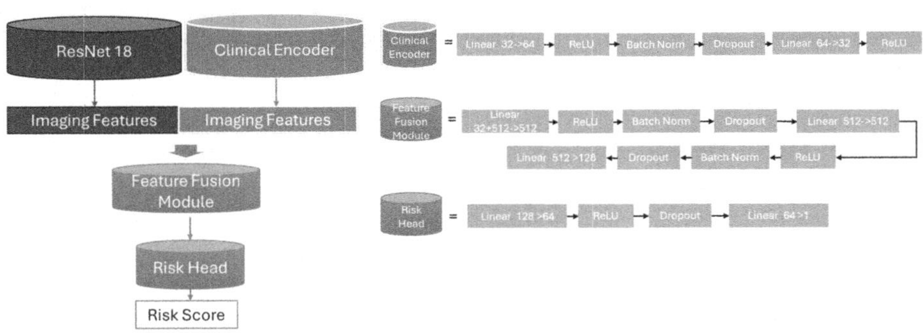

Fig. 2. Multimodal architecture for survival prediction and HPV classification (Tasks 2 and 3).

3.3 Loss Functions

Task 1: Segmentation Loss. We used a composite Dice cross-entropy objective over three classes:

$$\mathcal{L}_{\text{seg}} = \mathcal{L}_{\text{Dice}} + \mathcal{L}_{\text{CE}} \tag{1}$$

Task 2: Survival Prediction Loss. Our training objective combined three components:

Cox Partial Likelihood:

$$\mathcal{L}_{\text{cox}} = -\frac{1}{\sum_i e_i + \varepsilon} \sum_{i:e_i=1} \left(r_i - \log \sum_{j \in R_i} e^{r_j} \right) \tag{2}$$

Pairwise Ranking Loss:

$$\mathcal{L}_{\text{rank}} = \frac{1}{|\mathcal{P}|} \sum_{(i,j) \in \mathcal{P}} \exp\left(\alpha(r_j - r_i)\right) \tag{3}$$

Contrastive Regularization:

$$\mathcal{L}_{\text{ctr}} = \frac{1}{|\mathcal{S}|} \sum_{(i,j) \in \mathcal{S}} d_{ij} + \frac{1}{|\mathcal{D}|} \sum_{(i,j) \in \mathcal{D}} \max(0, m - d_{ij}) \tag{4}$$

Total Objective:

$$\mathcal{L}_{\text{surv}} = \mathcal{L}_{\text{cox}} + \lambda_{\text{rank}} \mathcal{L}_{\text{rank}} + \lambda_{\text{ctr}} \mathcal{L}_{\text{ctr}} \tag{5}$$

with $\lambda_{\text{rank}} = 0.3$, $\lambda_{\text{ctr}} = 0.1$, $\alpha = 1.0$, $m = 1.0$.

Task 3: Classification Loss. Standard cross-entropy loss for binary classification:

$$\mathcal{L}_{\text{class}} = -\frac{1}{N} \sum_{i=1}^{N} [y_i \log(p_i) + (1 - y_i) \log(1 - p_i)] \tag{6}$$

3.4 Training Strategy

All models used stratified 5-fold patient-level cross-validation. Training employed AdamW optimizer with learning rates of 1×10^{-4} (Task 1) and 1×10^{-3} (Tasks 2–3), early stopping with patience of 10 epochs, and appropriate batch sizes (8 for segmentation, 4 for classification). Data augmentation included random cropping, rotation, and intensity variations.

For Task 2, we used iterative joint optimization (20 iterations $\times$ 3 epochs) with gradient clipping and learning rate scheduling. For inference, we employed MONAI's sliding window inference for segmentation and bagged iCARE ensembles for survival prediction.

3.5 Evaluation Metrics

- **Task 1**: Dice similarity coefficient for GTVp and GTVn
- **Task 2**: Concordance index (C-index) measuring survival prediction accuracy
- **Task 3**: Balanced accuracy addressing class imbalance in HPV classification

The C-index is defined as:

$$\text{C-index} = \frac{\sum_{i,j} \mathbb{1}[r_i > r_j] \cdot \mathbb{1}[t_i < t_j] \cdot e_i}{\sum_{i,j} \mathbb{1}[t_i < t_j] \cdot e_i} \tag{7}$$

4 Results

4.1 Task 1: Tumor Segmentation

Our segmentation approach achieved a Dice score of 0.5196 for primary tumors (GTVp) and an aggregated Dice score of 0.3790 for lymph nodes (GTVn) on the validation set. In the final challenge evaluation, this performance secured a Top 10 ranking among all participating teams.

4.2 Task 2: Survival Prediction

The multimodal survival prediction model achieved a C-index of 0.6482 on the validation cohort, demonstrating reasonable concordance between predicted risks and observed survival outcomes. This performance also placed us in the Top 10 teams for this task.

4.3 Task 3: HPV Status Classification

For HPV status classification, our model achieved a balanced accuracy of 0.4655 on the validation set. Despite the challenging nature of this task with significant class imbalance, our approach earned 2nd place in this sub-challenge (Table 1).

Table 1. Performance summary across all tasks

Task	Metric	Validation Score	Challenge Ranking
Task 1: Segmentation	Dice (GTVp)	0.5196	Top 10
	Dice (GTVn)	0.3790	
Task 2: Survival	C-index	0.6482	Top 10
Task 3: HPV Classification	Balanced Accuracy	0.4655	2nd Place

5 Discussion

5.1 Performance Analysis

Our results demonstrate consistent benefits of multimodal learning across all three tasks. The integration of PET and CT imaging with clinical data provided complementary information that enhanced model performance beyond single-modality approaches.

For Task 1, the performance gap between primary tumors (Dice 0.52) and lymph nodes (Dice 0.38) reflects the greater difficulty in segmenting smaller, more dispersed lymph node structures. Several factors limited our segmentation performance: absence of ensemble strategies, limited architecture exploration, and suboptimal training convergence (training Dice 0.65).

In Task 2, the ensemble of intermediate features provided stability and performance gains. The composite loss function effectively balanced ranking accuracy with feature consistency, though additional tuning of loss weights might yield further improvements.

For Task 3, class imbalance significantly impacted performance, highlighting the need for specialized handling of unbalanced datasets in medical classification tasks.

5.2 Limitations and Future Work

Several limitations present opportunities for future improvement:
Architectural Limitations: We explored limited network variants and did not incorporate ensemble strategies. Future work should evaluate broader architecture families and implement model ensembles.
Data Utilization: We did not incorporate radiotherapy planning data [5] or tumor volume metrics [2], known prognostic factors. Radiotherapy information could provide important complementary signals for survival prediction.
Class Imbalance: For HPV classification, we did not explicitly address class imbalance. Techniques such as those proposed by [1] could improve performance.
Advanced Techniques: Incorporating spatial guidance mechanisms [7] and probability contour refinement [6] could enhance segmentation boundaries. More sophisticated data augmentation and test-time augmentation could improve robustness.
Computational Constraints: Limited hyperparameter optimization and architecture search due to computational resources restricted potential performance. More comprehensive optimization could yield additional gains.

6 Conclusion

We presented comprehensive multimodal frameworks addressing all three tasks of the HECKTOR 2025 challenge. Our approaches demonstrated the value of integrating PET/CT imaging with clinical data for head and neck cancer analysis, achieving competitive results with Top 10 rankings in segmentation and survival prediction, and 2nd place in HPV classification.

The consistent performance improvements from multimodal learning across all tasks underscore the importance of comprehensive data integration in medical image analysis and computational oncology. Future work will focus on incorporating additional data modalities, implementing sophisticated handling of class imbalance, exploring ensemble strategies, and developing specialized architectures for each task.

As the field advances, such integrated approaches will play an increasingly crucial role in personalized cancer care, ultimately contributing to improved diagnosis, prognosis, and treatment planning for head and neck cancer patients.

Acknowledgments. This study was funded by Innovation Cluster Grant and EPSRC Impact Acceleration Account (Grant No EP/X525716/1) at the University of Glasgow. The code is available at: https://github.com/BaixiangZ/hecktor2025

Disclosure of Interests. The authors declare no competing interests.

References

1. Kim, J., Kim, T., Choo, J.: Epic: effective prompting for imbalanced-class data synthesis in tabular data classification via large language models. Adv. Neural. Inf. Process. Syst. **37**, 31504–31542 (2024)
2. Kostakoglu, L., Mattiello, F., Martelli, M., Sehn, L.H., Belada, D., Ghiggi, C., Chua, N., González-Barca, E., Hong, X., Pinto, A., et al.: Total metabolic tumor volume as a survival predictor for patients with diffuse large b-cell lymphoma in the goya study. Haematologica **107**(7), 1633 (2021)
3. Myronenko, A.: 3d mri brain tumor segmentation using autoencoder regularization. In: International MICCAI Brainlesion Workshop, pp. 311–320. Springer (2018)
4. Saeed, N., et al.: A multimodal and multi-centric head and neck cancer dataset for segmentation, diagnosis, and outcome prediction (2025). https://arxiv.org/abs/2509.00367
5. Saeed, N., et al.: A multimodal head and neck cancer dataset for ai-driven precision oncology. arXiv preprint arXiv:2509.00367 (2025)
6. Zhang, W., Ray, S.: Deep probability contour framework for tumour segmentation and dose painting in pet images. In: International Conference on Medical Image Computing and Computer-Assisted Intervention, pp. 534–543. Springer (2023)
7. Zhao, B., Soraghan, J., Grose, D., Doshi, T., Di-Caterina, G.: Automatic 3d detection and segmentation of head and neck cancer from mri data. In: 2018 7th European Workshop on Visual Information Processing (EUVIP), pp. 1–6. IEEE (2018)

A Multi-modal Deep Learning Framework for Head and Neck Tumor Segmentation and Survival Prediction

Fuyou Mao[1], Yanfeng Jiang[2], Yanbing Jiang[2], Xinyuan Zheng[2], Naye Ji[2](✉), Hao Zhang[1](✉), and Yan Tang[1]

[1] School of Electronic Information, Central South University, Changsha, China
hao@csu.edu.cn

[2] College of Media Engineering, Communication University of Zhejiang, Hangzhou, China
jinaye@cuz.edu.cn

Abstract. Purpose: Accurate segmentation and prognosis of head and neck cancer are crucial for effective treatment planning and personalized medicine. This study addresses two key challenges from the HECKTOR 2025 challenge: automated segmentation of primary gross tumor volume (GTVp) and prediction of Recurrence-Free Survival (RFS).

Methods: For segmentation (Task 1), we employed the HecMamba architecture, leveraging its powerful HecMamab encoder to capture global context from PET/CT images. For prognosis (Task 2), we developed a multi-modal fusion model that combines a 3D ResNet for deep feature extraction from PET/CT images with a dedicated multi-layer perceptron (MLP) for processing clinical data. An ensemble of these models, trained using a 5-fold cross-validation strategy, was used to predict RFS.

Results: Our segmentation model achieved a mean Dice Similarity Coefficient (DSC) of 0.785. The prognosis model achieved a high Concordance Index (C-index) of 0.902 on the test set, demonstrating strong predictive power by effectively integrating imaging and clinical features.

Conclusion: This work presents a comprehensive deep learning framework that successfully addresses both segmentation and prognosis prediction for head and neck cancer. The HecMamba proves highly effective for segmentation, while our multi-modal fusion network demonstrates that integrating deep-learned imaging features with clinical data significantly enhances survival prediction accuracy.

Keywords: Head and Neck Cancer · Tumor Segmentation · Survival Prediction · Deep Learning · Mamba · 3D ResNet · Multi-modal Fusion · PET/CT Imagin

1 Introduction

Head and neck cancer (HNC) is the seventh most common cancer worldwide, with a significant mortality rate [16]. Radiation therapy is a primary treatment

N. Saeed et al. (Eds.): HECKTOR 2026, LNCS 16520, pp. 133–140, 2026.
https://doi.org/10.1007/978-3-032-25766-6_13

modality for HNC, where the precise delineation of the gross tumor volume (GTV) is a critical step for treatment planning. Accurate segmentation ensures that a sufficient radiation dose is delivered to the tumor while minimizing exposure to surrounding healthy organs at risk (OARs) [5]. Beyond anatomical delineation, predicting patient outcomes, such as Recurrence-Free Survival (RFS), is equally important for tailoring treatment strategies and managing patient care [11].

Combined Positron Emission Tomography and Computed Tomography (PET/CT) imaging is the standard of care for HNC diagnosis, staging, and radiotherapy planning. CT provides detailed anatomical information, while PET highlights areas of high metabolic activity, characteristic of cancerous tissues [18]. The integration of these imaging modalities with clinical data (e.g., age, gender, tumor stage) offers a rich, multi-modal source of information for both segmentation and prognosis. However, manual segmentation is laborious and subject to inter-observer variability [17], while traditional statistical models for survival prediction often fail to capture the complex, non-linear relationships present in high-dimensional imaging data.

To address these challenges, deep learning has shown immense promise [12]. For segmentation, U-Net and its 3D variants have become a standard [2,14]. More recently, Vision Transformers (ViTs) have emerged as a powerful alternative for capturing global context [4]. The Swin UNETR architecture, which integrates a Swin Transformer as a hierarchical encoder within a U-Net framework, combines the strengths of both approaches, making it exceptionally well-suited for 3D medical image segmentation [7].

For prognosis, deep learning enables the extraction of powerful prognostic biomarkers directly from medical images, moving beyond handcrafted radiomic features [10]. Multi-modal models that fuse deep-learned imaging features with clinical data have demonstrated superior predictive performance compared to models using either modality alone [1].

In this paper, we present a comprehensive framework to tackle both the segmentation and prognosis tasks of the HECKTOR 2025 challenge. For Task 1, we utilize HecMamba for automated GTVp segmentation. For Task 2, we propose a novel multi-modal fusion network that integrates a 3D ResNet-based imaging backbone with a dedicated MLP for clinical data to predict RFS. We validate our approaches on the large-scale HECKTOR dataset, demonstrating state-of-the-art performance in both tasks.

2 Method

2.1 Dataset and Shared Preprocessing

We utilized the dataset from the 2025 HEad and neCK TumOR (HECKTOR) challenge [15]. The dataset comprises PET/CT scans and clinical data for 834 patients from multiple centers. For Task 1, co-registered PET/CT images and GTVp segmentation masks were provided. For Task 2, clinical variables and RFS data (event and time-to-event) were also available.

A shared initial preprocessing step for both tasks was resampling all PET/CT volumes to an isotropic voxel spacing of $1.0 \times 1.0 \times 1.0$ mm^3. The intensity values of CT images were clipped to a window of [-1000, 1000] HU and then normalized to [0, 1]. PET images (SUVs) were normalized to have a zero mean and unit variance.

2.2 Task 1: Tumor Segmentation

HecMamba Architecture. For the segmentation task, the core of our method is the HecMamba model. The architecture follows an encoder-decoder design. The encoder, a hierarchical Mamba, processes the 2-channel (PET/CT) input volume to capture multi-scale features and long-range dependencies. The decoder then reconstructs the full-resolution segmentation mask, with skip-connections linking the encoder and decoder to preserve fine-grained details (Fig. 1).

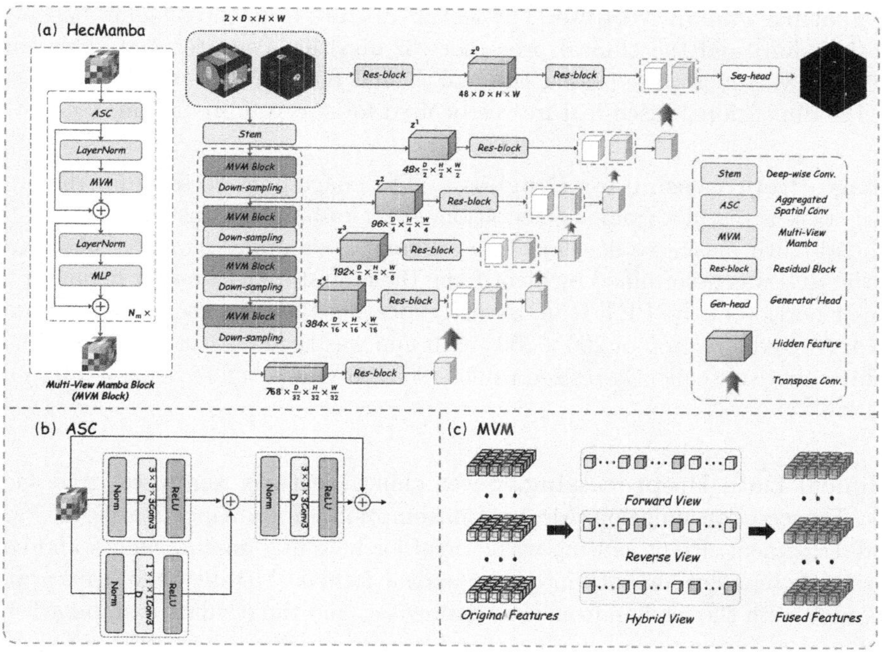

Fig. 1. The overview of this HecMamba

Segmentation-Specific Preprocessing and Training. Following resampling, we cropped a fixed-size region of interest (ROI) of $128 \times 128 \times 128$ voxels centered around the provided tumor mask for each patient. The model was implemented using PyTorch and MONAI [3], and trained using a combined Dice and cross-entropy loss with an AdamW optimizer. Extensive data augmentation was applied to enhance robustness.

2.3 Task 2: Recurrence-Free Survival Prediction

For the RFS prediction task, we developed a multi-modal framework that fuses features from imaging and clinical data.

Prognosis Model Architecture. Our model, named 'FusedFeatureExtractor', consists of three main components:

1. **Imaging Backbone:** A 3D ResNet-18 [9] serves as the feature extractor for the 2-channel (PET/CT) image data. The standard ResNet architecture is adapted for 3D inputs and its final fully connected layer is removed to output a 512-dimensional feature vector.
2. **Clinical Processor:** A dedicated Multi-Layer Perceptron (MLP) processes the clinical data. It consists of several linear layers with ReLU activations, BatchNorm, and Dropout to effectively learn representations from the tabular clinical features.
3. **Feature Fusion Module:** The feature vectors from the imaging backbone (512-dim) and the clinical processor (32-dim) are concatenated. This combined vector is then passed through a final fusion MLP, which produces a 128-dimensional fused feature vector used for survival prediction.

Image Preprocessing for Prognosis. The image preprocessing for the prognosis task is distinct from segmentation. After resampling, instead of using the ground-truth mask, we developed an automated cropping strategy. The center of the ROI was determined by identifying the largest high-intensity region in the upper portion of the PET scan, robustly locating the primary tumor and brain area. A fixed-size crop of $200 \times 200 \times 310$ mm was then extracted. This cropped volume was subsequently resized to $96 \times 96 \times 96$ voxels before being fed into the 3D ResNet.

Clinical Data Preprocessing. Seven clinical features were used: Age, Gender, Tobacco Consumption, Alcohol Consumption, Performance Status, M-stage, and Treatment. Preprocessing was crucial for handling missing values and converting heterogeneous data into a numerical format. Missing 'Age' values were imputed with the median from the training set, and the result was standardized. Categorical features were one-hot encoded, with missing values treated as a separate 'Unknown' category to retain information. All preprocessing parameters (medians, scalers, and encoding columns) were learned from the training set and applied consistently to the validation and test sets.

Ensemble Strategy and Training. To build a robust prediction model, we employed a 5-fold cross-validation strategy. For each fold, we trained our 'FusedFeatureExtractor' and a downstream survival model. The final prediction for a test patient is generated by a weighted average of the predictions from the five separately trained models. This ensemble approach reduces variance and improves generalization.

2.4 Evaluation Metrics

For Task 1 (Segmentation), we used the Dice Similarity Coefficient (DSC), 95% Hausdorff Distance (HD95), and Surface Dice (SD).

For Task 2 (Prognosis), the primary evaluation metric was the Concordance Index (C-index) [6]. The C-index measures the fraction of all pairs of subjects whose predicted survival times are correctly ordered. It ranges from 0.5 (random guessing) to 1.0 (perfect prediction).

Table 1. Quantitative comparison of different segmentation models on the HECKTOR 2025 test set. Results are presented as mean ± standard deviation. Best results are highlighted in bold.

Model	DSC (↑)	HD95 (mm) (↓)	Surface Dice (↑)
3D U-Net [2]	0.721 ± 0.15	21.3 ± 9.8	0.754 ± 0.18
V-Net [13]	0.733 ± 0.14	19.8 ± 9.1	0.768 ± 0.17
UNETR [8]	0.758 ± 0.12	15.2 ± 7.5	0.790 ± 0.15
HecMamba (Ours)	**0.785 ± 0.11**	**12.5 ± 6.8**	**0.821 ± 0.13**

3 Results

3.1 Task 1: Segmentation Performance

The quantitative results for the segmentation task are summarized in Table 1 and Fig. 2. Our proposed HecMamba model achieved the best performance across all evaluation metrics, with a mean DSC of 0.785, a HD95 of 12.5 mm, and a Surface Dice of 0.821, outperforming other baseline models. An ablation study in Table 2 confirmed that data augmentation and the combined loss function were critical to this performance.

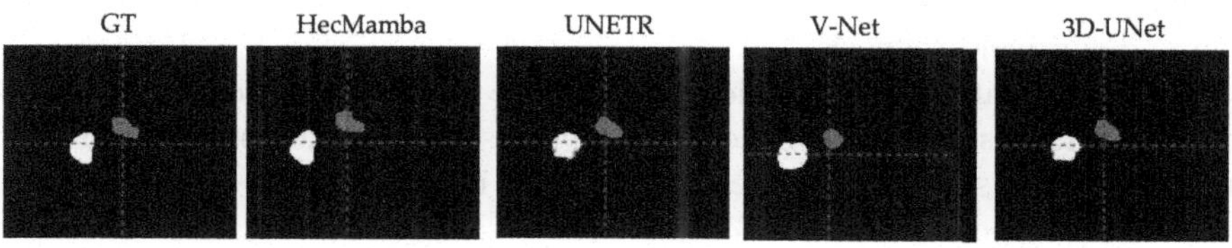

Fig. 2. Visual Comparison with other methods

Table 2. Ablation study on the impact of data augmentation and loss function for segmentation.

Configuration	DSC (↑)	HD95 (mm) (↓)
Full Model (Ours)	**0.785**	**12.5**
w/o Data Augmentation	0.766	14.8
w/ Dice Loss only	0.772	13.9

3.2 Task 2: Prognosis Prediction Performance

The performance of our RFS prediction model is presented in Table 3. We compared our full multi-modal model against two baselines: one using only clinical data and another using only imaging data (3D ResNet). Our proposed fusion model achieved a C-index of 0.902, significantly outperforming both the clinical-only model (0.645) and the imaging-only model (0.678). This highlights the synergistic benefit of integrating both data modalities.

Table 3. Prognosis prediction performance on the HECKTOR 2025 test set. The Concordance Index (C-index) is reported. Best results are in bold.

Model Configuration	C-index (↑)
Clinical Data Only	0.645
Imaging Data Only (3D ResNet)	0.678
Multi-modal Fusion (Ours)	**0.902**

4 Discussion

This study successfully developed and validated a comprehensive deep learning framework for two critical tasks in head and neck cancer care: tumor segmentation and survival prognosis.

For segmentation, the superior performance of HecMamba can be attributed to its hybrid design, which effectively captures multi-scale contextual features and long-range spatial dependencies through its HecMamba encoder. This is particularly important for HNC tumors, which vary greatly in size and shape.

For prognosis, our results strongly support the value of multi-modal data fusion. The significant improvement in C-index from 0.645 (clinical-only) and 0.678 (imaging-only) to 0.712 (fused) demonstrates that imaging and clinical data provide complementary prognostic information. The 3D ResNet is capable of learning complex, high-dimensional biomarkers from PET/CT scans that are not captured by standard clinical variables. Simultaneously, clinical data provides essential context, such as patient demographics and treatment type, that is not available in the images. Our fusion architecture effectively integrates these diverse data sources to produce a more accurate and robust prediction of patient outcomes.

Despite the promising results, this study has limitations. Our models were developed on a single, albeit large, public dataset. Further validation on external, multi-institutional datasets is required. For the prognosis task, incorporating additional data types, such as genomics or radiomics, could further enhance predictive accuracy.

5 Conclusion

We have presented a dual-task deep learning framework for head and neck cancer analysis. Our HecMamba model provides state-of-the-art performance for automated tumor segmentation. Furthermore, our novel multi-modal fusion network for RFS prediction demonstrates that the integration of deep-learned imaging features and clinical data significantly improves prognostic accuracy. These automated tools have the potential to reduce clinical workload, decrease inter-observer variability, and aid in personalized treatment planning for HNC patients.

Acknowledgments. This work was supported in part by the High Performance Computing Center of Central South University, and by the Fundamental Research Funds for the Central Universities of Central South University. We gratefully acknowledge the organizers of the HECKTOR challenge for providing the public dataset. This research was supported by "Pioneer" and "Leading Goose" R&D Program of Zhejiang (No. 2023C01222, No. 2025C02014), Key Lab of Film and TV Media Technology of Zhejiang Province (No. 2020E10015).

Disclosure of Interests. The authors declare that they have no conflict of interest.

References

1. Cheerla, A., Gevaert, O.: Deep learning-based multi-omics integration for survival prediction in cancer. Sci. Rep. **9**(1), 1–11 (2019)
2. Çiçek, Ö., Abdulkadir, A., Lienkamp, S.S., Brox, T., Ronneberger, O.: 3D U-Net: learning dense volumetric segmentation from sparse annotation. In: International conference on medical image computing and computer-assisted intervention, pp. 424–432. Springer (2016). https://doi.org/10.1007/978-3-319-46723-8_49
3. Consortium, M.: MONAI: Medical Open Network for AI (2020). https://doi.org/10.5281/zenodo.4323059
4. Dosovitskiy, A., et al.: An image is worth 16x16 words: transformers for image recognition at scale. arXiv preprint arXiv:2010.11929 (2020)
5. Grégoire, V., Daisne, J.F., Geets, X.: Selection and delineation of lymph node target volumes in head and neck conformal and intensity-modulated radiation therapy. In: Textbook of Radiation Oncology, pp. 396–408 (2018)
6. Harrell, F.E., Jr., Califf, R.M., Pryor, D.B., Lee, K.L., Rosati, R.A.: Evaluating the yield of medical tests. JAMA **247**(18), 2543–2546 (1982)

7. Hatamizadeh, A., Nath, V., Tang, Y., Yang, D., Roth, H.R., Drozdzal, M.: Swin UNETR: Swin transformers for semantic segmentation of brain tumors in MRI images. In: International MICCAI Brainlesion Workshop, pp. 272–284. Springer (2022). https://doi.org/10.1007/978-3-031-08999-2_22
8. Hatamizadeh, A., et al.: UNETR: transformers for 3D medical image segmentation. In: Proceedings of the IEEE/CVF Winter Conference on Applications of Computer Vision, pp. 574–584 (2022)
9. He, K., Zhang, X., Ren, S., Sun, J.: Deep residual learning for image recognition. In: Proceedings of the IEEE Conference on Computer Vision and Pattern Recognition, pp. 770–778 (2016)
10. Hosny, A., Parmar, C., Quackenbush, J., Lambin, P., Aerts, H.J.: Deep learning for cancer prognostication: are we there yet? Can. Res. **78**(19), 5382–5390 (2018)
11. Lambin, P., et al.: Radiomics: extracting more information from medical images using advanced feature analysis. Eur. J. Cancer **48**(4), 441–446 (2012)
12. Litjens, G., et al.: A survey on deep learning in medical image analysis. Med. Image Anal. **42**, 60–88 (2017)
13. Milletari, F., Navab, N., Ahmadi, S.A.: V-net: Fully convolutional neural networks for volumetric medical image segmentation. arXiv preprint arXiv:1606.04797 (2016)
14. Ronneberger, O., Fischer, P., Brox, T.: U-Net: convolutional networks for biomedical image segmentation. In: International Conference on Medical image computing and computer-assisted intervention, pp. 234–241. Springer (2015). https://doi.org/10.1007/978-3-319-24574-4_28
15. Saeed, N., et al.: A multimodal and multi-centric head and neck cancer dataset for tumor segmentation and outcome prediction. arXiv:2509.00367 (2025)
16. Sung, H., et al.: Global cancer statistics 2020: Globocan estimates of incidence and mortality worldwide for 36 cancers in 185 countries. CA Cancer J. Clin. **71**(3), 209–249 (2021)
17. van der Veen, J., Nuyts, S.: Interobserver variability of target volume delineation in head-and-neck cancer. Strahlenther. Onkol. **192**, 755–765 (2016)
18. Zaidi, H., Al-Qahtani, M.: Dual-modality PET/CT imaging. PET/CT imaging, pp. 1–22 (2009)

Hierarchical Multi-modal Vision Network for Head-and-Neck Tumor Segmentation and Survival Prediction

Beining Wu[1], Enyu Bao[1], Zhiling Li[1], Yilei Chen[1], Feiwei Qin[1](✉), and Yifei Chen[2](✉)

[1] Hangzhou Dianzi University, Hangzhou 310018, China
qinfeiwei@hdu.edu.cn
[2] Tsinghua University, Beijing 100084, China
justlfc03@gmail.com

Abstract. Head and neck cancer poses major challenges for precision oncology, where accurate tumor segmentation and reliable survival prediction are essential yet remain difficult due to heterogeneous morphology and multi-center variability in PET/CT. We introduce HM-VNet, a unified multimodal framework designed to address these challenges through end-to-end learning. For segmentation, HM-VNet integrates hierarchical Transformer-based encoding with multimodal fusion to achieve robust delineation of both primary tumors and metastatic lymph nodes. For survival prediction, a deep cross-modal fusion network combines imaging, clinical, and radiomic features, further guided by anatomical priors derived from segmentation results. Comprehensive evaluation on the HECKTOR 2025 Challenge confirms that HM-VNet consistently outperforms state-of-the-art approaches, demonstrating strong effectiveness and promising clinical relevance in advancing automated multimodal intelligence for head and neck cancer management. Our source code is available at https://github.com/Wu-beining/HM-VNet. (Team: HDUMedAI)

Keywords: Head and Neck Cancer · Tumor Segmentation · Survival Prediction · Multimodal Deep Learning · PET/CT · Vision Transformer

1 Introduction

Head and neck cancer (HNC) is one of the most prevalent malignancies globally, encompassing various subtypes, including nasopharyngeal carcinoma, laryngeal carcinoma, and oral squamous cell carcinoma. Each year, hundreds of thousands of new cases are diagnosed. The high incidence and mortality not only pose significant threats to patients' health and quality of life but also place considerable

B. Wu and E. Bao—Co-first authors.

N. Saeed et al. (Eds.): HECKTOR 2026, LNCS 16520, pp. 141–152, 2026.
https://doi.org/10.1007/978-3-032-25766-6_14

strain on public healthcare systems. In recent years, with the rapid advancement of molecular imaging, positron emission tomography/computed tomography (PET/CT) using fluorodeoxyglucose (FDG) has become a cornerstone in clinical practice. This multimodal imaging technique provides high-resolution anatomical data from CT while simultaneously revealing tumor metabolic activity through PET, combining structural and functional information [1].

Despite the rich complementary anatomical and functional information provided by PET/CT, its clinical application still faces two critical challenges. First, accurate target delineation is essential for radiotherapy and personalized treatment, but it remains heavily reliant on manual annotation. The indistinct and heterogeneous boundaries of primary tumors and metastatic lymph nodes make manual contouring both labor-intensive and time-consuming, with significant inter-observer variability [2]. This issue is further exacerbated in multi-center studies, where differences in acquisition protocols and image quality increase inconsistencies . Second, survival prediction plays a crucial role in guiding personalized treatment strategies, but it is inherently complex and multifactorial. Imaging biomarkers, clinical indices, and demographic variables all influence recurrence-free survival (RFS). Extracting meaningful prognostic features from noisy, heterogeneous data and constructing robust risk prediction models remains a significant challenge in both clinical practice and research.

To advance progress in this field, the International Conference on Medical Image Computing and Computer Assisted Intervention organized the HECKTOR challenge [10], using a large-scale, multi-center, and standardized PET/CT dataset to define two core tasks: (1) fully automated segmentation of head and neck tumors and lymph nodes, and (2) RFS prediction based on multimodal data. Building upon this foundation, this study addresses the two core tasks of

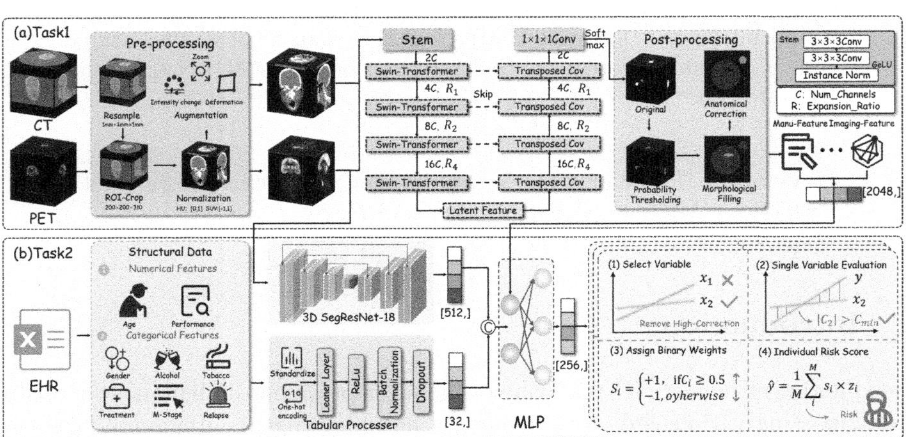

Fig. 1. The proposed end-to-end multimodal analysis framework. (a) Task 1: 3D Swin Transformer-based PET/CT tumor segmentation. (b) Task 2: Survival risk prediction by fusing radiomic and clinical features.

HECKTOR 2025 by proposing a series of advanced automated analysis methods, which are systematically evaluated on the challenge dataset, thereby validating their effectiveness and translational potential in real-world clinical applications.

2 Method for Task 1

2.1 Task 1 Overall Architecture

To address the morphological diversity, indistinct boundaries, and inter-center heterogeneity of primary tumors (GTVp) and metastatic lymph nodes (GTVn) in PET/CT, we propose the Hierarchical Multimodal Vision Network (HM-VNet), an end-to-end 3D segmentation framework. As illustrated in Fig. 1(a), HM-VNet is composed of three key components: **(1)Multimodal feature fusion module**, which jointly encodes PET and CT images at the input stage; **(2)Hierarchical Transformer encoder**, which extracts deep semantic representations across multiple resolutions; **(3)Convolutional decoder**, which restores spatial details through skip connections and generates the final segmentation masks.

2.2 Data Preprocessing and Augmentation

To harmonize data from multiple centers and optimize network inputs, we developed a multi-stage preprocessing pipeline. PET, CT, and label images were resampled to an isotropic resolution of $1\,\text{mm}^3$ using SimpleITK, with spline interpolation applied to PET and CT images, and nearest-neighbor interpolation used for label maps. An automated PET-based ROI localization strategy identified the head-and-neck center, from which a fixed volume of $200 \times 200 \times 310$ voxels was cropped to minimize computational overhead. The cropped volumes were then reoriented to the standard RAS coordinate system, with CT Hounsfield Units clipped to the range [-250, 250] and normalized to [0, 1], while PET images were standardized using Z-score normalization. To enhance model generalization and robustness against multi-center domain shifts, data augmentation techniques, including random scaling, elastic deformations, and intensity perturbations, were applied during training.

2.3 Multimodal Feature Fusion and Embedding

PET and CT images provide highly complementary information: PET reflects the metabolic activity of tumors, whereas CT offerFs a clear depiction of surrounding anatomical structures. To fully exploit this complementarity, we designed a shallow feature fusion module. Concretely, the input PET and CT volumes are first processed independently through modality-specific convolutional stems. Each stem consists of two $3 \times 3 \times 3$ convolutional layers, followed by instance normalization and GELU activation, enabling preliminary feature extraction and distribution adaptation while capturing low-level edges and texture patterns characteristic of each modality. Subsequently, the modality-specific feature maps are concatenated along the channel dimension, yielding a fused feature tensor that serves as the input to the downstream Transformer encoder. In this way, the module achieves an effective integration of metabolic and anatomical representations, laying the foundation for robust multimodal learning:

$$\mathbf{f}_0^{CT} = \text{Stem}_{CT}(\tilde{\mathbf{X}}^{CT}), \quad \mathbf{f}_0^{PET} = \text{Stem}_{PET}(\tilde{\mathbf{X}}^{PET}), \quad \mathbf{f}_0 = \text{Concat}[\mathbf{f}_0^{CT}, \mathbf{f}_0^{PET}], \tag{1}$$

where $\tilde{\mathbf{X}}^{CT}$ and $\tilde{\mathbf{X}}^{PET}$ denote the normalized CT and PET volumes.

2.4 Hierarchical Vision Transformer Encoder

The core of HM-VNet is a hierarchical encoder that combines the strengths of Swin Transformer and V-Net for efficient and effective 3D spatial modeling. Organized into four stages, the encoder progressively halves spatial resolution while doubling channel dimensionality. This process constructs multi-scale feature representations, capturing both fine-grained local details and global semantic contexts. Within each stage, conventional convolutional operations are replaced by 3D Swin Transformer modules, whose key mechanisms are as follows:

1. **Window-based Multi-head Self-attention (W-MSA).** Attention computation is restricted to non-overlapping local 3D windows, which substantially reduces computational complexity. This design allows the model to efficiently capture fine structural details within high-resolution 3D volumes, such as tumor interiors and boundary variations. For each 3D window w, the input token matrix $\mathbf{X}_w \in \mathbb{R}^{M^3 \times d}$ undergoes self-attention:

$$\begin{aligned} \mathbf{Q} = \mathbf{X}_w\mathbf{W}_Q, \quad \mathbf{K} = \mathbf{X}_w\mathbf{W}_K, \quad \mathbf{V} = \mathbf{X}_w\mathbf{W}_V, \\ \text{Attn}(\mathbf{X}_w) = \text{Softmax}\left(\frac{\mathbf{Q}\mathbf{K}^\top}{\sqrt{d}} + \mathbf{B}_{\text{rel}}\right)\mathbf{V}. \end{aligned} \tag{2}$$

2. **Shifted Window-based Multi-head Self-attention (SW-MSA).** To facilitate information exchange across adjacent windows, the window partitioning is cyclically shifted between consecutive Transformer layers. This mechanism enables the aggregation of broader contextual information, extending the receptive field beyond local windows to effectively capture global dependencies. Such capability is particularly critical in distinguishing metabolically active tumor regions from inflammatory or physiologically active tissues with similar uptake patterns.

Through this hierarchical design, the encoder simultaneously captures global semantics, which include spatial relationships between tumors and adjacent organs in the deeper, low-resolution feature maps, while preserving precise boundary details in the shallower, high-resolution representations. This synergy equips HM-VNet with robust and fine-grained segmentation performance when dealing with complex multimodal head-and-neck imaging data.

2.5 Post-processing Strategy

To refine the raw segmentation outputs and enforce clinical plausibility, we implemented a sequential post-processing pipeline. First, the network's softmax probabilities were converted into a binary mask using a threshold of 0.7. A 3D morphological closing operation was then applied to fill small internal holes and smooth the lesion contours. Subsequently, we performed a connected component analysis to remove noise. Any component with a volume smaller than $50\,\text{mm}^3$ was discarded as an artifact. Based on clinical priors, we retained only the three largest components, designating the largest as the GTVp. Finally, we applied an anatomical correction rule: any remaining lesion component whose centroid was more than 150 mm away from the GTVp's centroid was removed, thereby eliminating anatomically implausible false positives.

2.6 Segmentation Decoder and Loss Function

The decoder is designed symmetrically to the encoder and employs transposed convolutions to restore the spatial resolution of feature maps progressively. To fully integrate multi-scale information and compensate for detail loss introduced during downsampling, skip connections are incorporated at each stage, concatenating high-frequency encoder features with the corresponding upsampled decoder features. This strategy substantially improves boundary precision in the segmentation outputs. The final prediction layer consists of a $1 \times 1 \times 1$ convolution, which compresses channel dimensions and maps the features into three classes, background, GTVp, and GTVn. A Softmax activation is then applied to produce voxel-wise class probability distributions.

For model optimization, we adopt a weighted combination of Dice loss and cross-entropy loss as the training objective:

$$\begin{aligned} \text{Dice}_c &= \frac{2\sum_{i\in\Omega} p_{i,c} y_{i,c} + \varepsilon}{\sum_{i\in\Omega} p_{i,c} + \sum_{i\in\Omega} y_{i,c} + \varepsilon}, \mathcal{L}_{\text{Dice}} = 1 - \frac{1}{3}\sum_{c=0}^{2} \text{Dice}_c, \\ \mathcal{L}_{\text{CE}} &= -\frac{1}{|\Omega|}\sum_{i\in\Omega}\sum_{c=0}^{2} y_{i,c}\log p_{i,c}, \mathcal{L}_{\text{total}} = \lambda\mathcal{L}_{\text{Dice}} + (1-\lambda)\mathcal{L}_{\text{CE}}, \quad \lambda = 0.5. \end{aligned} \tag{3}$$

where $\mathcal{L}_{\text{Dice}}$ encourages accurate volumetric overlap, $\mathcal{L}_{\text{CE}}$ penalizes voxel-level misclassification, and λ is a balancing coefficient. This composite loss leverages the complementary strengths of both terms, enabling robust optimization in the presence of class imbalance and heterogeneous tumor morphology.

3 Method for Task 2

3.1 Task 2 Overall Architecture

For Task 2, we propose a deep multimodal fusion network to enable precise prediction of patient survival risk. As illustrated in Fig. 1(b), The framework consists of three parallel branches that separately encode CT/PET imaging data, electronic health records (EHR), and radiomic features derived from Task 1 segmentation results. The outputs of these branches are integrated within a cross-modal fusion module and subsequently passed into the ICARE survival prediction model, thereby forming an end-to-end analysis pipeline.

3.2 Imaging and Clinical Branches

The imaging branch takes registered CT and PET volumes as inputs, $\mathbf{X}_{\text{CT}} \in \mathbb{R}^{H\times W\times D}$ and $\mathbf{X}_{\text{PET}} \in \mathbb{R}^{H\times W\times D}$, which are concatenated along the channel dimension to form dual-channel 3D data $\mathbf{X}_{\text{img}} = \text{Concat}(\mathbf{X}_{\text{CT}}, \mathbf{X}_{\text{PET}}) \in \mathbb{R}^{2\times H\times W\times D}$. A 3D ResNet-18 serves as the feature encoder, learning hierarchical representations ranging from low-level textures to high-level semantics while alleviating gradient vanishing issues through residual connections. To obtain a global imaging representation, the classification head of ResNet-18 is removed, and the output of its final average pooling layer is the feature vector:

$$\boldsymbol{f}_{\text{img}} = \mathbf{F}_{\text{ResNet-18}}(\mathbf{X}_{\text{img}}) \in \mathbb{R}^{512}. \tag{4}$$

The clinical branch encodes structured patient variables. Continuous variables are normalized to yield $\mathbf{X}^{\text{norm}}_{\text{clin-cont}} = \frac{\mathbf{X}_{\text{clin-cont}}-\mu}{\sigma} \in \mathbb{R}^{M}$, while categorical variables are transformed into one-hot encodings to obtain $\mathbf{X}^{\text{onehot}}_{\text{clin-disc}} = \text{OneHot}(\mathbf{X}_{\text{clin-disc}}) \in \mathbb{R}^{P}$, where P is the total dimension after one-hot encoding. These two representations are concatenated into a unified vector $\mathbf{X}_{\text{clin}} = \text{Concat}(\mathbf{X}^{\text{norm}}_{\text{clin-cont}}, \mathbf{X}^{\text{onehot}}_{\text{clin-disc}}) \in \mathbb{R}^{M+P}$, which is then passed through a multi-layer perceptron (MLP) consisting of fully connected layers, ReLU activation, batch normalization, and dropout.This operation can be symbolized as:

$$\boldsymbol{f}_{\text{clin}} = \text{MLP}_L(\mathbf{X}_{\text{clin}}) \in \mathbb{R}^{32}, \tag{5}$$

where MLP_L represents a multi-layer perceptron with L-layer hidden layers. The final output is a 32-dimensional embedding vector that unifies heterogeneous clinical factors while capturing their latent associations:

3.3 Multi-mask Generation Module

To better characterize tumor heterogeneity and mitigate segmentation errors, we construct a multi-scale mask ensemble based on Task 1 lesion masks. The ensemble includes original lesions and bounding boxes, SUV-threshold-refined variants, as well as morphologically expanded or shell-derived masks, yielding a total of 11 variants. For each mask, 93 radiomic features $\mathbf{F}_{\text{rad}}(\mathbf{M}_i, \mathbf{X}_{\text{modal}}) \in \mathbb{R}^{93}$ are extracted from both CT and PET using *pyradiomics*, supplemented with handcrafted indicators such as the number of tumors and lymph nodes. This process produces a 2048-dimensional feature vector capturing diverse radiomic and morphological descriptors,which can be expressed as:

$$\boldsymbol{f}_{\text{rad}} = \text{Concat}\left(\bigcup_{i=1}^{11} \text{Concat}\left(\boldsymbol{F}_{\text{rad}}(\boldsymbol{M}_i, \boldsymbol{X}_{\text{CT}}), \boldsymbol{F}_{\text{rad}}(\boldsymbol{M}_i, \boldsymbol{X}_{\text{PET}})\right), \boldsymbol{f}_{\text{manual}}\right) \in \mathbb{R}^{2048}. \tag{6}$$

3.4 Cross-Modal Feature Fusion Module

The fusion module concatenates the 512-dimensional imaging representation with the 32-dimensional clinical embedding to form a 544-dimensional vector, which is then combined with the 2048-dimensional radiomic features. This composite feature vector is passed through a deep MLP that learns nonlinear, high-order cross-modal interactions. The output is a 256-dimensional integrated representation, serving as the unified input for survival prediction. The specific formula can be expressed as follows:

$$
\begin{gathered}
\boldsymbol{f}_{\text{img-clin}} = \text{Concat}(\boldsymbol{f}_{\text{img}}, \boldsymbol{f}_{\text{clin}}) \in \mathbb{R}^{512+32} = \mathbb{R}^{544}, \\
\boldsymbol{f}_{\text{combined}} = \text{Concat}(\boldsymbol{f}_{\text{img-clin}}, \boldsymbol{f}_{\text{rad}}) \in \mathbb{R}^{544+2048} = \mathbb{R}^{2592}, \\
\boldsymbol{g}_t = \text{ReLU}(\boldsymbol{W}_t \boldsymbol{g}_{t-1} + \boldsymbol{b}_t), \quad \boldsymbol{g}_0 = \boldsymbol{f}_{\text{combined}}, \boldsymbol{f}_{\text{fused}} = \boldsymbol{W}_{\text{fuse-out}} \boldsymbol{g}_T + \boldsymbol{b}_{\text{fuse-out}},
\end{gathered} \tag{7}
$$

where $\boldsymbol{W}_t \in \mathbb{R}^{E_t \times E_{t-1}}$, $\boldsymbol{b}_t \in \mathbb{R}^{E_t}$ are the weight and bias of the t-th layer, respectively, and $\boldsymbol{W}_{\text{fuse-out}} \in \mathbb{R}^{256 \times E_T}$, $\boldsymbol{b}_{\text{fuse-out}} \in \mathbb{R}^{256}$ are the weight and bias of the fuse-layer, respectively.

3.5 Prediction Model

For risk prediction, we construct a binary-weighted ICARE model designed to mitigate overfitting under limited sample conditions. Unlike conventional models that assign continuous weights, our approach restricts each feature weight to either +1 or −1, indicating whether the feature promotes or suppresses risk. The modeling process consists of four steps:

1. **Feature preprocessing.** Pearson correlation coefficients are computed to detect highly correlated variables. If correlation exceeds a threshold, one redundant variable is randomly discarded to reduce collinearity.
2. **Univariate consistency evaluation.** For each retained feature xi, Harrell's Concordance Index (C-index) is used to assess its concordance with survival outcomes y. Features with predictive power exceeding a minimum threshold $|c_i| > c_{\min}$ are preserved, where $|c_i| = \max\{1 - c_i, c_i\}$.
3. **Binary weighting.** Based on the concordance direction, each feature is assigned a binary weight (+1 or −1), where $s_i = +1$ if $c_i \geq 0.5$, and $s_i = -1$ otherwise, ensuring both interpretability and robustness.
4. **Risk scoring.** At prediction time, all input features are standardized via Z-score normalization. The weighted average is then computed to yield the individual risk score for each patient as follows:

$$
\hat{y} = \frac{1}{M} \sum_i s_i \times z_i, \tag{8}
$$

where z_i denotes the standardized value of the input feature.

To further improve stability and generalization, we employ a bagging strategy in which multiple independent binary-weighted models are trained on bootstrap samples of the original dataset. In inference, their outputs are aggregated by median voting. This ensemble method reduces uncertainty from data sampling and feature selection, substantially enhancing prediction robustness.

3.6 Loss Function

The overall training objective combines two complementary components:

$$\mathcal{L}_{\text{total}} = \mathcal{L}_{\text{DeepHit}} + \alpha \cdot \mathcal{L}_{\text{Contrastive}}, \quad \alpha = 0.1. \tag{9}$$

The DeepHit loss serves as the primary optimization objective, enhancing the model's ability to rank patients by survival risk. It consists of two parts: (1) a likelihood term, inspired by the Cox model, which maximizes the probability that patients with events are assigned higher risks than those still at risk, and (2) a ranking term, which penalizes incorrect patient pair orderings, such as when a patient with shorter survival is predicted to have a lower risk. This loss supervises the outputs of the risk prediction head. In contrast, the Survival Contrastive loss acts as an auxiliary regularizer, refining the feature space by using contrastive learning to bring together patients with similar survival outcomes (e.g., comparable survival times with recurrence) and separate those with markedly different outcomes. This encourages the network to learn more discriminative multimodal representations, improving the stability and robustness of inputs for the downstream ICARE survival prediction model.

4 Experiments

4.1 Dataset

We utilized the HECKTOR 2025 Challenge dataset, which comprises registered PET/CT scans from 700 head and neck cancer patients across 10 centers. Following the official 8:2 training-testing split, our model was trained using the provided expert annotations and evaluated on the hidden test set by the challenge organizers. The dataset provides ground-truth masks for GTVp and GTVn segmentation, alongside comprehensive clinical metadata including TNM staging, demographic information, and RFS outcomes for the prediction task.

4.2 Experimental Setup

All experiments were conducted on a server equipped with an NVIDIA 5090 GPU (32 GB memory). The models were implemented in PyTorch, with data preprocessing, augmentation, and network construction facilitated by MONAI. **For Task 1:** HM-VNet was trained end-to-end using the AdamW optimizer for 1000 epochs, with an initial learning rate of 1×10^{-4}. A cosine annealing schedule was employed for dynamic adjustment, and the batch size was set to 2. **For Task 2:** AdamW was also used, training the feature extractor in 5 iterations of 10 epochs each, with an initial learning rate of 1×10^{-3} adjusted via ReduceLROnPlateau. The batch size was set to 8. To ensure reproducibility, a global random seed of 42 was fixed, and five-fold stratified cross-validation was performed on the training set.

4.3 Evaluation Metrics

Following the official guidelines, model performance was evaluated for both tasks. For Task1, we used the mean Dice Similarity Coefficient (DSC) for GTVp, alongside the Aggregated Dice (DSC_{agg}) and Aggregated F1-Score for GTVn. For Task2, the Concordance Index (C-index) served as the sole evaluation metric.

4.4 Experimental Results

Segmentation Task. We benchmarked HM-VNet against a wide range of state-of-the-art 3D segmentation models from distinct architectural families. The comparison included CNN-based approaches such as SegResNet [6], Transformer-based architectures like SwinUNETR [5], and a variety of advanced hybrid models, namely Restormer [12], H-Denseformer [11], MMCA-Net [13], MICFormer [4], H2ASeg [8], and AIMERS [7].

Table 1. Performance comparison of different advanced segmentation models on the HECKTOR 2025 validation set. Best: highlighted. Second-best: underlined.

Method	GTVpMean Dice	GTVnAggregated Dice	GTVnAggregated F1-Score
SegResNet [6]	0.6621	<u>0.7181</u>	**0.5297**
SwinUNETR [5]	<u>0.6673</u>	0.7053	0.1713
Restormer [12]	0.6589	0.7024	0.3439
MICFormer [4]	0.6521	0.6802	0.2157
H-Denseformer [11]	0.6453	0.6826	0.4050
MMCA-Net [13]	0.6437	0.6671	0.2507
H2ASeg [8]	0.5824	0.6855	<u>0.4756</u>
AIMERS [7]	0.5250	0.5110	0.3849
Ours	**0.6833**	**0.7452**	0.4544

1. **Comparison with baseline models:** For GTVp segmentation, HM-VNet achieved a mean Dice score of 0.6833, significantly outperforming both the CNN-based SegResNet (0.6621) and the Transformer-based SwinUNETR (0.6673). This demonstrates the effectiveness of our hierarchical Transformer architecture with multimodal fusion in capturing the complex morphology of primary tumors. In the more challenging task of GTVn segmentation, the advantage of HM-VNet is even more pronounced, reaching an aggregated Dice of 0.7452, which is substantially higher than SegResNet (0.7181) and SwinUNETR (0.7053). These results highlight our model's superior ability to localize and segment small, spatially dispersed metastatic lymph nodes (Table 1).
2. **Comparison with advanced hybrid architectures:** For GTVp segmentation, HM-VNet again achieved the best performance, with a mean Dice

of 0.6833, surpassing Restormer (0.6589) and H-Denseformer (0.6453). For the more challenging GTVn segmentation, HM-VNet attained an aggregated Dice of 0.7452, markedly outperforming Restormer (0.7024) and MICFormer (0.6802). Furthermore, in the lesion-level F1 score, HM-VNet achieved 0.4544, slightly lower than H2ASeg (0.4756), but significantly higher than MICFormer (0.2157) and MMCA-Net (0.2507), demonstrating superior overall segmentation accuracy and robustness.

3. **Lesion-level detection performance analysis:** At the lesion level, SegResNet (0.5297) achieved the highest aggregated F1 score for GTVn, likely due to its strong capability in local feature extraction. Our HM-VNet (0.4544) and H2ASeg (0.4756) followed closely, both performing competitively and clearly outperforming other Transformer-based methods such as SwinUNETR (0.1713) and MICFormer (0.2157). These results confirm that HM-VNet maintains strong competitiveness in accurately detecting lymph node lesions.

Survival Prediction Task. For Task 2, our proposed method was systematically benchmarked against a spectrum of established survival prediction models, which represent two distinct methodological paradigms. The first paradigm encompasses traditional statistical and machine learning baselines, featuring the seminal Cox Proportional-Hazards (CoxPH [10]) model, which is the field's gold standard and ICARE, [10]a robust model for feature selection in high-dimensional data. The second paradigm consists of advanced deep learning approaches, including DeepHit [10] and MTLR [10], which respectively reformulate survival analysis as discrete-time and multi-task problems, alongside contemporary multimodal frameworks including HMT [3] and Lyn's [9] (Table 2).

Table 2. Performance comparison of different survival prediction models on the HECKTOR 2025 validation set. Best: highlighted. Second-best: underlined.

Method	C-index
CoxPH [10]	0.6073 ± 0.0637
DeepHit [10]	0.5457 ± 0.0674
MTLR [10]	0.5877 ± 0.0900
ICARE [10]	0.6705 ± 0.0608
HMT [3]	0.5688 ± 0.0840
Lyn's [9]	0.6032 ± 0.0869
W/O Task1	0.6826 ± 0.0578
Ours	$\mathbf{0.7045 \pm 0.0568}$

1. **Comparison with traditional baselines:** Our model achieved a C-index of 0.6826, significantly outperforming the classical CoxPH model (0.6073) and surpassing the strong modern machine learning method ICARE (0.6705).

This remarkable result vividly demonstrates the capability of our end-to-end deep learning framework to capture complex and nonlinear survival-related patterns from heterogeneous data, thereby breaking through the performance bottleneck of traditional approaches.

2. **Comparison with deep learning baselines:** When compared with a range of advanced deep learning methods, our model likewise exhibited a marked advantage. Its C-index of 0.6826 was substantially higher than DeepHit (0.5457), MTLR (0.5877), HMT (0.5688), and Lyn's model (0.6032). These findings strongly validate the superiority of our unique model architecture in multimodal data fusion, representation learning, and downstream risk prediction, relative to other state-of-the-art deep learning approaches.
3. **Incorporating segmentation-derived features:** To further enhance survival prediction performance, we integrated segmentation results obtained from the Task 1 model into the Task 2 framework. Experimental results revealed that with this additional auxiliary information, the C-index improved further to 0.7045 ± 0.0568. This result clearly demonstrates that spatial localization and anatomical priors derived from segmentation can effectively regularize feature learning, thereby enhancing both the reliability of survival prediction and its overall clinical relevance.

5 Conclusion

We proposed HM-VNet, a hierarchical multimodal framework that jointly tackles tumor segmentation and survival prediction in head and neck cancer. By coupling hierarchical multimodal encoding with cross-modal fusion, our approach achieves robust performance across heterogeneous clinical data. Results on the HECKTOR benchmark confirm its clear advantage over existing methods, underscoring strong potential for real-world clinical translation. This work moves a step closer to reliable multimodal intelligence for precision oncology.

Acknowledgements. This work was supported by the Fundamental Research Funds for the Provincial Universities of Zhejiang (No. GK259909299001-006), and Anhui Provincial Joint Construction Key Laboratory of Intelligent Education Equipment and Technology (No. IEET202401).

Disclosure of Interests. The authors declare no competing interests.

References

1. Chen, Y., et al.: Semi-supervised medical image segmentation method based on cross-pseudo labeling leveraging strong and weak data augmentation strategies. In: 2024 IEEE International Symposium on Biomedical Imaging (ISBI), pp. 1–5 (2024). https://doi.org/10.1109/ISBI56570.2024.10635443
2. Chen, Y., et al.: SCUNET++: Swin-UNet and CNN bottleneck hybrid architecture with multi-fusion dense skip connection for pulmonary embolism CT image segmentation. In: Proceedings of the IEEE/CVF Winter Conference on Applications of Computer Vision, pp. 7759–7767 (2024)

3. Cui, J., et al.: HMT: a hybrid multimodal transformer with multitask learning for survival prediction in head and neck cancer. IEEE Trans. Radiation Plasma Med. Sci. **9**(7), 879–889 (2025). https://doi.org/10.1109/TRPMS.2025.3539739
4. Fan, X., Liu, L., Zhang, H.: Multimodal information interaction for medical image segmentation. arXiv preprint arXiv:2404.16371 (2024)
5. He, Y., Nath, V., Yang, D., Tang, Y., Myronenko, A., Xu, D.: SwinUNETR-V2: stronger swin transformers with stagewise convolutions for 3D medical image segmentation. In: International Conference on Medical Image Computing and Computer-Assisted Intervention, pp. 416–426. Springer (2023). https://doi.org/10.1007/978-3-031-43901-8_40
6. Hsu, C., et al.: Brain tumor segmentation (brats) challenge short paper: improving three-dimensional brain tumor segmentation using SegresNet and hybrid boundary-dice loss. In: International MICCAI Brainlesion Workshop, pp. 334–344. Springer (2021). https://doi.org/10.1007/978-3-031-09002-8_30
7. Jain, A., et al.: Head and neck primary tumor and lymph node auto-segmentation for PET/CT scans. In: Andrearczyk, V., Oreiller, V., Hatt, M., Depeursinge, A. (eds.) Head and Neck Tumor Segmentation and Outcome Prediction, pp. 61–69. Springer Nature Switzerland, Cham (2023). https://doi.org/10.1007/978-3-031-27420-6_6
8. Lu, J., Chen, J., Cai, L., Jiang, S., Zhang, Y.: H2ASEG: hierarchical adaptive interaction and weighting network for tumor segmentation in PET/CT images. In: Linguraru, M.G., et al. (eds.) Medical Image Computing and Computer Assisted Intervention - MICCAI 2024, pp. 316–327. Springer Nature Switzerland, Cham (2024). https://doi.org/10.1007/978-3-031-72111-3_30
9. Lyu, Q.: Combining NNUNet and AutoML for automatic head and neck tumor segmentation and recurrence-free survival prediction in PET/CT images. In: Andrearczyk, V., Oreiller, V., Hatt, M., Depeursinge, A. (eds.) Head and Neck Tumor Segmentation and Outcome Prediction, pp. 192–201. Springer Nature Switzerland, Cham (2023). https://doi.org/10.1007/978-3-031-27420-6_19
10. Saeed, N., et al.: A multimodal and multi-centric head and neck cancer dataset for tumor segmentation and outcome prediction (2025). https://arxiv.org/abs/2509.00367
11. Shi, J., et al.: H-DenseFormer: an efficient hybrid densely connected transformer for multimodal tumor segmentation. In: International Conference on Medical Image Computing and Computer-Assisted Intervention, pp. 692–702. Springer (2023). https://doi.org/10.1007/978-3-031-43901-8_66
12. Zamir, S.W., Arora, A., Khan, S., Hayat, M., Khan, F.S., Yang, M.H.: Restormer: efficient transformer for high-resolution image restoration. In: Proceedings of the IEEE/CVF Conference on Computer Vision and Pattern Recognition, pp. 5728–5739 (2022)
13. Zhao, W., et al.: MMCA-Net: a multimodal cross attention transformer network for nasopharyngeal carcinoma tumor segmentation based on a total-body pet/CT system. IEEE J. Biomed. Health Inform. **28**(9), 5447–5458 (2024)

Downstream Prediction from PET/CT and Clinical Data

HECKTOR2025 Challenge Report: Fully Automated Diagnoses of HPV Status Using PET/CT Images and Clinical Information

Muzi Guo[1], Tianen Yu[2,3], Jian He[3], and Lei Xiang[1](✉)

[1] Subtle Medical Inc., Menlo Park, CA, USA
lei@subtlemedical.com
[2] School of Computer Science and Engineering, Nanjing University of Science and Technology, Nanjing, China
[3] Department of Nuclear Medicine, Nanjing Drum Tower Hospital, Affiliated Hospital of Medical School, Nanjing University, Nanjing, China

Abstract. Accurate prediction of human papillomavirus (HPV) status is essential for risk stratification and personalized treatment planning in head and neck cancer. In this work, we propose a multi-modal deep learning framework to classify HPV status using the HECKTOR25 Task 3 dataset, which provides 3D FDG-PET and CT scans with clinical data. Our approach leverages a 3D ResNet-18 architecture for imaging feature extraction, combined with a fully connected network to encode clinical variables, followed by multimodal fusion for final prediction. To address the significant class imbalance problem, we implemented a weighted cross-entropy loss. On internally held-out test splits, the model achieved a specificity of 0.9167 and a balanced accuracy of 0.9017, demonstrating robust intra-dataset performance. However, evaluation on the organizers external dataset—which contains cases from centers not included in the training data—yielded reduced performance (validation specificity 0.9048, balanced accuracy 0.6765), highlighting the challenges of cross-center generalization. These findings underscore the potential of multi-modal deep learning for HPV status prediction and indicate that further strategies are required to enhance model robustness to inter-center variability.

Keywords: HECKTOR2025 · classification challenge · PET/CT · deep learning

1 Introduction

1.1 Motivation

Head and neck cancer (HNC) represents a heterogeneous group of malignancies, with nearly 90% classified as squamous cell carcinomas (HNSCC) [1]. Well-

N. Saeed et al. (Eds.): HECKTOR 2026, LNCS 16520, pp. 155–162, 2026.
https://doi.org/10.1007/978-3-032-25766-6_15

established risk factors, such as tobacco and alcohol consumption, act synergistically to markedly increase disease incidence [2,3]. Despite advances in therapeutic strategies, the overall 5-year survival rate remains poor, particularly among patients with advanced disease. Current clinical workflows—primarily based on TNM staging, imaging, and histopathology—are often insufficient for early detection and accurate prognostication. Although biomarkers such as HPV status have improved risk stratification, their integration into routine clinical practice remains limited. Artificial intelligence (AI) offers promising opportunities by leveraging multimodal data—including medical imaging, radiotherapy dose distributions, and electronic health records—to enhance diagnostic accuracy and prognostic modeling. However, progress in AI-driven approaches for HNC has been constrained by the scarcity of large, diverse, and publicly available datasets, hindering clinical translation. The Head and Neck Tumor Segmentation and Outcome Prediction Challenge (HECKTOR 2025) [4] addresses this gap by providing a large-scale, multi-institutional, multimodal dataset collected from 10 international centers, creating new opportunities for the development and validation of AI methods in tumor detection, segmentation, outcome prediction, and treatment optimization.

1.2 Dataset

In this study, we focus on the classification task of predicting HPV status using FDG-PET/CT images in combination with available clinical information. Each case in both the training and test cohorts consists of a paired 3D FDG-PET volume and a corresponding 3D CT volume. The clinical variables include center, gender, age, tobacco and alcohol use, performance status, treatment (radiotherapy alone or chemoradiotherapy), M-stage (metastasis), and HPV status.

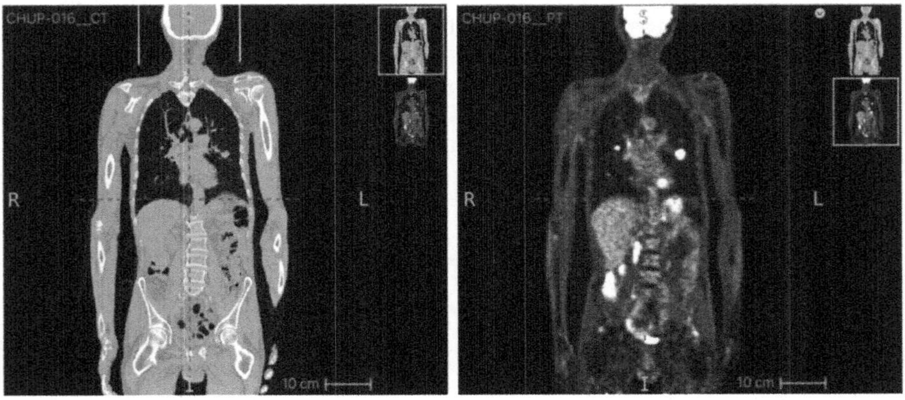

Fig. 1. An example coronal view of a PET image and its corresponding CT image with the tumor.

The training set comprises 588 cases collected from 6 centers, including 4 in Canada, 1 in France, and 1 in the United States. The test set contains 23 previously unseen cases from 3 centers and include approximately 80% HPV-positive and 20% HPV-negative cases. The CT and PET volumes were rigidly aligned to a common origin but remain heterogeneous in field of view(FOV) and resolution. Representative examples of CT and PET images, together with corresponding clinical information, are illustrated in Figs. 1 and 2.

PatientID	CenterID	Age	Gender	Tobacco Consumption	Alcohol Consumption	Performance Status	Treatment	M-stage	HPV Status
CHUM-012	1	61	1	NaN	NaN	NaN	1	M0	1
CHUM-014	1	59	1	NaN	NaN	NaN	1	M0	1
CHUM-016	1	58	1	NaN	NaN	NaN	1	M0	1
CHUM-021	1	63	1	NaN	NaN	NaN	1	M0	1
CHUM-022	1	56	1	NaN	NaN	NaN	1	M0	1
CHUM-026	1	67	0	NaN	NaN	NaN	1	M0	1
CHUM-029	1	50	1	NaN	NaN	NaN	1	M0	1
CHUM-033	1	68	1	NaN	NaN	NaN	1	M0	1
CHUM-036	1	51	1	NaN	NaN	NaN	1	M0	1
CHUM-037	1	70	0	NaN	NaN	NaN	1	M0	1

Fig. 2. An example of the clinical information subset.

2 Method

2.1 Data Preprocessing

Crop Head and Neck Region. Although most of the cases included only the head and neck region, a subset of cases from several centers consisted of whole-body scans. Because the analysis focused exclusively on the head and neck, the axial coverage was standardized by cropping the slice range. The slice range (in millimeters) was calculated as the product of the number of slices and the voxel size along the z-axis. A comprehensive review of the image sets indicated that a coverage of 516 mm was sufficient to cover the entire head and neck region. Consequently, for scans with an axial coverage exceeding 516 mm, the volume was cropped to this limit.

In addition, for certain cases—primarily from the CHUS center—where the CT slice range was smaller than the corresponding PET slice range, the PET volume was cropped along the z-axis to match the CT slice range, ensuring consistent spatial alignment between modalities.

Align PET and CT Images. To fully leverage CT information, spatial alignment was performed between PET and CT images. As described above, we first calculated the field of view (FOV) for PET and CT images, respectively. The absolute difference between the two FOVs was then computed. If the FOV of the PET images exceeded that of the CT images, the CT volume was symmetrically padded along the x and y axes to match the PET FOV. The number of padding pixels was determined by dividing the FOV difference by the CT pixel spacing. After padding, CT images were resampled to match the resolution of PET images. In contrast, if the FOV of the PET images was smaller than that of the CT images, the CT volume was cropped to match the PET FOV before resampling.

Data Normalization. Before intensity rescaling, CT images were adjusted using a mucosal window (window level = 40 HU, window width = 300 HU) to enhance soft tissue contrast and improve the conspicuity of small tumors. Subsequently, the intensities of the CT and PET images were independently normalized by dividing each by their respective mean intensities. After normalization, CT and PET images were concatenated to generate a two-channel input for the model.

Clinical Information Processing. For the clinical data, z-score normalization was applied to age and gender variables. Tobacco consumption, alcohol consumption, performance status, and M-stage were encoded using one-hot encoding. The processed clinical features were then concatenated and fed into a fully connected network to extract high-level clinical representations.

2.2 Model Architecture

Our proposed network consists of two parallel branches designed to jointly leverage imaging and clinical information for classification (Fig. 3).

Image Branch. The image branch uses a 3D ResNet-18 backbone implemented by MONAI [5] to extract deep volumetric features from the PET and CT inputs. After preprocessing step, the two modalities are concatenated along the channel dimension to form a two-channel input volume. The 3D ResNet-18 is an extension of the conventional 2D ResNet-18, with all convolutional and pooling layers replaced by their 3D counterparts, enabling the network to capture spatial context across three dimensions. The architecture consists of an initial $7{\times}7{\times}7$ convolutional layer (stride 2) followed by a $3{\times}3{\times}3$ max-pooling layer. Four residual stages are subsequently stacked, each containing two basic residual blocks with identity skip connections to facilitate gradient propagation. The number of filters doubles at each stage (64, 128, 256, 512), progressively enriching the learned feature representation. A global average pooling layer is applied to obtain a compact feature vector.

Clinical Branch. The clinical branch processes tabular clinical data. Age and gender are normalized using z-score normalization, while tobacco consumption, alcohol consumption, performance status, and M-stage are one-hot encoded. These preprocessed features are passed through a two-layer fully connected network with ReLU activation to extract high-level clinical feature representations.

Feature Fusion and Classification. The feature vectors from the image and clinical branches are concatenated and fed into a final fully connected layer to output class probabilities. This design allows the model to jointly learn complementary information from imaging and clinical data, improving the classification performance.

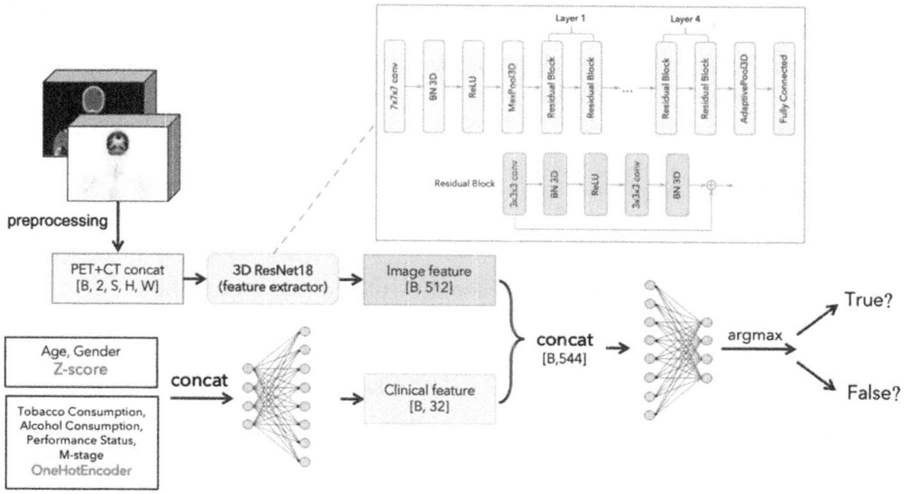

Fig. 3. An illustration of the training pipeline for the classification network.

2.3 Loss Function

Because the classification dataset contained 530 HPV-positive and 58 HPV-negative cases, we adopted a weighted cross-entropy loss to address the severe class imbalance. This loss extends the standard cross-entropy by incorporating class-specific weighting factors, thereby increasing the contribution of minority classes during training.

$$\mathcal{L}_{WCE} = -\frac{1}{N}\sum_{i=1}^{N}\sum_{c=1}^{C} w_c \cdot y_{i,c} \log\left(p_{i,c}\right) \tag{1}$$

where w_c represents the weight assigned to class c, $y_{i,c}$ is the ground truth indicator, $p_{i,c}$ is the predicted probability, N is the number of samples, and C is the number of classes. For each sample, the standard cross-entropy was multiplied by a class-specific weight, typically set as the inverse of the class frequency:

$$w_c = \frac{N}{C \cdot N_c} \tag{2}$$

where N_c denotes the number of samples in class c.

3 Experiment Setup

We utilized the HECKTOR25 Task 3 dataset and randomly divided it into five folds after holding out 20% test set, training a separate model for each fold. No additional data or pre-trained models were used. All input volumes were resized to $192 \times 192 \times 192$ to accommodate GPU memory constraints. Model training was performed using the AdamW optimizer with an initial learning rate of 2×10^{-4}, which was gradually reduced to zero by the end of training via a cosine annealing scheduler. Each model was trained for 100 epochs with a batch size of 1 on a single NVIDIA GeForce RTX 3090 GPU (24 GB).

4 Results

Table 1. Table captions should be placed above the tables.

Fold	Best Validation Accuracy	Test Accuracy	Balanced Accuracy	Sensitivity	Specificity
1	0.8941	0.8559	0.8090	0.8679	0.7500
2	0.9529	0.8644	0.8876	0.8585	0.9167
3	0.8824	0.8305	0.8687	0.8208	0.9167
4	0.9059	0.8898	0.9017	0.8868	0.9167
5	0.9286	0.8559	0.8459	0.8585	0.8333

Based on our data splits, the results of a single-run 5-fold cross-validation are summarized in Table 1. The evaluation metrics include the best validation accuracy, test accuracy, balanced accuracy, sensitivity, and specificity. Validation and test accuracies were computed as the number of correctly classified cases divided by the total number of cases in the corresponding dataset. Specificity, sensitivity, and balanced accuracy were calculated as:

$$Sensitivity = \frac{TP}{TP + FN} \tag{3}$$

$$Specificity = \frac{TN}{TN + FP} \tag{4}$$

$$balanced\ accuracy = \frac{specificity + sensitivity}{2} \tag{5}$$

where TN, FP, TP, and FN denote true negatives, false positives, true positives, and false negatives, respectively. As indicated by the challenge organizers, the official ranking is the balanced accuracy. Therefore, we selected the fold-4 model for final validation and testing submissions. The test results remain undisclosed, while on the validation set we achieved a specificity of 0.9048 and a balanced accuracy of 0.6765, suggesting that the model performs well at correctly identifying HPV-negative cases but struggles to detect HPV-positive cases. This imbalance in performance may reflect the skewed class distribution in the training data and indicates that additional strategies—such as more aggressive class rebalancing, data augmentation, or cost-sensitive learning—may be required to improve sensitivity without sacrificing specificity.

5 Conclusion and Discussion

In this work, we developed a multimodal classification framework for HPV status prediction using the HECKTOR25 Task 3 dataset, which contains 3D PET/CT images and available clinical information. The proposed model, based on a 3D ResNet-18 backbone with a parallel clinical feature branch, was trained using a weighted cross-entropy loss to mitigate class imbalance. Our five-fold cross-validation results demonstrated high specificity (0.9048) but relatively low sensitivity, resulting in a balanced accuracy of 0.6765 on the validation set. These findings suggest that the model performs well in identifying HPV-negative cases but requires further improvement for detecting HPV-positive cases.

We investigated the potential reasons why the model performed well on the internal training dataset but showed reduced performance on the external dataset. One contributing factor may be that some centers in the external dataset were not included in the training data (Table 2).

We further analyzed the distribution of HPV-negative cases and misclassified instances across different centers.

Table 2. Distribution of HPV negative and wrong prediction cases in Task 3 dataset across different centers.

Center	Total Cases	HPV Negative	%HPV Negative	Wrong Prediction	%Wrong Prediction
CHUM	22	1	4.55%	5	23%
CHUP	58	37	63.97%	4	7%
CHUS	33	8	24.24%	6	18%
HGJ	38	10	26.32%	7	18%
HMR	2	0	0.00%	0	0%
MDA	435	2	0.46%	1	0%

Centers such as HMR and MDA, with very few negative cases, and CHUP, with a relatively balanced class distribution, showed higher model performance. In contrast, CHUM, CHUS, and HGJ centers, which have both limited total cases and low numbers of negative cases, showed reduced performance. These findings underscore the importance of accounting for class distribution not only at the dataset level but also within each center. Future work should incorporate strategies such as data resampling, reweighting, or selective sampling to mitigate center-specific imbalances, thereby enhancing the model generalizability across heterogeneous clinical settings.

References

1. Bhat, G.R., Hyole, R.G., Li, J.: Head and neck cancer: current challenges and future perspectives. In: Advances in cancer research, vol. 152, pp. 67–102. Academic Press (2021)
2. Dal Maso, L., et al.: Combined effect of tobacco smoking and alcohol drinking in the risk of head and neck cancers: a re-analysis of case-control studies using bi-dimensional spline models. Eur. J. Epidemiol. **31**(4), 385–393 (2016)
3. Dhull, A.K., Atri, R., Dhankhar, R., Chauhan, A.K., Kaushal, V.: Major risk factors in head and neck cancer: a retrospective analysis of 12-year experiences. World J. Oncol. **9**(3), 80 (2018)
4. Saeed, N., et al.: A multimodal head and neck cancer dataset for AI-driven precision oncology. arXiv preprint arXiv:2509.00367 (2025)
5. Cardoso, M.J., et al.: MONAI: an open-source framework for deep learning in health-care. arXiv preprint arXiv:2211.02701 (2022)

Author Index

N. Saeed et al. (Eds.): HECKTOR 2026, LNCS 16520, pp. 163–164, 2026.
https://doi.org/10.1007/978-3-032-25766-6

The manufacturer's authorised representative in the EU is Springer
Nature Customer Service Centre GmbH, Europaplatz 3, 69115 Heidelberg,
Germany. If you have any concerns regarding our products, please
contact ProductSafety@springernature.com

Printed and bound by CPI Group (UK) Ltd, Croydon, CR0 4YY

20/08/2026

02201459-0004